NATIONAL GEOGRAPHIC

TRAVELER
Miami
& the Keys

NATIONAL GEOGRAPHIC
TRAVELER
Miami
& the Keys

Mark Miller

National Geographic
Washington, D.C.

Contents

**Page 1: South Beach
surfer, Miami
Pages 2–3: Ocean Drive,
South Beach, Miami
Left: Diver and
loggerhead turtle**

How to use this guide

See back flap for keys to text and map symbols.

The *National Geographic Traveler* brings you the best of Miami & the Keys in text, pictures, and maps. Divided into three main sections, the guide begins with an overview of history and culture. Following are 11 area chapters with sites selected by the author for their particular interest and which are treated in depth. Each chapter opens with its own contents list for easy reference.

The areas, and sites within the areas, are arranged geographically. Some areas are further divided into two or three smaller areas. A map introduces each area, high-lighting the featured sites. Walks and drives, plotted on their own maps, suggest routes for discovering an area. Features and side-bars offer detail on history, culture, or contemporary life. A More Places to Visit page rounds off some chapters.

The final section, Travelwise, lists essential information for the traveler—pre-trip planning, getting around, useful websites, and what to do in emergencies—plus a selection of hotels, restaurants, shops, and activities.

To the best of our knowledge, site information is accurate as of the press date. However, it's always advisable to call ahead.

Color coding

70

Each area is color coded for easy reference. Find the area you want on the map on the front flap, and look for the color flash at the top of the pages of the relevant chapter. Hotel and restaurant listings in the **Travelwise** are also color coded to each area.

Visitor information

Museum of Contemporary Art
www.mocanomi.org
🖼 33 F5
✉ 770 N.E. 125th St. between N.E. 7th Court & 8th Ave., just off I-95
☎ 305/893-6211
🕐 Closed Mon.
💲 $–$$

Practical information is given in the side column by each major site (see key to symbols on back flap). The map reference gives the page number where the site is shown on a map, followed by the grid reference.

Further details include the site's address, telephone number, days closed (where applicable), and entrance fee ranging from $ (under $4) to $$$$$ (over $20). Visitor information for smaller sites is listed in italics and parentheses in the text.

TRAVELWISE

Color-coded area name

Town/area name

Hotel name & price range

Address, telephone & fax numbers, website

Brief description of hotel

Hotel facilities & credit card details

Restaurant name & price range

Address, telephone number & website

Brief description of restaurant

Restaurant facilities & credit card details

Hotel & restaurant prices

An explanation of the price ranges used in entries is given in the Hotels & restaurants section (beginning on p. 244).

AREA MAPS

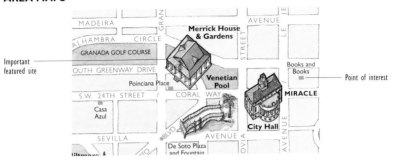

Important featured site

Point of interest

● A locator map accompanies each area map and shows the location of that area in Miami.

AREA/EXCURSIONS MAPS

Map reference

Point of interest

Important point of interest

● A locator map accompanies each area map and shows the location of that area of Miami, the Keys, or surrounding district.

WALKING TOURS

Start point

Building outline

Direction of route

Walk route

Red numbered bullets link sites on map to descriptions in the text.

● An information box gives the starting and ending points, time and length of the walk, and places not to be missed along the route.

NATIONAL GEOGRAPHIC

TRAVELER

Miami
& the Keys

About the author

Mark Miller earned a degree in American Social History from Stanford University, entered journalism as a newspaper copyboy, and subsequently reported for Reuters and the CS Radio network, where he also produced documentaries.

He has contributed to Society books and publications, including *National Geographic,* since 1977, his assignments ranging across North America from Alaska to Florida's Dry Tortugas, as well as to the Caribbean and Europe.

Miller lives in Los Angeles, where he is a partner of 12 Films, a documentary film production company.

Travelwise is by Elizabeth Carter. Food journalist and experienced restaurant/hotel inspector, Elizabeth was drawn to Miami through her passion for Spanish culture. She writes regularly for *Food Illustrated* magazine. She is based in Britain but, with her American husband, has maintained a home in South Florida for a number of years.

History & culture

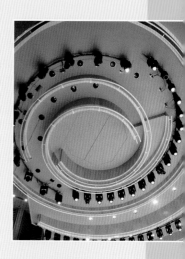

Inside the Adrienne
Arsht Center for the
Performing Arts

Miami today

IN 1994 SOME 34 HEADS OF STATE FROM CENTRAL AND SOUTH AMERICA convened at the Biltmore Hotel in Coral Gables for what was called the Summit of the Americas. (Fidel Castro was conspicuously absent.) The meeting had a post-Cold War viewpoint—that the future of the three Americas includes increasing economic and cultural interdependence. Greater Miami played host to the summit not simply because the United States wished to offer the Biltmore's hospitality to the presidents and prime ministers, but because the metropolis already symbolizes that interdependence more than any other city in the Western Hemisphere. And it is a fact that more Miamians speak Spanish than English.

The city inherited the mantle of "Capital of the Americas" as a result of politics—most notably, the historical accident that has kept Havana out of competition for the title since 1959—but mainly because of finance. Miami's money industry has ties extending south nearly to the Pole, and the city is the leading import/export hub in the region, a brokerage house for a bewildering variety of products and commodities shipped through the region. Perhaps even more important is the largely successful merging of Anglo-American business and culture with the customs of the Americas to the south, which demonstrates daily that while borders drawn by statesmen and enforced by arms are one thing, human ambitions and the historical momentum they generate are quite another.

The epic saga of Miami's Cuban community obscures the fact that the city has large and vital groups of expatriates from other southerly lands. Some arrived first class by air; others, like a good many Haitians, risked their lives in decrepit fishing boats. Some newcomers are among the richest and most influential people in Miami; others languish among the ranks of the poorest. (Despite formidable pockets of economic power, Dade County, which embraces Miami, is one of the poorest counties in America.)

For a traveler, Miami's internationalism translates into a metropolitan sprawl with an astonishing diversity of ethnic neighborhoods where homeland language and customs are preserved in family life, cafés and restaurants serve indigenous fare, and shops and markets trade in the essentials and whimsies of the communities' particular traditions and heritage. If you explore Greater Miami by car, besides the city's historic Cuban and Jewish districts you will find enclaves of African Americans, Bahamians, Colombians, Costa Ricans, Guyanese, Haitians, Jamaicans, Nicaraguans, Puerto Ricans, Peruvians, Trinidadians, Venezuelans, and Virgin Islanders. The transitions are seldom obvious, for in Miami the process of assimilation is one of blending—as Little Havana, for example, has taken in a new generation of political refugees from Nicaragua.

It takes a wide net to embrace Miami's cultural heritage—the Historical Museum of Southern Florida (see p. 39) in Downtown Miami showcases a human saga spanning ten millennia and a geographic area embracing the Caribbean and touching Central and South America. The "folklife" section of the museum's excellent website (www.hmsf.org/collections-south-florida .htm) documents the traditional arts of more than 60 cultural groups living in South Florida, including the indigenous Miccosukee, whose world endures on a small reservation in the Everglades.

With over 140 commercial banks, Miami is indeed an international financial capital, and it is not an exaggeration to call it the Capital of the Caribbean. To those more interested in culture, however, the city's other nickname, "Gateway to the Americas," is more evocative of Miami's peculiar appeal.

Caribbean colors and costumes, art deco architecture and vintage convertibles—in this case a shark-finned Cadillac—are virtual trademarks of South Miami Beach's trend-conscious Ocean Drive.

INTRODUCING MIAMI

There is no American metropolis like Miami. Most of its 2.4 million people consider themselves fortunate, despite a six-month threat of hurricanes, to live so close to South Florida's captivating wetlands and jungles and the bewitching Florida Keys.

Relative to other American urban areas, Greater Miami is a youngster, taking root only at the end of the 19th century. Its polyglot character reflects a heritage peculiar to this region—as an outpost of Spanish colonials, a vacation mecca, and a sun-drenched retirement haven for work-weary Northerners. Then came the exodus of Cubans following Fidel Castro's takeover, a phenomenon that quickly transformed a slow-paced, leisure-oriented city into the "capital of Latin America."

Miami is probably best known by stereotypes. Films, television, and hard-boiled fiction generally portray it as a flamingo-colored city of outlaws. For years, Miami Beach was known

Enormous cruise ships ply the waters of Biscayne Bay in Miami, recognized as the cruise capital of the world.

as God's waiting room, where elderly Jewish folk lived out their years in residential hotels. Other notions persist—of a nightlife capital where club-crawling hedonists pursue ephemeral pleasures (true); of drug trafficking (true); of anti-Castro sentiment (true); of an excess of pink things (not true except perhaps in Miami Beach's Art Deco District, where refurbished moderne and streamline hotels and apartments sport vivid pastels).

Greater Miami lies hard by some of the most inviting seashore in the Americas, caressed by gentle surf and balmy trade winds. In November, as autumn chills northern places, Miami's "high" season commences, bringing daytime temperatures in the low 80s, and overnight lows in the 70s. Warm days and nights year-round are what makes South

Miami Beach the closest thing to a 24-hour city in the land. Biscayne Bay, which separates Miami from Miami Beach's barrier island, is a sailor's delight, with dozens of small islands left in a wild state. Along its shore, public parks preserve thousands of forested acres and grassy beaches.

Greater Miami supports a full complement of performing arts troupes and theater companies, orchestras, museums, and universities. Ethnic neighborhoods offer immersion in Caribbean and Latin American culture. A colony of pink flamingos, florid embodiments of a subtropical ambience, graces the infield of Hialeah Park's old racetrack, which is no longer used. Communities such as Coconut Grove and Coral Gables explain why some 700 people move to Florida every day: neighborhoods of gardened homes, tree-shaded boulevards, appealing civic architecture and grand plazas, and tropical gardens lapped by azure waters—the apotheosis of the Florida Dream.

Dancing waiters and bar staff provide entertainment at Mango's Tropical Cafe, a popular Caribbean restaurant and bar on Ocean Drive in South Beach.

The most enjoyable sojourns here indulge the senses. Take time to experience what state officials proudly call "The Real Florida"— the beaches, reefs, and shoreline jungles of Biscayne Bay, and the dreamy wilds of the Everglades, a place unlike any other on Earth, where you can rent a canoe and explore a primordial waterworld so serene, the loudest sound is often the beating of your heart. Taste New World cuisine, immerse yourself in warm Gulf Stream waters, dig your toes into the sand that crunched beneath the boots of Florida's first European visitor, Juan Ponce de León, and idle away a day on a shore so paradisiacal it seemed to the Spanish adventurer proof certain that his long-sought Fountain of Youth lay close at hand.

MIAMI DISTRICTS TODAY

Along with its beaches and hotels, Miami is home to a diverse range of ethnic communities and intriguing architectural styles. No one quite agrees on the names of Miami's major districts, let alone their boundaries, but here, in brief, are its main areas.

distinctive neighborhoods such as Bayside and Morningside, whose Mediterranean Revival and bungalow-style residences, built before 1940, grace palm-lined avenues.

Little Haiti

Just west of Upper Eastside, this fragment of the Caribbean is decorated with Haitian art and commerce. Its Buena Vista neighborhood has more Mediterranean-style residences. Adjoining is Miami's Design District (around N.E. 40th Street), whose showrooms, galleries, and furniture and fabric stores cater to designers and architects.

Allapattah

This working-class neighborhood of 40,000 (about 70 percent Hispanic), northwest of downtown, includes Miami's industrial, medical, and government buildings. Locals shop in the wholesale outlets that are supplied by garment-making factories. Cooks favor the Produce Market, Miami's largest. Photographers roam the Miami River here for picturesque exotica—funky bistros, old ships, auto repair shops, even rusty iron junkyards.

Downtown

You can't miss downtown's skyline, one of America's most handsome, especially at night when spotlights paint skyscrapers in vivid colors. It is anchored by commercial and residential high-rises, the appealing Miami-Dade Cultural Center, and Bayside Marketplace, a popular shopping, dining, and entertainment complex on Biscayne Bay.

Little Havana

A political and economic beachhead for arriving Cubans since 1959, now seeing Latinos from elsewhere, Little Havana lies just southwest of downtown. Shops and restaurants include Nicaraguan, Mexican, and Colombian enterprises. Miami's Cuban population has expanded from here, but this remains the sentimental heart of the community.

Upper Eastside

Miami's northeastern reach flanks Biscayne Boulevard (US 1) north of downtown. An ethnically mixed district, its charm lies off the boulevard's deteriorating motel row in

Overtown

Situated between Allapattah and downtown, this predominantly African-American community of about 8,000 struggles to overcome unemployment, homelessness, and crime. Community pride and civic programs have helped instill hope for rejuvenation. Overtown's theme park celebrates Miami's African-American heritage, an inspiring saga too often obscured by the community's day-to-day travails.

Flagami

Jutting west from Little Havana near the international airport, its contrived name a salute to Miami's first railroader, Flagami's fast-growing grid of houses and small businesses is a middle-income, Anglo-American and Hispanic community of about 45,000. Its supper clubs and lounges draw patrons citywide, and windsurfers take advantage of the lakes in its Blue Lagoon district.

Coral Gables

In Coral Gables the classic beauty and

Retirees, like these card players, still make up a sizable proportion of Miami Beach's permanent residents.

grandeur of historic Spain mix with the vibrancy of a large American metropolis set in the tropics. With 42,000 residents, including many rich Latin émigrés, and more than 140 multinational corporations, the city has grown into Latin America's unofficial business capital in the U.S. Additionally, the private University of Miami's main campus is located here.

Coconut Grove
Sophisticated, comfortable, culturally diverse, overgrown with vegetation, "the Grove" is one of Miami's most appealing suburbs. Its bohemian flair invites comparisons with New York's Greenwich Village and London's Chelsea. The 18,000 people who live here are proud of it. Many of its most luxurious addresses are condominiums overlooking Biscayne Bay, where wooded shores seclude some of South Florida's most sumptuous residences.

Coral Way
This commercial area north of Coconut Grove embraces the neighborhoods of Brickell, Coral Gate, Douglas, Parkdale-Lyndale, Shenandoah, Silver Bluff, and the Roads. Here on weekends, apartment-dwellers cruise and dream of house-owning. Why? The Brickell district holds some of America's most critically acclaimed condominium designs. Older houses in Shenandoah and Silver Bluff display a diversity of handsome architecture.

Miami Beach
There are no 2 square miles anywhere like these on the American Riviera, a dazzling sweep of sand and Gulf Stream-warmed blue shallows flanked by over 800 art deco buildings, and some of the nation's most determinedly posh hotels. Here also is North America's preeminent nightclub scene, whose notoriously photogenic habitués decorate dance floors by night and sidewalk café tables by day. ∎

History

MIAMI'S CLIMATE AND NATURAL RESOURCES HAVE BEEN ATTRACTING attention since the time of the ancient Greeks. It has been coveted by the Spanish and the English, served as a haven for runaway slaves, and inspired everything from a railroad magnate's ambitions to some of the country's most imaginative architecture. It has been home to pirates, Prohibition rumrunners, and celebrities, to hurricanes, Seminole wars, and a burgeoning tourist industry.

PREHISTORY

It is believed that the first Miamians were the Tequesta, hunter-gatherers and fisherpeople who settled at the mouth of the Miami River and on Biscayne Bay's coastal islands as early as 10,000 years ago. The Miami River—El Rio Nombrado de Agua Dulce on Spanish maps—ran clear, and at least one great freshwater spring gushed from the floor of shallow Biscayne Bay, creating upwelling offshore fonts and making it possible, even up to the late 1800s, to dip a cup into the sea and drink from it. Perhaps because of this phenomenon, the notion arose that "miami" is Tequesta for "sweet water"—*agua dulce*—as freshwater was once called. Others trace the name to the Seminole language and translate it as "big water." Hunting parties into the Everglades brought back deer, bears, and wild pigs. Men fished from dugout canoes for shark and sailfish, porpoises, stingrays, and manatees. Women and children gathered clams, conchs, oysters, and turtle eggs from the riverbanks and beaches.

Europeans started to write accounts of this region in the 1500s, but the Tequestas' sheltered world saw few changes until one day in 1566, when they encountered their first European, Pedro Menendez de Aviles, appointed by Spain as the first governor of "La Florida." He arrived with a company of soldiers and a Jesuit priest bent on saving heathen souls. Brother Francisco Villareal promptly founded a mission but failed to imbue the Tequesta with Christian fervor. Yet the Spaniards left a more fateful legacy: Old World diseases against which Miami's native populations had no immunity.

FIRST EUROPEAN EXPLORERS

In April 1513, Christopher Columbus's ambitious lieutenant, Juan Ponce de León, landed somewhere to the north near present-day St. Augustine, around Easter Sunday—*la pascua florida* in Spanish; perhaps why the explorer named his "island" La Florida. The next half-century saw mistreatment of Florida's native peoples at the hands of the conquistadores.

Menendez's visit to the Miami Tequesta in 1566 was a peacemaking overture—he would soon sign a treaty with the Calusa, whose domain included the Keys. He traded with cloth and hardwares, more valuable to the tribes than the gold bars and Spanish shipwreck survivors. He put up watchtowers from the Carolinas to Biscayne Bay to warn treasure galleons of lurking pirates, and enlisted the Tequesta as allies, ending their enslavement of shipwrecked Spaniards. La Florida joined Spain's New World empire, though the swampy peninsula appeared to offer little more than turtle eggs and mosquito bites, and was valued mainly for its strategic location above the main sea lane of the Gulf of Mexico.

By the mid-1700s, St. Augustine was still a beleaguered garrison of about 2,000, its economy dependent upon supplying the military. Spain's mission system was a failure. Meanwhile the Spanish Crown was refusing to allow desperately needed trade with the English colonies, barring non-Catholics from becoming colonists, and failing to convince entrepreneurs to bet their futures on La Florida. Capital flowed instead to Mexico and Cuba.

The 1763 treaty ending the French and Indian War delivered La Florida to the British, whose settlement schemes also foundered. Following the American Revolution, Great Britain traded Florida

Right: Flooding after the 1926 hurricane damaged or destroyed nearly every building in Downtown Miami.

back to Spain for possession of the Bahamas, and in 1784 the Spanish instituted a new settlement program. A 175-acre tract on Bahía Biscaino was granted to Pedro Fornells, and an Englishman named John Egan was awarded 100 acres on the north bank of the Rio Nombrado, making the unlikely pair Miami's first documented residents.

Better known for his quest for the Fountain of Youth than his naming of Florida, Juan Ponce de León may have been the first European to visit Miami's shores.

BEGINNING OF AMERICAN SETTLEMENT

What kings and ministers decree is one thing; what people do is another. Americans began to see their destiny in terms of expansion, and resented European adventurers on the continent. In Spain's corridors of power, sober minds saw La Florida's sale to the United States as the logical option, but logic was losing ground to greed, a force more handily exploited by mercantile minds than bureaucratic ones. Pirates had turned the south coast and the Keys into a no-man's-land of tropical treachery, where cutthroats preyed on American ships, convincing Washington that a Spanish Florida meant anarchy. Meanwhile, Spain's policy of giving sanctuary to escaped American slaves enraged Southern planters, who sent raiding parties from Georgia. In 1811, a band of Yankee irregulars attacked

St. Augustine and set about razing plantations until British warships chased them off. The outbreak of the War of 1812 obliged Madrid to let Great Britain take up positions in Florida, further arousing American ire; its outcome stripped La Florida of British naval protection. American adventurers—more pirate than patriot—continued to raid Spanish settlements. In 1821, its options evaporated, Spain ceded the peninsula to the United States, and the Stars and Stripes flew over the new Florida Territory.

By 1825 Cape Florida, Key Biscayne, had a lighthouse, although mariners complained that its beacon was so ineffectual there was greater danger they would run ashore while searching for it. Congress passed the Homestead Act, opening up Florida to settlers. The dark side of this policy was the strong-arm removal of Indians from their lands and forced relocation to reservations in the West. Their futures bleak, thousands united under the Seminole banner. In 1835, the settlers went to war, led by Maj. Francis Dade, for whom today's Dade County (of which Miami is the seat) is named. For the next 22 years, Florida was a guerrilla war zone.

MIAMI'S BEGINNINGS

Miami languished through the Civil War as an uncontested Confederate backwater, but after the South's defeat, it sprang back to life. In 1870, an Ohioan named William Brickell built a home and trading post on the Miami River. A fellow Clevelander, Ephraim Sturtevant, acquired land on Biscayne Bay. Clearing mangrove tangles a few miles south, settlers established a post office where mail was postmarked "Coconut Grove." Word of South Florida's tropical weather spread, luring adventurous travelers to Miami's first inn, the Bay View House, built on a rise now embraced by Peacock Park. The Biscayne Bay Yacht Club started up in 1887, and the following year a school opened. It was not until 1891, however, that the area found a civic leader with a vision for its future. Ephraim Sturtevant's daughter, Julia Sturtevant Tuttle, had visited in 1875 and returned from Ohio the widowed mother of a son and daughter. She purchased 640 acres—one square mile—on the north bank of the river and moved into the abandoned buildings of Fort Dallas. Surveying the shoreline, she determined to develop it into a major city.

A key requirement was a rail link to the rest of America. Tuttle sought out Henry Flagler. His Florida East Coast Railway had reached West Palm Beach some 70 miles north, but Miami struck him as an unworthy destination. A freak freeze during the winter of 1894–95 changed his mind. Most of Florida's citrus trees were stunted, but Miami's escaped the chill. The story is that Tuttle and her friends, William and Mary Brickell, brought healthy orange blossoms to the mogul, declaring Miami a meteorological oasis of sunshine and warmth. The ploy worked; on April 15, 1896, the first of Flagler's trains steamed into town. Flagler opened the luxurious Royal Palm Hotel for tourists lured south by promotions of "America's Sun Porch." He built houses for workers, dredged a ship channel in Biscayne Bay, and donated land for public schools. In July 1896, voters approved the city's incorporation. There was talk of naming it Flagler, but the 368 who cast ballots codified a name then more than two generations old, and Miami became an official Florida city.

MIAMI & THE SPANISH-AMERICAN WAR

The city was barely two years old in April 1898, when the United States took up arms against Spain over the issue of Cuba's independence. During the three months of the "Splendid Little War," as Secretary of State John Hay called it, Miami (population about 1,200) grew up fast. Initially the Army rejected the city as a base for training an invasion force, a decision bemoaned by every local businessman from Flagler on down. The mogul became an enthusiastic supporter, dismissing the onset of Miami's sweltering summers by assuring Army brass that a "constant sea breeze" guaranteed "the comfort of officers and men." There was no "pleasanter location on the Atlantic Coast." At his own expense, he broke ground for "Camp Miami." It was an offer impossible to refuse. Soon more than 7,000 recruits were living in canvas tents set up in what today is Downtown Miami near the Freedom Tower, sweltering in wool uniforms. Officers were put up at the airy Royal Palm.

For Miami merchants, it was indeed a splendid little war. Drugstores switched from selling lemonade by the glass to delivering it by the barrel; larger enterprises saw proportionate jumps in revenue. In North Miami, a hard-drinking red light district flowered. But Flagler's lie that Miami possessed an "inexhaustible supply of purest water" evaporated in the heat of typhoid fever that killed 24 recruits. Hundreds were felled by dysentery, and the mosquito-tormented soldiers nicknamed the base "Camp Hell." Flagler assured Washington that their "discomforts" were "grossly exaggerated." Luckily for all, the war ended, and Camp Hell was disbanded after a mere six weeks.

The military's sojourn in Miami, however, accelerated the city's development by clearing land, laying track, paving streets, digging wells, and constructing buildings. Even more important in terms of Miami's future was the war reporting that introduced the hitherto little known city to the nation. Thousands of young men returned to far more prosaic hometowns with a lingering sense of wonder and an unsatisfied curiosity.

MODERN MIAMI

For all its progress, as the 20th century dawned Miami was still little more than a strip of civilization sandwiched between Biscayne Bay and the Everglades wilderness 3 miles west. But America's demand for residential land increased, triggering development fever and conservationist fervor, two forces that immediately clashed and have figured in Miami-area politics ever since. Draining of the Everglades commenced in 1906. A decade later Royal Palm Park was dedicated, planting the seed of Everglades National Park. Carl Fisher, a wealthy industrialist from Indiana, crossed the new 2-mile wooden bridge to "Ocean Beach," a spit of sand and coral rock paralleling Miami's shoreline across Biscayne Bay. Gazing at the wilderness of bay cedar, seagrape, mangrove, sea oats, and prickly pear cactus, he had a vision of hotels, golf clubs, and polo fields, a pleasure Mecca incorporated in 1915 as Miami Beach.

By 1920 Miami's population stood at nearly 30,000—a 440-percent increase over the 1910 census. Word spread that an investment in

Henry Flagler's trains brought guests right to the door of the Royal Poinciana Hotel in 1896.

Florida land guaranteed fabulous returns—that today's swamp was tomorrow's subdivision. Thousands moved to Miami and its soggy environs, setting off the frenzied buying and selling of the Florida land boom. In 1925 developers sought permits for 971 subdivisions. Nearly 175,000 deeds were recorded in new sister communities like Coral Gables, Miami Shores, Hialeah, Miami Springs, Boca Raton, and Opa-Locka. The boom ended the following year with tax scandals and a devastating hurricane. The 1929 stock market collapse administered the coup de grace.

Miami's location, however, continued to entice visionaries such as Fisher, and Juan Trippe, founder of Pan American Airways. By 1935 Trippe's flying boats linked Miami to 32 Central and South American countries, bathing the city in the romantic glow of the glamorous new world of transoceanic aviation. World War II transformed the city back into a military town, turning hotels into barracks; beaches were used for drill, preparing 500,000 soldiers and 50,000 officers for combat. As with the Spanish-American War, thousands of young men and women would remember their time in the sun, and many would come back to stay.

CUBAN EXODUS

The postwar years were good to Greater Miami. The influx of newcomers continued, and tourism increased exponentially, spurring construction booms that produced pleasure palaces like Miami Beach's 1,206-room Hotel Fontainebleau, whose glittery opulence symbolized the region's status as the capital of hemispheric hedonism. The city appeared to have matured into a community best known for retirees and sun-seeking tourists, but history was about to deal it a wild card in the person of Fidel Castro. As the year 1958 came to a close, the 32-year-old rebel commander's guerrilla war waged against long-time Cuban dictator Fulgencio Batista sent the strongman fleeing into exile.

For Cuban refugees, Miami is the goal.

Castro's transformation of Cuba into a Communist state commenced with public executions and moved swiftly on to the confiscation of private industry and property. By the summer of 1960, the island's social elite and mercantile class—fearing political persecution and Communist indoctrination of their children—began to leave in droves, most aboard one of the half-dozen daily "Freedom Flights," a 250-mile hop from Havana to Miami. There were no round-trips on this route.

When the first refugees arrived, Miami's population was about 700,000. For every resident of Hispanic heritage—estimated then to number around 50,000—there were three African Americans, and about ten more in the demographic category of "All others," most of them white. By the mid-1970s Miami's Cuban refugee population stood at more than 300,000; today, Cuban Americans account for about 675,000 of Greater Miami's almost two million residents. Indeed, Miami is where more than half of all Cubans in the United States have chosen to live.

The profound transformation worked on the city's character by the Cubans' exodus, however, was less a result of numbers than of their backgrounds. Many were business people, professionals, or entrepreneurs whose enterprises ranged from small shops to sugar plantations, rum distilleries, and cigar factories. Many had worked in government and law enforcement, or taught in schools and universities. There were those for whom Castro's policies held the most draconian possibilities, and they arrived determined to reestablish themselves.

Their efforts reenergized the city while recreating neighborhoods reflecting the culture of pre-revolution Cuba. Streets were renamed after Cuban martyrs, moribund Cuban social clubs were revitalized, and trade organizations were set up. Cuban-owned small businesses, a mainstay of pre-Castro Cuba, sprang up all over Miami. Cuban grocery stores opened, while other stores added Cubano versions of coffee,

cheese, and bread to their shelves to serve their new clientele. The refugees' need for places to live generated a boom in housing renovation and construction. Cuban restaurants delighted tourists by offering an exotic alternative to Miami's familiar kosher delis, seafood emporiums, and traditional steak houses.

Today, more than 40 years after fleeing the island, Cuban Americans dominate Miami's roster of notables. In early 1999, the *New York Times* reported that "The mayors of the city

and county of Miami, the county police chief and the county state attorney are all Cuban-born or of Cuban descent. So are the president of the largest bank, the owner of the largest real estate developer, the managing partner of the largest law firm, nearly half of the county's 27-member delegation in the state Legislature and two of its six members of Congress.

"About the only accomplishment Cuban Americans cannot claim," the *Times* went on to observe, "is regaining their country."

Poverty, despair, and disappointment are the flip side of Miami's fabled immigrant success story, now into its fifth decade.

Cubans remain the region's single largest Latin American group, making up about 50 percent of the total Hispanic population, which accounts for more than half of Miami-Dade County's residents. In recent years, however, the influx of non-Cuban Hispanic immigrants has turned talk of Miami's "Cubanization" to its "Latin Americanization." The change is evident even in Little Havana, where store windows display Salvadoran corn pancakes, and restaurant waitresses are likely to be from Honduras or Peru. In contrast to a decade ago, the music and talk broadcast by Miami's highest-rated station is not Cuban, but Colombian—proving that the notion of the melting pot here remains a vital part of American life. ■

Culture

DO YOU ENJOY AUTHENTIC CARIBBEAN FESTIVITIES? YOU'LL FIND EVERY-thing here from Cuban block parties to Haitian nightclubs, from *moros y cristianos* (black beans and rice) with fried plantains to local blue crabs drenched in butter and garlic. For more traditional tastes, there are Western art galleries, orchestras, ballet, and off-Broadway productions, not to mention speedboat races and fishing tournaments.

FINE ARTS

Owing to the aggressive forays of Spanish adventurers in the New World commencing in the 16th century, South Florida's European-American history is a lengthy saga relative to other regions in North America. The lineage of Miami's cultural institutions runs back nearly as far, to the first missions established by Catholic priests who dreamed of imbuing Florida's native people with Christian faith and customs, and teaching them to speak and read Spanish so that they might someday be relied upon as kindred souls and loyal subjects of Madrid. It proved an unrealistic ambition, at least in those days, but the friars' determina-tion presaged a tradition among Miami-area settlers to found institutions of civilization in the tangled tropical jungles as soon as they could, as proof, perhaps mainly to themselves, that they had subdued the wilderness surrounding them.

The first artist of any note to work in Florida was America's great painter of wild birds, John James Audubon, who briefly explored the Keys in the 1830s. It was not until the arrival of railroads in the later years of the 19th century and the land booms of the early 20th century, however, that the Miami area acquired a moneyed class from which came its founding patrons of the arts. These families gave their names, their money, and often their private holdings to endow small yet elegant collections such as Miami's Bass Museum of Art (see p. 93), a treasury of old master paintings, sculptures, textiles, period furniture, objets d'art, and ecclesiastical arti-facts generally regarded as the finest of their kind in southeast Florida. Like many leading American pioneers in far-flung places, they promoted the establishment of schools and colleges whose roles in the community went beyond education to celebrate and nurture their community as well. Thus, within the walls of Greater Miami's leading learning institutions—the University of Miami, the Wolfson Campus of the Miami-Dade Community College, and Florida International University (see p. 59), most notably—you'll find some of the region's premier public art collections.

The successive influxes of the ethnic groups that characterize the metropolis today added a variety of culturally and ethnically themed museums, libraries, and memorials found in few other American cities. The flow-ering of Greater Miami's Jewish community, for example, is celebrated at Miami Beach's Jewish Museum of Florida (see p. 94). The continuing exodus of Cubans from their island home has transformed Miami into a surrogate Havana, where galleries, libraries, museums, restaurants, and nightclubs focus exclusively on Cuban art, literature, history, cuisine, and music. The arrival of other Caribbean émigrés, most notably Haitians, is reflected in the shops of Miami's Little Haiti district, and in the rise of ethnic theater com-panies, often itinerant troupes without a stage of their own, and the growing presence of Caribbean music on Miami's radio stations.

Miami's awareness of its political and financial roles as the unofficial capital of the Caribbean (some would say of Latin America as well) is the reason the city's downtown Miami Art Museum at the Miami-Dade Cultural Center is devoted to Western Hemispheric art since World War II, and why the Wolfson Campus of the Miami-Dade Community College, once primarily a show-case for innovative Miami area artists, maintains a noted collection of international works in its Interamerican Art Gallery. It is

The renowned sculptor Eduardo da Rosa, in front of one of his works in his Miami studio

a phenomenon reflecting the city's status as a cultural crossroad.

Open the Tropical Life section of the *Miami Herald* (which publishes a Spanish-language edition, *El Nuevo Herald*) and you'll find notices spanning the spectrum of the region's cultural colors: a panel discussion by Holocaust scholars and survivors; an exhibition of African-American artists working in Miami; a symposium on Eastern European issues; galleries featuring folk art produced in Miami by Caribbean newcomers. If there is a theme that unifies all this diversity, it is one of hope and faith in the future. Even Miami Beach's famed art deco hotel architecture is much more than merely an ornamental vogue. Originally built for sojourners from the Northeast, many of whom had fled European oppression, the buildings' jaunty upbeat styles, owing little to the past, still seem optimistic about this great metropolis's destiny, and that of the people who choose to live here.

PERFORMING ARTS

The sense of being at a geographic threshold that so many people feel upon arriving in Miami—a place where embarkation to far-away places hangs in the air and hints at exotic possibilities—has encouraged an unusually exuberant creative tradition in the region's roster of performing arts troupes. In the beginning, the impetus for putting up concert halls and theaters was civic pride among Miami's founding families, who wanted their cousins in the long-established cities of the Northeast to take seriously their outpost of progress under the palms. As elsewhere in young communities in the late 19th century, in Miami it was more often the custom for friends to gather in a parlor around a piano and entertain themselves by singing Broadway tunes, reciting poetry, and acting out plays. Ambitions soon extended beyond citrus growing, shipping, fishing, city building, and railroading, however, to garnish the growing settlement with more than homespun performances. An official brass band was formed to welcome travelers who rode the rails south to the sun. On occasion, Miami's wealthiest winter visitors invited musicians south for private concerts in estates such as Coconut Grove's palatial Vizcaya. Some

In 2006, the popular and highly regarded Miami City Ballet moved to its current home—the impressive Ziff Ballet Opera House, part of the Adrienne Arsht Center for the Performing Arts.

of the performers, seduced by the region's balmy weather and Miami's exotic fringe of azure sea, dazzling white sand, and gently rustling palms, saw not only a delightful comfort to be enjoyed, but opportunity to go from a back seat in an orchestra at home to the podium.

The influx of Northerners into the Miami area, many of them newcomers of European heritage and thus as fond of opera and classical music as Miami's native-born Yankees were of ragtime and vaudeville, created in the city

audiences who might not be wealthy but were sophisticated in their appreciation of the performing arts. Opera singers, string quartets, and orators were invited down from the Northeast to perform—invitations made all the more attractive by the prospect of exchanging winter chill for tropical sunshine. As often, these talented visitors stayed to become pioneers of the musical or thespian variety.

Greater Miami has proved to be as nurturing to start-up companies as it is to orchids. The Miami City Ballet held its inaugural performance in Miami in 1986; today it is one of the ten best-funded troupes in the United States (with a fiscal year 2007–2008 budget of approximately $12 million and enjoys the support of more than 14,000 season subscribers. In 2006 the opera moved to what is now called the Adrienne Arsht Center for the Performing Arts, an acoustically advanced hall with dramatic common areas.

The great odyssey of Cubans to South Florida, along with the city's proximity to the cultures of the Tropic of Cancer, is reflected in the variety and quality of its troupes. The *Miami Herald's* Tropical Life section on any day demonstrates the remarkable diversity of performances, from flamenco ballet to dancers interpreting the music of Eastern Europe, the Caribbean, West Africa, Israel, and Central and South America. On weekend evenings in Miami's Little Havana district (see pp. 49–60), a half-dozen clubs throb to the big-band sound of pre-Castro Cuban jazz, and contemporary music by young Cuban American musicians fusing the styles of both cultures.

Taking it easy and listening to live music at Miami's century-old Tobacco Road bar

For the same reasons, including long-standing cultural links with the Northeast in general and New York City's theater industry in particular, Greater Miami's playhouses draw on a small army of seasoned, well-schooled actors and an astonishingly fecund cadre of playwrights. The result is a year-round calendar of significant new works, as well as polished productions of perennially popular musicals and plays reflecting the region's kaleidoscopic creative multiculturalism.

Previewing Greater Miami's performing arts scene

Several excellent websites offer information on Miami's performing arts palette. One of the best is Event Guide Miami *(www.miami.event guide.com)*, a comprehensive day-by-day listing of happenings in the Greater Miami area. The alternative newspaper *Miami New Times* is a must-read during your stay. Its website *(www.miaminewtimes.com)* features reliable readers' recommendations on local bests. The *Miami Herald (www.herald.com)* offers a broad range of event notices and insights into Greater Miami's ethnic jambalaya. A large number of Greater Miami's performing arts organizations have websites enabling you to peruse upcoming playbills and, in many cases, buy tickets online.

OTHER CULTURAL ATTRACTIONS OF NOTE

Subtropical weather and the Caribbean influence have filled Greater Miami's calendar with a never-ending pageant of festivals and cultural events. Their variety reflects the region's diversity: concerts, operas, ballets, flower shows, speedboat races, fishing tournaments, marathons.

Be sure to explore ethnic districts on foot if your schedule permits doing so—they're full of exotica. Book and music stores sell the songs and stories of the Caribbean, Africa—even pre-war Europe—and offer uniquely personal insights into the unusual bloodlines of this one-of-a-kind American metropolis.

The region's unusual tradition of whimsical experimentation in architecture is seen in few other American cities, and is a continuing phenomenon inspired by the hopefulness and optimism so many feel here. Take the time to visit some of Greater Miami's distinctive neighborhoods, such as El Portal, and adjoining communities such as Coral Gables and Opa-locka.

Pick up one of Miami's informative daily or weekly newspapers and open its pages (and your mind) to the unfamiliar. Here, if the trade winds bring a purple sky that rains on your beach party, you still have plenty of places to go and countless things to do.

The best source for festival information is the *Travel Planner,* updated annually and distributed free by the Greater Miami Convention & Visitors Bureau. Use the bureau's website *(www.gmcvb.com)* to obtain a copy by mail. ■

Miami is one of America's best known, least understood cities. Like New York and Los Angeles, it conjures up images (some accurate, some not) of a place unlike any other city in the United States.

Miami's central districts

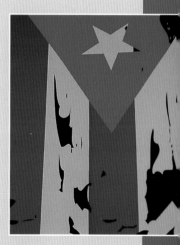

Cuban flag poster

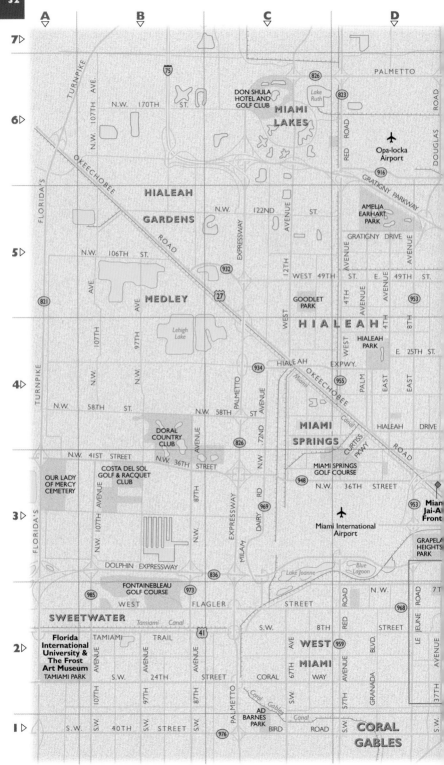

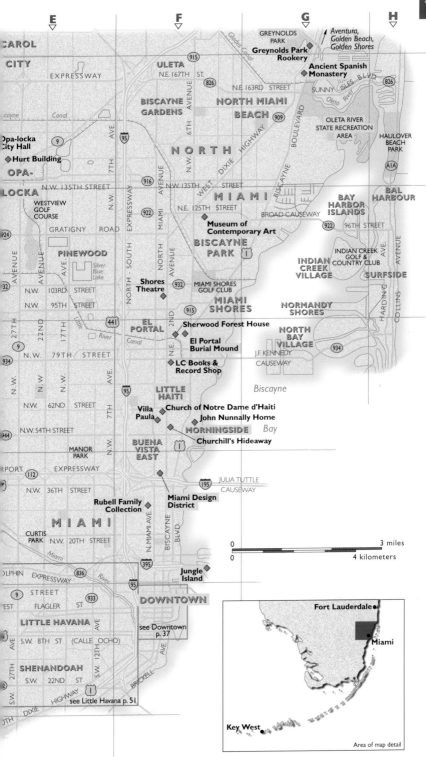

E F G H

CAROL
CITY
EXPRESSWAY

ULETA
N.E. 167TH ST.

GREYNOLDS PARK
Greynolds Park
Rookery

*Aventura,
Golden Beach,
Golden Shores*

Ancient Spanish
Monastery

BISCAYNE
GARDENS

NORTH MIAMI
BEACH

N.E. 163RD STREET

SUNNY ISLES BLVD.

Opa-locka
City Hall
Hurt Building

OPA-
LOCKA

N.W. 135TH STREET

WESTVIEW
GOLF
COURSE

GRATIGNY ROAD

PINEWOOD

Silver
Blue
Lake

N.W. 103RD STREET

N.W. 95TH STREET

N O R T H

M I A M I

N.E. 125TH STREET

BROAD CAUSEWAY

Museum of
Contemporary Art

BISCAYNE
PARK

MIAMI SHORES
GOLF CLUB

OLETA RIVER
STATE RECREATION
AREA

HAULOVER
BEACH
PARK

BAY
HARBOR
ISLANDS

96TH STREET

INDIAN CREEK
GOLF &
COUNTRY CLUB

INDIAN
CREEK
VILLAGE

BAL
HARBOUR

SURFSIDE

NORMANDY
SHORES

Shores
Theatre

EL
PORTAL

Sherwood Forest House

El Portal
Burial Mound

LC Books &
Record Shop

MIAMI
SHORES

NORTH
BAY
VILLAGE

J.F. KENNEDY
CAUSEWAY

Biscayne

LITTLE
HAITI

Villa
Paula

Church of Notre Dame d'Haiti
John Nunnally Home

MORNINGSIDE

Churchill's Hideaway

Bay

BUENA
VISTA
EAST

MANOR
PARK

RPORT EXPRESSWAY

N.W. 36TH STREET

Rubell Family
Collection

Miami Design
District

JULIA TUTTLE
CAUSEWAY

M I A M I

CURTIS
PARK

N.W. 20TH STREET

DOLPHIN EXPRESSWAY

STREET

FLAGLER ST

DOWNTOWN

*see Downtown
p. 37*

Jungle
Island

LITTLE HAVANA

S.W. 8TH ST. (CALLE OCHO)

SHENANDOAH

S.W. 22ND ST

see Little Havana p. 51

0   3 miles
0   4 kilometers

Fort Lauderdale

Miami

Key West

Area of map detail

Miami's central districts

THOUGH FLAMBOYANT MIAMI BEACH TENDS TO GARNER MORE ATTENTION than its mainland sister city, the heart and soul of what makes Greater Miami a truly international metropolis and the commercial center of South Florida lie in Miami's central districts. Here you'll find some of the region's oldest neighborhoods, often a short walk from the highest concentrations of immigrant newcomers, creating the city's exotic juxtapositions of cultures. Here, too, are most of the financial interests that use Miami as a base for hemispheric operations, and the power base of Miami's determined, passionately political Cuban-American leadership.

The steady influx of immigrants makes accurate population counts difficult, but most assessments suggest that fewer than a quarter of central Miami's residents remain in the category of non-Latin whites who originally settled the community. Estimates of the central districts' non-Cuban Caribbean citizenry— primarily Haitians, Puerto Ricans, Jamaicans, Bahamians, and Dominicans—currently range in the vicinity of a quarter-million, creating an inner city tableau in which one out of every three faces is Caribbean.

Miami's central districts hold some of the city's best known tourist attractions and cultural institutions, most of its most significant archaeological sites, and prime examples of the fanciful residential "theme" architectures that characterize the entire region. Miami's heart also wears the region's social problems on its sleeve: minority unemployment and despair, homelessness and pockets of economic blight. But Miami has a long record of overcoming hardships, and everywhere in Miami's center you'll find construction and renovation work under way, propelled perhaps less by the region's resilient economy than by Miamians' conviction that their city is destined to become a cosmopolitan and influential hemispheric capital.

A note on navigating Miami's central districts: The city's streets are generally numbered according to an east–west, north–south orientation. Although you will almost certainly encounter exceptions, most avenues, courts, places, and roads run north–south, while most streets, drives, lanes, and terraces run east–west. The division between east and west is Miami Avenue; Flagler Street divides north from south. Street prefixes reflecting the compass rose—N., S., E., W., N.W., N.E., S.W., and S.E.—are assigned according to the road's position relative to the intersection of Miami and Flagler. Avenues, beginning with First, count upward the farther west and southwest they lie from Miami Avenue. Streets, starting with First, are numbered progressively according to their distance from Flagler Street. Downtown Miami is largely arranged according to a grid of right angles, permitting easy around-the-block recoveries from missed turns while exploring by car. But beware: Many streets, avenues, etc. are numbered but also have names (for example, in Miami, S.W. 13th Street is also known as Coral Way, and US 1 is known as Biscayne Boulevard in the north, Brickell Avenue in the center, and South Dixie Highway in the south). ■

Left: Cuban- and Anglo-Americans make up the bulk of Miami's population, but the city has drawn residents from all over South and Central America and the Caribbean. Right: Colorful wall folk art adorns many buildings in Little Haiti.

Downtown Miami

Opinions of Downtown Miami differ. Grand from a distance, the financial district's skyscrapers are not particularly people-friendly when confronted close-up. Travelers can be disoriented (and disappointed) by the downtown area's seeming lack of a center or a unifying social current. There is no Boulevard St.-Germain here, no Upper West Side to stroll on weekends; and come evening, downtown sidewalks become deserted and not the safest place to wander.

Fireworks explode over Downtown Miami during the Fourth of July celebrations.

There is less disagreement about downtown's dimensions, which are generally said to fall between N.E. 15th Street and S.E. 14th Street, and run from the Biscayne Bay waterfront to I-95. Within this 28-block-wide embrace lies a district that can be rewarding to those who explore it on foot. You'll find street vendors selling brewed coffee and Caribbean-style pastries, cakes, juices, and fruit drinks. Spanish-language music radio blares from the entrances of low-priced emporiums occupying sidewalk-level storefronts (many specializing in consumer electronics, luggage, clothing, and jewelry and catering mainly to a year-round traffic of Latin American shoppers), creating a peculiar blend of North and Latin American retailing. Venture a few blocks west of Biscayne Boulevard (the main thoroughfare closest to the waterfront) and you find yourself in a cultural mélange—Haitian here, Jamaican there, now Puerto Rican, now Central or South American—a mix of frenetic shops, hole-in-the-wall lunch counters, and Cuban cafeterias serving powerful *café Cubano* by the cup, on the sidewalk.

Downtown is polyglot; Spanish is ubiquitous and Creole is heard often, as are Hebrew and Brazilian Portuguese. On some streets, Rastafarians brush elbows with Orthodox Jews, and their sidewalk shops occasionally adjoin. It is a city evolving toward a cosmopolitan character that holds a vision of a uniquely American future.

Walk east on Flagler Street from its intersection with Miami Avenue, and you will encounter handsome relics of Miami's past, architectural jewels such as the Walgreen's drugstore chain's streamline moderne flagship (now a Sports Authority store) at N.E. Second Avenue and, beside it, the ornate 1926 Florentine Renaissance Ingraham Building, its lobby a study in art deco. Some call the 1939 Depression moderne Alfred I. duPont Building, at 169 E. Flagler, Miami's answer to New York's Rockefeller Center. (The exquisite murals arching above the ornate lobby were inspired by Florida's history and the era's dogged determination to believe in a better future.) At 174 E. Flagler you'll encounter the Spanish-Moorish Olympia Building. Inside, the Gusman Center for the Performing Arts occupies a movie theater built in 1925 by the Paramount

Pictures studio in the style of a Mediterranean courtyard, now a prime venue for screenings during Miami's annual film festival.

The cacophonous throng of humanity swirls around downtown until mid-afternoon, then quickly thins as shadows of high-rise buildings lengthen. By evening the only people you're likely to find here are tourists looking lost. ■

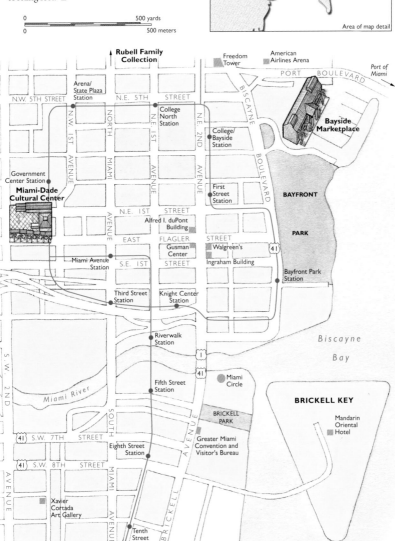

MIAMI

MIAMI BEACH

CORAL GABLES

Port of Miami

Area of map detail

| 0 | 500 yards |
| 0 | 500 meters |

Rubell Family Collection

Freedom Tower

American Airlines Arena

PORT BOULEVARD

Port of Miami

Arena/ State Plaza Station

N.W. 5TH STREET

N.E. 5TH STREET

College North Station

College/ Bayside Station

BISCAYNE

Bayside Marketplace

N.W. 1ST AVENUE

NORTH

N.E. 1ST

N.E. 2ND AVENUE

MIAMI AVENUE

BOULEVARD

Government Center Station

Miami-Dade Cultural Center

First Street Station

BAYFRONT

N.E. 1ST STREET

Alfred I. duPont Building

EAST FLAGLER STREET

Gusman Center

Walgreen's

41

PARK

Miami Avenue Station

S.E. 1ST STREET

Ingraham Building

Bayfront Park Station

Third Street Station

Knight Center Station

Riverwalk Station

Biscayne

I

Bay

41

S.W. 2ND

Miami River

Fifth Street Station

Miami Circle

BRICKELL KEY

BRICKELL PARK

Mandarin Oriental Hotel

41 S.W. 7TH STREET

SOUTH

Greater Miami Convention and Visitor's Bureau

Eighth Street Station

MIAMI AVENUE

41 S.W. 8TH STREET

AVENUE

Xavier Cortada Art Gallery

AVENUE

Tenth Street Promenade Station

BRICKELL

Brickell Banking/ Commercial District

MIAMI-DADE PUBLIC LIBRARY

Miami-Dade Cultural Center

Miami-Dade Cultural Center

DOWNTOWN'S LONG-DISCUSSED LACK OF A CENTER WAS addressed in the late 1970s and 1980s by a much-debated redevelopment project that amounted to a total makeover of its western flank. The centerpiece (and most successful aspect) of this ambitious undertaking is the 3.3-acre Philip Johnson-designed Miami-Dade Cultural Center complex between First and Flagler Streets, home to the Miami Art Museum, the Historical Museum of Southern Florida, and the city's premier repository of books and historical documents, the Miami-Dade Public Library. Johnson's creation was labeled "neo-Mediterranean," and in fact the tiled plaza has the ambience of a public place alongside that Old World sea. Chairs and benches offer an opportunity for a peaceful respite away from downtown street and sidewalk traffic. The historical museum and the Miami Art Museum (Center for the Fine Arts) adjoin, and you should visit both.

MIAMI ART MUSEUM

Though its imposing facade might suggest an omnibus approach, the museum's collection showcases international art, from the perspective of the Americas, from World War II to the present. Exhibitions change regularly and their quality is high, with a growing reputation; in the museum's large pleasant galleries you will certainly see some things you recognize from books and art postcards, but there are also many surprises—unfamiliar works

HISTORICAL MUSEUM OF SOUTHERN FLORIDA

The task is formidable: to chronicle in a comprehensible way some ten millennia of human life along these shores. The museum does it brilliantly, using traditional and state-of-the-art interactive exhibitions and installations, such as an old Miami streetcar. You can explore the galleries on your own or on a guided tour (check schedules when you arrive). Exhibits depict Miami and its environs centuries before Europe knew of the New World (including the Miami Circle; see p. 48). In the **Folklife Collection** you can trace the human odysseys that brought so many cultures to the Florida peninsula, right up through this century's Jewish and Cuban communities.

One popular exhibit recounts the unusual influence that railroads had in bringing Miami and the rest of South Florida into the American cultural mainstream. The emphasis of the museum is on understanding the social forces that produced this region's unusual history and unique character. One of its more appealing and memorable aspects is a collection of more than a million historical images—from primitive

by modern masters and artists surely destined for similar recognition in the future. This is an especially fine archive of work from Central and South America, the Caribbean islands, Europe, Asia and the Middle East, and also from South Florida.

Miami Art Museum
www.miamiartmuseum.org
✉ 101 W. Flagler St.
☎ 305/375-3000
🕐 Closed Mon.
$ $–$$

Historical Museum of Southern Florida
www.hmsf.org
✉ 101 W. Flagler St.
☎ 305/375-1492
🕐 Closed major holidays
$ $

A fanciful bronze statue in the Miami-Dade Cultural Center's historical museum depicts a Seminole Indian youth with South Florida's largest reptile.

Miami-Dade Public Library

www.mdpls.org

✉ 101 W. Flagler St. at N.W. Ist Ave.

☎ 305/375-2665 (Miami Beach branch: 2100 Collins Ave., tel 305/535-4219)

🕐 Closed Sun. July–Sept.

painted portraits to historical family photographs—whose countenances gaze out from a past still echoing in the faces streaming along the sidewalks outside. Don't overlook the museum's gift shop, whose thoughtfully chosen inventory reflects these themes. The exhibitions, which change often, include some shows designed to be especially appealing

Miami's public art programs decorate parks and squares with unusual sculpture. One example, "Dropped Bowl," frames a downtown spire.

to younger visitors. Call ahead to reserve a place on group tours in languages other than English, and for walking tour prices and times.

MIAMI-DADE PUBLIC LIBRARY

You need not be a scholar to appreciate and enjoy this handsome library, which holds more than four million books and artifacts. Scholars work here, often in its special collections.

There's art as well in the first floor auditorium and in the lobby on the second floor. While on the first floor, look up at the domed ceiling of the cupola to see trompe l'oeil clouds and a pungent quote from Shakespeare's *Hamlet* on words and meaning, both works of public art by the distinctive California-based modernist Edward Ruscha (roo-SHAY). A big draw is changing exhibitions in the auditorium, usually of photographs and paintings relating to Miami's past and present. Many photos are drawn from the library's **Romer Collection** (archived in the Helen Muir Florida Collection), a resource of 17,500 prints and negatives documenting Miami history. (View some wonderful images of old Miami online at www.mdpls.org/databases/ Romer_Site/search_romer.asp.) You might have time to attend screenings at the library's **Louis C. Wolfson Media Center,** an archive of cinema and television founded by one of Florida's leading movie-theater chain owners. Don't be embarrassed to duck inside simply for the relief of its air-conditioning. ∎

Painting Miami

Downtown's skyscrapers are illuminated in color after dark to celebrate a season or a holiday, salute a charity or foreign dignitary, encourage a local athletic club, or just inspire a sigh. There are 40 permanently illuminated high-rises in

Miami. Some, such as the Bank of America Tower, change colors up to 100 times a year. Red and orange probably mean a salute to the Miami Heat basketball team. Orange and aqua are the colors of the Miami Dolphins football team. ∎

Rubell Family Collection

ANOTHER ARCHIVE OF THE NEW IS THE EXTRAORDINARY treasury of contemporary art collected by Don and Mera Rubell, which some critics insist is among the most significant contemporary fine art collections in the world. (The Rubells, originally from New York, also own Miami Beach's stylishly upscale Albion Hotel; a family member, Steve Rubell, was a co-founder of Manhattan's famed Studio 54 nightclub.)

Below: A visitor contemplates a contemporary work at the Rubell museum.

The collection bills itself as exhibiting "provocative works from the 1960s to the present," and delivers by featuring the likes of Jeff Koons, Keith Haring, Cindy Sherman, Jean-Michel Basquiat, Paul McCarthy, and Charles Ray, along with notable newcomers. It is certainly the most audacious private collection open to the public in Miami, with its works being displayed in a very large split-level warehouse-like industrial space in the Wynwood Arts District. What you'll find is a museum of works representing virtually every artist who has achieved note in the last two decades.

As the writer Tom Wolfe noted in his book *The Painted Word*, modern art sustains a contentious intellectual offshoot by its astonishing ability to evoke emotion and provoke debate about what is art—evidenced in the Rubells' museum by a formidable library of writings about the phenomenon. The collection is open Friday through Sunday in the afternoon, or by appointment. ■

Rubell Family Collection
www.rubellfamilycollection
.com

🅰 33 F3
✉ 95 N.W. 29th St., between N.W. 1st & N. Miami Aves.
☎ 305/573-6090
🕐 Open Wed.–Sat., 10 a.m. to 5 p.m.
💲 $–$$

Suggesting early 20th-century depictions of future cities, a computer-controlled MetroMover train traverses Downtown Miami.

Downtown Miami by MetroMover

It's free and takes less than an hour, but two scenic loops on the city's elevated MetroMover trains will enable you to reconnoiter the whole of downtown—the area between the bay and N.W. First Avenue, and the north–south stretch bounded by N.E. 15th and S.W. 14th Streets—and get a clear sense of the Central Business District's layout, making subsequent trips through the grid less confusing.

Taking the air-conditioned, driverless, computer-operated coaches is easier and often cooler than roaming downtown on foot. Be sure to take the easy-to-read Miami-Dade County Transit Map with you to track your journey (available without charge at the Government Center station at 138 N.W. Third Street, at all visitor information centers, and at *www.co.miami-dade.fl.us/transit/Transit_Schedules.asp*), an essential guide to the county's wide-ranging bus system. There are two MetroMover loops, and you should take both for a comprehensive tour.

INNER LOOP

The Inner Loop circles the business district, and permits transfer to a spur running north near the bayfront to N.W. 15th Street. On your way there you will pass **Bayfront Park** (see p. 44). Just north of the College/Bayside

station (after you switch trains) is the **Freedom Tower,** rising above Biscayne Boulevard; it was completed in 1924, and once served as home to the long-gone *Miami News.* Offices here processed requests for political asylum during the first wave of Cuban immigration (see pp. 22–25). Its neighborhood is trying to transition from being down-at-the-heel to modern and dynamic. The highlight is the 14-story, 20,000-seat bayfront **American Airlines Arena,** whose opening ceremony was a Gloria Estefan concert on December 31, 1999. The Miami Heat professional basketball team plays here. Its unusual design, a whirlwind of concrete and steel, is the work of Miami's high-profile architectural firm, Arquitectonica.

Just past the Park West station the route skirts **Bicentennial Park.** To the north is the massive **Port of Miami,** serving Miami's heavy cruise ship traffic, with shops and

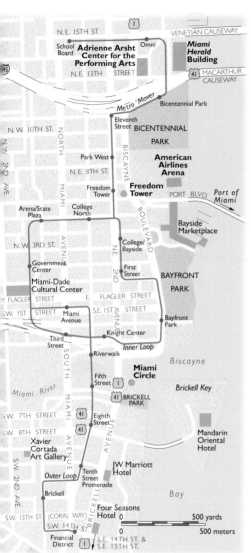

 See also area map p. 37
► Government Center station (at Miami-Dade Cultural Center)
↔ 4.4 miles
⏱ 1 hour
► Government Center station

NOT TO BE MISSED
- Bayfront Park (depart train)
- Freedom Tower (view from train only)
- Adrienne Arsht Center for the Performing Arts
- Bayside Marketplace

BRICKELL AVENUE OUTER LOOP

Your destination is the **Financial District** station near Brickell and S.W. 14th Street. (Transfer to the Financial District train at the Third Street station.) Once a boulevard of grand estates, Brickell is still trod by moguls; not railroaders anymore, but financiers inhabiting the office and luxury condominium towers shading the street. South of the Riverwalk station there is a good view up and down the Miami River, where the Tequesta first settled. You can even see the grass covering a 2000-year-old, 38-foot Indian ruin that was discovered in 1998 and awaits public viewing (see p. 48). The few older wooden houses along the way are survivors of Miami's first suburb. The train reverses direction at the Financial District station.

If you have a half-hour to spare and feel like taking a pleasant walk through an upscale neighborhood of posh condominiums, walk east from the MetroMover's Financial District station to Bayshore via 14th Street—here designated S.E. 14th Street, as are all local streets on the bay side of Brickell below the Miami River. Follow S.E. 14th's arc south to S.E. 15th Street, which loops west back to Brickell, a few blocks south of the Financial District station. ∎

restaurants. As you glide over Interstate 395, which crosses Biscayne Bay to Miami Beach over the MacArthur Causeway, look inland to check out the beautiful new **Adrienne Arsht Center for the Performing Arts,** a two-block-square opera, ballet, and symphony complex that opened in 2006.

Ahead are the **headquarters of the *Miami Herald*** and its Spanish-language alter ego, *El Nuevo Herald.*

Tragedy
begets beauty
in Bayfront Park:
The *Challenger*
disaster inspired
this eye-lifting
sculpture by
Japanese master
Isamu Noguchi.

Bayfront Park

IN 1926, THIS ROLLING, TREE-SHADED GREEN FLANKING Biscayne Boulevard was built up with fill dredged from Biscayne Bay. Here, in 1933, an assassin fired his revolver at Franklin Delano Roosevelt, missing the newly elected president but fatally wounding Chicago mayor Anton Cermak. Pleasanter political memories are evoked by the Claude and Mildred Pepper Fountain. (Congressman Pepper, who died in his 90s, ended his long career as a champion of the rights of America's aged.)

Bayfront Park
- Map p. 37
- Between S.E. 2nd & N.E. 2nd Sts.

The fountain is a magnet for the romantic, particularly on warm evenings. The imposing figure from another time guarding the park's eastern edge is that of Cristóbal Colón, better known as Christopher Columbus. His statue is a 1953 gift to Miami from the Italians, Colón's countrymen.

Another memorial, a stark and subdued double helix, rises at the park's southeastern edge. Created by Japanese sculptor Isamu Noguchi, the monument commemorates the seven astronauts who died in 1986 when NASA's space shuttle *Challenger* exploded soon after its launch from Cape Canaveral. Noguchi, an inspired minimalist, presided over the

park's 1987 makeover. The intricate brickwork of Biscayne Boulevard, reminiscent of promenades on the beach in Rio de Janeiro, is the work of Brazilian landscape architect Robert Burle Marx.

The park still hosts a cross-section of Miami life—families on picnics, Caribbean steel drummers, strolling lovers, tourists, elderly chess players, and people exercising dogs. Its open-air amphitheater often reverberates with music, and every night a laser light show pierces the Miami sky with glowing beams of vivid electronic colors. Even if nothing is happening, you will remember the views of Biscayne Bay and the Port of Miami from the park's waterside promenade. ■

A wall mural on Little Havana's main street depicts life in pre-Castro Cuba, evoking the nostalgic yearning of many Cuban exiles to return to their homeland.

Little Havana

This 30-block neighborhood, centering around S.W. Eighth Street (Calle Ocho), is to Miami what Little Italy is to New York: an ethnic beachhead where immigrants began the American chapter of their saga, cushioned by familiar traditions.

Little Havana begins near Brickell Avenue's Banker's Row and runs west, crossing the Miami River and petering out in residential neighborhoods around Florida International University near Sweetwater. Many of Little Havana's better known attractions are on or near S.W. Eighth between S. Miami Avenue and S.W. 27th Avenue. (Calle Ocho refers to S.W. Eighth Street in particular and the surrounding Little Havana district in general, as Wall Street denotes all of Lower Manhattan's financial district.) The Cubans were followed here by Central and South American immigrants, notably Nicaraguans, Salvadorans, and Dominicans. Their restaurants are interspersed among long-established Cuban bistros, fruit stands *(puestos de frutas)*, and shoe-shine stands *(limpiabotas)*. Sidewalk coffee windows *(cafetines)* serve up appetizing *media noche* sandwiches and tall glasses of *mojitos*, and espressolike *cafecitos* that pump up enthusiasm for *juegos de domino*,

sidewalk domino games played by men in Panama hats.

Some critics have called Calle Ocho's downscale business strip seedy, and feel its virtues as a tourist attraction have been oversold. Newcomers expecting a Disneyland version of Old Havana or an ethnic enclave with the exotic density of San Francisco's Chinatown will be disappointed.

Still, Little Havana's vibrancy can be beguiling, especially on weekends, when its clubs are thronged by aficionados of Latin music and dancing and its best restaurants do reservations-only business.

Calle Ocho's heart beats strongly between S.W. 12th and S.W. 27th Avenues, a stretch officially designated the Latin Quarter. You should be aware, however, as on many urban streets, there is risk in wandering away from busy lighted areas at night, or parking in places that become deserted after dark. Use common sense. ■

Calle Ocho walk

If you can look at Little Havana and empathize with its evident nostalgia for a way of life lost to its residents some 40 years ago, you will forgive Calle Ocho's aesthetic shortfalls—the occasionally bogus "Caribbean" decoration, the hand-lettered signage—and admire its sanguine humanity.

To start your walking tour in the heart of Little Havana, take Metrobus No. 8 from Miami Avenue and Flagler Street near the Miami-Dade Cultural Center. A good place to get off the No. 8 for your stroll east is at Calle Ocho's intersection with 36th Avenue.

As you amble east along S.W. Eighth Street, you will see sidewalk cafés (cafeterias) and lunch counters (fondas) where locals sip café Cubano, an espresso-style jolt, from shot glass-size paper cups. Consider making a dinner reservation for later in the evening at **Versailles ❶** (3555 S.W. 8th St., tel 305/444-0240; see p. 245), which draws patrons from all over town. The fare is traditional (rich, spicy, and sweet), including everything from arroz con pollo (rice with chicken) to roast pork to flan in oversized portions. Versailles is the Cuban community's most endearing restaurant, and political events tied to Elian Gonzalez and the latest Cuban rafter have often taken place here. But Anglos will also enjoy the festive ambience of a pre-Castro Havana, and everyone enjoys the walls of mirrors and etched glass that enable indirect people-watching.

Two blocks east lies the gothic **Woodlawn Park Cemetery ❷,** which has a black marble tribute to the Unknown Cuban Freedom Fighter and the graves of three former Cuban presidents. The cemetery, which opened in 1913, also has a memorial to the victims of South Florida's tragic 1935 hurricane, the Category 5 Labor Day storm that ravaged the Florida keys and points north, claiming over 400 victims in its path.

Women pushing babies in strollers carry string-tied pink boxes from pastry shops (dulcerías). At S.W. 32nd Avenue you will find plenty to tempt you. One of the best bakeries

Wall mural in Calle Ocho

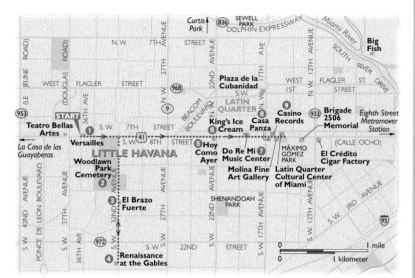

is **El Brazo Fuerte** ❸ *(1697 S.W. 32nd Ave., tel 305/444-7720),* where, save for the fresh bread and Cuban crackers, virtually everything is sugar-coated, caramelized, or topped with meringue. Try a *pastelito,* whose sweet dough is stuffed with meat, guava, or cream cheese, or one of the custard Napoleons called *señoritas,* or *masareales,* guava pastries so sweet they can make you light-headed.

Lunch carts, called *fritangas,* selling roasted meat *(carne asada)* with tortillas, beans, and rice, are wheeled along mostly by Nicaraguan newcomers. Usually on their bill of fare are *baho,* a meat-and-vegetable stew, and *nacatamal,* a tamale filled with rice, pork, potatoes, green olives, and prunes and wrapped in a banana leaf. For something cool, order a *guarapo,* sweetened by a syrupy

🅝 See also area map p. 33
▶ Intersection of S.W. 8th St. & 36th Ave.
↔ 6.75 miles
🕒 3 hours
▶ MetroMover's 8th St. station

NOT TO BE MISSED

- Versailles
- El Brazo Fuerte
- Hoy Como Ayer
- King's Ice Cream

extract from sugarcane stalks, or a *cocofrio,* whipped up from coconut milk.

For nouvelle Cuban cuisine, you can try **Renaissance at the Gables** ❹ *(2340*

Beating the Miami heat

Those unused to South Florida's summer heat and humidity may find it daunting. Don't bring your woolens. Dress appropriately in clothing that doesn't betray dampness. An excellent solution: the elegant *guayabera,* the traditional Cuban smock shirt ubiquitous in Miami, even in business settings. Typically made from sheer white linen and cut generously

large, a guayabera also makes a practical souvenir. Calle Ocho's best known source is La Casa de las Guayaberas *(5840 S.W. 8th St., tel 305/266-9683).* A handkerchief is handy for blotting away perspiration. Last, just ignore the heat. Don't even mention it. Miamians know that surrendering to it—sweating without fretting—is the first step toward conquering it. ■

CALLE OCHO WALK

Grief over a homeland lost, and for many who perished trying to regain it, is often in evidence in Little Havana.

S.W. 32nd Ave., tel 305/445-1313), which features live entertainment Wednesday through Saturday nights.

Back on Calle Ocho, watch for **Hoy Como Ayer** ⑤ (2212 S.W. 8th St., tel 305/541-2631), where on Thursday, Friday, and Saturday nights various Latin bands perform the music of yesteryear. Dark, hot, and thumping with Latin beats and sexy patrons, this is one of Little Havana's most popular bars. Even Mick Jagger and Bono have reportedly visited.

Find **King's Ice Cream** ⑥ (1831 S.W. 8th St., tel 305/643-1842), and order a scoop of something mysterious, like *guanabana* or *mamey,* or perhaps something slightly more familiar, like coconut or mango. Next door, at No. 1829, is the **Do Re Mi Music Center** ⑦ (tel 305/541-3374), an emporium of Cuban music, including reissues from pre-Castro decades, when Havana nightclubs reverberated with big-band jazz. Calle Ocho is Miami's top bazaar for music from Latin and South America, and also from Spain. Flamenco dancers perform at tiny

Casa Panza ⑧, a husband-and-wife affair (1620 S.W. 8th St., tel 305/643-5343) known for superb Spanish fare. The festivities carry on late into the night, or rather well into the morning, seven days a week.

Nearby **Casino Records** ⑨ (1646 S.W. 8th St., tel 305/642-7522) displays recordings according to their country of origin. You can catch the MetroMover from the Eighth Street station (59 S.E. 8th St.).

After a couple of more blocks you will reach **Brigade 2506 Memorial**, a poignantly simple tribute to the scores of Cuban exiles who lost their lives in the Bay of Pigs invasion in 1961 (see p. 53). Across from it lies **Máximo Gómez Park**, nicknamed Domino Park for the game that is played here by visitors, most of whom are old men (see p. 57).

Retrace your route if you are returning to Versailles for dinner. Just west of the restaurant, the **Teatro Bellas Artes** (3713 S.W. 8th St., tel 305/325-0515) is known for its Saturday midnight revue of beautiful, lip-synching cross-dressers who sway to Latin pop hits. ■

Brigade 2506 Memorial

SOME MONUMENTS AGE QUICKLY, BUT WHERE CALLE Ocho crosses S.W. 13th Avenue—the latter better known in Little Havana as Memorial Boulevard—even after more than four decades, a simple stone monument with an eternal flame stirs strong emotions. If there had been additional troops of equal determination backing up the 2506th brigade, the outcome might well have been different. However, within three days the force of about 1,300 Cubans who had committed themselves to overthrowing Fidel Castro found themselves terribly alone, especially in the hours after landing near Cuba's south coast Bahia de Cochinos (Bay of Pigs) on April 17, 1961. Newspapers were soon calling the adventure a fiasco.

Brigade 2506 Memorial

Map p. 51

It began in Miami, among Cubans determined to free their island from Castro's two-year-old grip. Encouraged, trained, and bankrolled by the CIA, and convinced that the American government was solidly behind them, they felt assured of air support and other aid. (During the 1960 presidential campaign, John F. Kennedy had proposed that America support Cuban exiles in an invasion.)

Most of the counterrevolutionaries had little or no combat experience or training. Many hit the beach wearing T-shirts and tennis shoes, carrying out-of-date rifles. The Cuban populace failed to rise up in support of them; the expected air support didn't come. Castro, a rifle in one hand and a cigar in the other, led his troops to battle. Ninety-four of the brigade were killed, the rest given 30-year prison sentences. Some two years later, they were back in Miami, ransomed by 62 million dollars in public and private funds. (Among the survivors was the father of pop star Gloria Estefan.) The inscription on the memorial recalls "the Martyrs of the Invasion Brigade of April 17, 1961." ∎

LITTLE HAVANA'S CHANGING FACES

As new immigrants arrive, Little Havana is becoming more cosmopolitan. By 2000, the U.S. Census revealed that Cuban Americans dropped to only 48 percent of the district's 93,000 residents. Nicaraguans made up 12 percent; Hondurans, 5 percent; Guatemalans, Puerto Ricans, and Colombians each 2 percent. Over the past decade, as Cuban Americans have assimilated into mainstream America, many have moved into Greater Miami neighborhoods while other Spanish-speaking immigrants from the Caribbean, Central and South America have taken their place. ∎

Plotting Castro's overthrow

During 1960 and 1961, Manuel Artime went often to the unremarkable little ranch-style house on Poinciana Avenue, between Le Jeune and Douglas, just inside Miami's city limits. Shaded by trees and secluded behind a high fence, it was rented by a tall man who wrote spy novels in his spare time. His name was E. Howard Hunt, a CIA agent with whom Artime and his comrades, including former Cuban officials, were designing a government to replace Fidel Castro's regime. Years later, Hunt recalled with amusement a neighbor lady who, noting the late-night gatherings of men always without women, gossiped to others her suspicions about his sexual orientation. "She got me a date with her recently divorced daughter," said the operative, who would later spend 32 months in prison for his role in the Nixon-era Watergate break-in. "Inasmuch as I was married, which of course I couldn't reveal to my neighbor, I guess the daughter—when I didn't make any advances—confirmed her mother's suspicions. Which was fine. It was an additional layer of cover, you could say." The house is now gone. ∎

New World cuisine

It was born in Greater Miami among chefs inspired by the region's emergence as a crossroads of diverse culinary traditions. Its catchwords are "fresh" and "healthy," its signature includes fresh fruit as a major component of meals, and the more exotic the better. You will find them served in fruit salads and salsas, chutneys and slaws, compotes and desserts. They're mixed into breads, ice cream, and mousses, pureed into sauces and spreads, even fermented into wine. Key limes, kiwis, mangoes, and kumquats are among the better known stars of this innovative cuisine.

Among less familiar exotics are:

Acerola—the "Barbados cherry" tastes like a tart strawberry. Just one packs between 20 and 50 times the vitamin C of an orange.

Atemoya—heart-shaped or round, its pale green, bumpy skin holds a juicy, white pulp with the taste of a piña colada.

Bignay—a sweet-tart taste bomblet resembling white grapes, loaded with vitamin A, it's a popular source of homemade quality wine.

Black sapote—a green-skinned cousin of the persimmon, sometimes called chocolate pudding fruit because of its rich, sweet, chocolate-brown flesh. Often served alone with a dash of vanilla or lemon juice, and used in mousses and to flavor ice cream.

Calomondin—resembling a tiny orange, related to the kumquat, it has an edible peel and a taste not unlike a lemon. Popular in preserves.

Carambola—also known as the star fruit for its shape when sliced crosswise, this golden fruit lends itself to artistic presentations. Depending on the variety, its crisp flesh hints of apple, grape, and citrus, sometimes sweet, sometimes tart.

Ciruela—a decorative red or orange fruit sized and shaped like a plum tomato. Its cream- or red-colored flesh reminds some of peanuts.

Guava—common around Greater Miami, this oversize member of the berry family comes in many shapes and varieties whose skin may be white, yellow, green, or pink. (The yellow kind are usually the sweetest.) Its flesh reminds

some of strawberry; others say pineapple or lemon. Miami menus are sweetened by guava nectar, preserves, sauces, and desserts. You can buy it canned or in tubes of paste. Take it home with you to try baking your own *pastalitos*.

Jackfruit—the world's biggest tree fruit can weigh in at 80 pounds. Bumpy-skinned and oval-shape, yellow or brown when ripe, its flesh suggests melon, mango, and papaya. Sometimes cooked like a vegetable, its chestnut-flavored seeds are roasted and used as seasoning.

Kiwi—a trademark staple of New World cuisine, often used as a decorative garnish. Egg-sized, with brown, fuzzy skin, its jade-green flesh is speckled with small black edible seeds and tastes like a mix of banana, peach, and strawberry. It is served in fruit salads, compotes, ice cream, and preserves.

Monstera—cucumber-shaped fruit that sheds pale green scales as it ripens. Its custardlike flesh has a sweet acidic taste hinting of ripe bananas, and is often used in desserts or eaten fresh.

Muscadine grape—A Florida native, larger than most grapes, with pale green, brown-speckled skin and a musky, fruity, tannic flavor. It is used for making juice, preserves, and a local wine called scuppernong.

Papaya—in the Greater Miami area, the most common variety is the small, yellowish pear-shaped Solo. Its sweet, aromatic flesh reminds people variously of peaches, apricots, or berries. Served sliced with a spritz of lime juice, and in salads, salsas, and desserts.

Sugar apple—also known as sweetsop, the skin of this nubby, heart-shaped fruit can be mauve, yellow-green, or red. Regardless, it bursts open as the fruit ripens, revealing citruslike segments of creamy, sweet flesh (sometimes white, sometimes yellow). It's often blended into ice cream. (Ask for this specialty when you visit King's Ice Cream on Calle Ocho, see p. 52.) ■

Presentation is an integral part of Miami's contemporary cuisine, as pleasing to behold as to taste.

Three Cuban Art Galleries

**Xavier Cortada
Art Gallery**

www.cortada.com

- 🗺 Map p. 51
- ✉ 104 S.W. 9 St..
- ☎ 305/858-1323
- 🕐 Open daily, but call
  to confirm

**Latin Quarter
Cultural Center
of Miami**

www.latinquartercultural
center.org

- 🗺 Map p. 51
- ✉ 1501 S.W. 8 St.
- ☎ 305/649-9797
- 🕐 Open Mon.–Sat.,
  11 a.m. to 7 p.m.
- 💲 Admission varies
  by event

DURING THE PAST DECADE LITTLE HAVANA HAS BEEN invigorated by art and artists. Although there's no singular "Miami" style, the emerging movement often evokes nostalgia for a lost Cuba, or other Latin American country.

The **Xavier Cortada Art Gallery** exhibits works by the eponymous artist. Cortada's style is an amalgamation of Cuban Modernism, a form of expressionism, and black outlines and bold tropical colors. His subjects range from the American dream to old Cuba, and from AIDS to sports and more. Besides in his studio and gallery, his work has been exhibited at the White House, the Florida Supreme Court, the Miami Art Museum, and on murals throughout the streets of Little Havana.

The **Latin Quarter Cultural Center of Miami** is another place to find South American art. In addition to the fine works it displays, the center's goal is to have a positive impact in the social pride of the community, particularly with children's and seniors' programs.

Once a month, on the last Friday, the streets of Calle Ocho reverberate with the creative energy of Viernes Culturales/Cultural Fridays. Held from 7 p.m. to 11 p.m., it's an open-air gallery and celebration with more than a hundred artists of various media, as well as musicians, food vendors, and 3,000 attendees.

At the **Molina Fine Art Gallery,** *(1634 S.W. 8th St., 305/642-0444)* visitors can study or purchase the Cuban artist's colorful oil paintings and prints. Luis Molina is celebrated for his Afro-Cuban folklore pieces that feature mulatto farmers as well as parrots, roosters, and other animals found on farms. Santeria, the religion in which African gods and goddesses mix with Catholic saints, is an important element in many of his works. Molina also participates in "Voices For Freedom," a movement that supports the dozens of intellectuals who were imprisoned by Fidel Castro in 2003. ∎

Xavier Cortada's "Bishop Verot" hangs at his Little Havana gallery.

Máximo Gómez Park

IF YOU HAPPEN BY CALLE OCHO AND S.W. 15TH AVENUE, and stay a while to watch the domino games played here, you will probably find the subject of Cuba's past and future being discussed amid the clatter of the wooden tiles, a popular Cuban pastime. More famous than impressive, this little enclosure, better known as Domino Park, is nevertheless a beloved icon of Little Havana's founding generation.

The players are generally older men in billowing hot-weather shirts or *guayaberas,* watched over by a tableau of Southern Hemispheric leaders depicted in the surrounding mural, added after the real-life versions gathered in Miami for the 1994 Summit of the Americas.

At the southwest corner of W. Flagler Street and S.W. 17th Avenue, on the redbrick **Plaza de la Cubanidad,** a fountain bears the inscription *"Las palmas son novias que esperan"* (The palm trees are lovers—some say girl-friends—who wait). So said José Martí, the 19th-century Cuban poet revered for his resistance to Spanish colonial rule. The palms still symbolize the yearning for an island free of despotism. ∎

A cup of José

If you're not averse to caffeine, don't leave Miami without stopping by a Little Havana side-walk cafeteria for a shot of *café Cubano.* This is major league stuff, brewed with sugar added to the grinds, then sweetened even more by adding sugar to the viscous espresso that results. If you ask for coffee in English, odds are you will be served a *colada,* an espresso in a cup barely large enough for your thumb. For something more like the standard *Norteamericano* "cuppa Joe," order *café con leche,* traditionally one part Cuban-style coffee to two parts milk. ∎

A serious game of dominoes next to a mural depicting Latin American statesmen

Máximo Gómez Park

Map p. 51

El Crédito Cigar Factory

ON FEBRUARY 3, 1962, PRESIDENT JOHN F. KENNEDY BANNED all trade with Cuba, his motive being to deprive Fidel Castro's cash-strapped economy of 35 million dollars in annual income and to hobble Cuban efforts to export revolution in the Americas.

El Crédito Cigar Factory
- Map p. 51
- 1106 S.W. 8th St.
- 305/858-4162 or 800/726-9481
- Closed Sun.

The embargo crippled Florida's cigarmaking industry, which then depended exclusively on Cuban tobacco. Warehouses held only a ten-month supply, after which some 6,000 people stood to lose their jobs. (The day before announcing the embargo, Kennedy, a cigar aficionado, sent an aide around Washington to buy up choice Cuban brands.) Many of South Florida's cigarmakers went bust. Among notable survivors is Calle Ocho's El Crédito Cigar Factory, where the aromatic products of this arcane trade are rolled by hand—cut with rounded blades, wrapped tightly, and pressed in vises—as they have been since the firm was founded in 1807 in Havana.

This is Miami's premier factory, employing about two dozen people who, using plastic presses, quietly roll cigars using Dominican tobacco (grown, it is said, from Cuban seeds), producing highly rated smokes such as El Crédito's La Gloria Cubana. There's a store at the factory where you can buy cigars individually or in bulk. In 2008 El Crédito celebrated its 40th anniversary in Miami's Little Havana. ■

Cigarmakers, like these at El Crédito, were once read to by a colleague to help pass the time.

The right way to smoke a cigar

- Clip the end closest to the label with a cigar cutter or sharp knife.
- Avoid damaging the wrapper leaf.
- To light the cigar, hold it horizontally and rotate the end over a match or butane flame until evenly burning.
- Place the cigar in your mouth and lightly draw smoke.
- Don't inhale; cigar smoke is meant to be savored and then released.
- Hold the cigar firmly in the mouth but don't clench it in your teeth.
- Avoid wetting the "foot" excessively with saliva.

- Smoke slowly, no more than two puffs a minute, lest the cigar become overheated and sour.
- A cigar should last between 30 and 90 minutes—about 50 puffs in all—spending more time in your hand than in your mouth.

"The true smoker," decreed August Barthélemy, author of *L'Art de fumer pipe et cigare* (1849), "abstains from imitating Vesuvius."
—Courtesy of Barnaby Conrad III, author of *The Cigar* (Chronicle Books, 1996) ■

Not seaworthy, but evoking wonder and amusement, this boat of stone blocks and wood beams decorates the Florida International University campus.

More things to do in & around Little Havana

THE FROST ART MUSEUM AT FLORIDA INTERNATIONAL UNIVERSITY

The Art Museum started in 1977 as a student gallery on the campus of this public university near Sweetwater. Two decades later, its austere but striking concrete building holds one of the Southeast's most smartly curated showplaces for Latin American and 20th-century American works. (Several times in recent years, readers of Miami's alternative *New Times* newspaper have voted it among Miami's best.) The collection of Cuban and Florida artists is one of the most interesting you will find anywhere in the state.

Treat yourself to a stroll in the 26-acre sculpture park, which holds monumental pieces by Alexander Calder, Anthony Caro, Willem de Kooning, and Isamu Noguchi, among other masters. A visit to the museum's website *(www .FrostArtMuseum.org)* reveals the exceptional richness of its holdings, due in large measure to the generosity of several major American collectors. If you plan a visit to Miami's Little Havana district, consider including this as one of your stops—it's a 20-minute drive west on S.W. Eighth Street, also known as Calle Ocho, Little Havana's main boulevard.

🅰 32 A2 ✉ FIU's University Park Campus, S.W. 107th Ave. & 8th St. ☎ 305/348-2890 🕐 Open Wed.–Fri. 10 a.m.– 5 p.m., Sat. noon–4 p.m.

LITTLE HAVANA'S ANNUAL BLOCK PARTY

If your Miami visit falls in late February and early March, you have an opportunity to experience Carnaval Miami International, the nation's largest Hispanic cultural festival. Carnaval's nine-day calendar of concerts, parades, and contests, including a golf tournament held on the verdant and challenging Biltmore Hotel course in Coral Gables, ends with Little Havana's swirling Kiwanis Club-sponsored block party, a celebration of art, dance, music, and food that crowds Calle Ocho with thousands of people between 4th and 27th Avenues.

If you attend the block party, consider taking the MetroMover to the Eighth Street station. It's a bit of a hike west to the center of the festival, but you will avoid the hassles of traffic and parking. Miami's No. 8 Metrobus leaves from the intersection of Miami Avenue and Flagler Street (just east of the Miami-Dade Cultural Center complex, see pp. 38–39) and proceeds into the heart of Little Havana. A good place to get off on Calle Ocho is its intersection with 36th Avenue, where you will find people waiting for tables outside the ever-popular Versailles Restaurant *(3555 S.W. 8th St., tel 305/445-7614)*. For information about the event, call 305/644-8888 and follow the recorded menu of instructions, or you can try

the Salsaweb Internet Company website
(www.carnavalmiami.com).

MIAMI RIVER

Its meander through Little Havana is picturesque, as the placid stream is frequently
navigated by tugboats, small Caribbean
freighters, fishing boats, and luxury cruisers,
its banks busied by boatyards, fisheries,
warehouses, and marinas. Here a thriving
bohemian creative community lives afloat in
houseboats. Early 20th-century draining cut
the Miami off from its source in the Everglades,
then near today's 32nd Avenue bridge; canals
now supply it with water. East of 24th Avenue,
the river follows its age-old path. The public
parks along it are favorite destinations of
strollers and bicyclists, who linger here to
watch the occasionally exotic traffic on the
water below. One of the most charming parks,
in its overgrown bucolic way, is **Sewell Park,**
a somnolent palmy hideaway that slopes down
on the south bank near the 17th Avenue
bridge. There are picnic tables and Miami's
only public boat-launching ramp just
upstream at **Curtiss Park** on the north bank
(take N.W. 20th St. west to N.W. 22nd Ave.).

If this part of town appeals to you, have
a look at the pretty little Miami River Inn
(see p. 245), a bed-and-breakfast on South
River Drive. The inn is a cluster of nicely
restored, early 20th-century, clapboard houses,
wooden-floored architectural jewels set
around a garden in an otherwise unimpressive
neighborhood. The inn's antique-filled rooms
are pleasantly old-fashioned, parking is secure,
there's a swimming pool, and guests may use
the fitness center at the nearby YMCA.
🏔 33 E3 **Miami River Inn** ✉ 118 S.W.
South River Dr. at S.W. 4th Ave. ☎ 305/
325-0045

TOWER THEATER

Located at the intersection near Máximo
Gómez Park in Little Havana, this movie
theater played a role in the lives of many
Cuban exiles arriving in Miami after 1959.
Built in 1926, remodeled in 1931 and 2000,
this art deco structure features a classical
chase light marquee and a 40-foot illuminated steel tower on the roof. In 2002, the
City of Miami authorized Miami-Dade
Community College (now Miami Dade
College) to manage and operate the theater.
The College welcomed the opportunity to
continue the Tower Theater's rich tradition
by promoting the arts in all their forms
within South Florida's multicultural, multi-
ethnic, and international community.
✉ 1508 S.W. 8th St. ☎ 305/643-8706,
www.mdc.edu/iac/towertheater/counter/
default.asp ■

Orange Bowl

Every New Year's weekend from 1935
to 1996, football fans flocked to the
University of Miami's famous stadium for
the annual Big Eight football classic; they
seldom failed to fill all of the 74,000-plus
seats of the horseshoe-shape enclosure,
which rose rather incongruously above Little
Havana's low rooftops. For many years the
university's team couldn't lose here, creating
an electrifying tension among the fans and
a spooky sense of predestined hopelessness
in visiting teams. The team now plays at
Dolphin Stadium. For 20 years, the Miami Dolphins professional football team also called the
Orange Bowl home, before moving to
Dolphin Stadium in 1986. Though the
Orange Bowl's scoreboard chronically mal-
functioned and its bathrooms often flooded,
Miamians still regarded the rusted relic
with affection, because its completion in
the gloomy years of the Depression era
brought Miami into the ranks of America's
major football capitals and brightened
local spirits.

But in March 2008, demolition of the
so-called Old Lady began; the land was set
aside for a proposed stadium of the Florida
Marlins, which are to be renamed the Miami
Marlins. The stadium was located at 1501
N.W. 3rd St., between 7th & Flagler Sts. and
S.W. 12th & 17th Aves. ■

A sailboat skirts the edge of the Gulf Stream off North Miami's Golden Beach.

North Miami

North of Flagler Street in Downtown Miami, street names acquire the prefix "North." Those on the Bay side of Miami Avenue are considered to be in the Northeast; those on the Everglades side are designated Northwest. But the reality is that the borders between Miami's various compass-point districts are not precise, nor (save for the convenience of map readers) do they need to be.

If you were asked to draw the northernmost boundaries of North Miami, you would probably get little argument if you traced a line west from Biscayne Bay in the environs of Aventura, Golden Beach, and Golden Shores, following the Dade-Broward County line to Florida's Turnpike, and then following that toll highway as it heads southwest, passing between Hialeah and the Everglades, and then runs due south to Sweetwater. Inside this quarter-circle arc lies Northwest Miami. It begins at I-95 and runs west for about 9 miles, where subdivisions and industrial strips finally give away to farmland "reclaimed" (conservationists say "stolen") from the Everglades.

Hialeah and Opa-locka are the Northwest's best known communities. The former is a patchwork of residential development and commercial land, its name associated by most people who do not live in Florida with the old Hialeah thoroughbred racetrack. Just north of Hialeah is Opa-locka, whose fanciful Moorish architecture arose from a developer's fascination with the *Arabian Nights,* Richard F. Burton's classic retelling of ancient Middle Eastern fables that blend everyday life with romantic fantasies. Drive west from Opa-locka Airport and you will find Miami Lakes, where the Everglades' forced retreat left a plain of ponds shimmering amid upscale golf courses and private residential developments.

Miami's northeastern quadrant is much smaller in area and much more residential, its houses ranging from modest bungalows built in land boom days to high-rise condominiums overlooking more golf courses and the yachty northern backwaters of Biscayne Bay and the Atlantic. You need an automobile to get to North Miami's far-flung parks, museums, neighborhoods, and curiosities, but the effort will dispel your first impression that its sole attractions are golf and powerboating. ■

Miami Design District

AS OFTEN HAPPENS IN AMERICAN CITIES, ARTISTS IN search of economical studio space sparked the revival of the part of Northeast Miami that runs roughly from N.E. Second Avenue to N. Miami Avenue and between 36th and 41st Streets. Only in the last decade have the flower-decorated streets shed a reputation for sidewalk peril, particularly at night, but like New York's East Village, it has acquired a corps of painters and sculptors, media artists and photographers who anchor it against any further drift toward decay.

**Miami Design
District**
www.miamidesigndistrict.net
33 F3

About the time the novelist F. Scott Fitzgerald (1896–1940) was writing his first novel in St. Paul, Minnesota, this neighborhood was known as Decorators Row, where interior designers and decorators came to showrooms that catered only to the trade. Today you can visit the district's antiques stores, fabric outlets, furnituremakers, and manufacturers' showrooms. Fortieth Street, between N.E. Second and N. Miami Avenues, has a reputation for elegant whimsy and exotica; let your tastes and interests guide you. If you're fond of antiques, visit the **Susan R Lifestyle Boutique** *(93 N.E. 40th St., tel 305/573-7463)* or **Artisan Antiques Art Deco** *(110 N.E. 40th St., tel 305/573-5619).*

In between showrooms are little hole-in-the-wall cafés where designers debate the merits of, say, Corbusier or the Bauhaus group. The flowered court of the **Michael's Genuine Food & Drink** *(130 N.E. 40th St., tel 305/573-5550)* offers a respite from street traffic, and so does the **Grass Restaurant & Lounge,** with its Caribbean and Indonesian setting *(28 N.E. 40th St., tel 305/573-3355).*

Most galleries and showplaces close at sundown. However, on the second Saturday evening of every month, from 7 p.m. to 10 p.m., design district galleries, shops, studios, and bistros hold open houses, often scheduled to coincide with the openings of artists' shows. ■

Museum of Contemporary Art

Museum of Contemporary Art
www.mocanomi.org
🅰 33 F5
✉ 770 N.E. 125th St. between N.E. 7th Court & 8th Ave., just off I-95
☎ 305/893-6211
🕐 Closed Mon.
💲 $–$$

LOCALS REFER TO THE 23,000-SQUARE-FOOT SHOWPLACE by its initials, "MoCA," and Miamians are especially fond of this already well-established museum, which opened in 1996.

Like Los Angeles's original "Temporary Contemporary" (another museum known locally as MoCA), the main gallery has an appealing studio-warehouse look, the kind of space artists covet. The Diego Rivera, and the internationally renowned Frank Stella. Whether or not they are to your taste, MoCA's unifying thread is quality and earnest intent. The museum is also committed to

big room represents the major leagues, drawing work from far and wide; a smaller separate space generally exhibits the newest of the new, often from local artists. Inside is contemporary fine art representing the world's avant-garde movements, which occasionally includes the usual multimedia installations and photography that expand the definition of art. The mainstay of the collection are paintings and sculptures, however. Among modern art icons, Julian Schnabel is well represented.

MoCA's major exhibitions have examined the work of diverse art world legends such as Mexican artist Frida Kahlo, her husband showing the work of Latino artists and filmmakers, whose works are screened, along with other avant-garde cinema, in MoCA's appealing courtyard.

Even if your time is limited, do try to visit the excellent gift shop, which holds a thoughtfully chosen inventory of art books, exhibition catalogs, and postcard reproductions of works in MoCA's permanent collection. Also check the schedule of guided architectural walking tours of North Miami's neighborhoods. The strolls explore some of Greater Miami's more appealing residential streets, particularly those in the Morningside district (see p. 64). ■

New fine art is MoCA's specialty.

Morningside

THE REVITALIZATION OF THE DESIGN DISTRICT COINCIDED with an interest in Miami's older residential neighborhoods, particularly those built during the city's boom era of the 1920s and the early Depression years. Almost forgotten were the bungalow enclaves of the Morningside subdivision flanking Biscayne Boulevard.

The 1920s' Jazz Age had a penchant for fantasies in architecture. It was not enough merely to build a home; it had to have a theme. Two leading styles of the period were mission revival, emulating the Spanish colonial churches of far-off California, and Mediterranean Revival, a catch-all for imitations of homes built near that fabled sea. These vogues were in full bloom across America when the building of Morningside commenced.

Morningside's theme homes have escaped the heavy hand of urban renewal, and today they are cherished by design-conscious homeowners. A few years back, restoration zealots lobbied successfully to have Morningside declared a historic zone. Among its notable homes are the Mediterranean

Revival-style **John Nunnally Home** and an early example of the mission style at 5940 N.E. Sixth Court, between N.E. 59th and N.E. 60th Streets, both private residences.

You can drive Morningside easily enough, although traffic barriers along Biscayne Boulevard block automobiles from entering some of these pretty streets. It is probably most convenient to park somewhere along Biscayne Boulevard and explore on foot. The subdivision is not terribly large, extending from the bay shore west to around Biscayne Boulevard, and running north–south from N.E. 60th to N.E. 50th Streets. (The Museum of Contemporary Art—see p. 63—occasionally offers guided architectural walking tours that include the Morningside area.) ■

El Portal Burial Mound

El Portal Burial Mound

33 F4

500 N.E. 87th St.

IN ANOTHER NORTH MIAMI NEIGHBORHOOD, KNOWN AS El Portal, the historical architecture is considerably older. For years, homeowners and city workers have been digging up arrowheads and stone points, bits of broken pottery, and pieces of conch shell shaped into tools, the detritus of some 1,800 years of Indian life here. The neighborhood is believed to be one of a dozen or more Tequesta village sites identified so far in Dade County. The public park here contains one of only two tribal burial grounds in the county currently open to the public.

Don't expect much; your imagination will have to kick in here as you approach an innocuous grassy knoll called the Little River Mound. (The small stream ripples by on its way through El Portal district, confined to one of Miami's many urban canals.) About 4 feet high and some 50 feet in circumference, the mound was the first archaeological site to be preserved in Dade County.

It is not, however, particularly well known. Archaeologists working with the county prize the site, which they believe was a place for mortuary ceremonial practice, probably part of a Tequesta village founded as far back as A.D. 500. The mound came later, probably between about 1200 and 1500, in an area cleared of the mixed hardwood and pine forest that once covered much of Dade County. Scholars debate the Tequestas' vintage; some fix their arrival in South Florida around 3,000 years ago, while conceding the merit in others' contentions that human habitation (not necessarily Tequesta) commenced much earlier. The tribe's scant archaeological remains, mostly pottery shards and shells, don't reveal many clues.

There is no charge for entering the burial ground, which lies near the Little River canal east of I-95 near 79th Street and North Miami Avenue. For a glimpse of yet another site of archeological importance, look south from downtown's Brickell Avenue drawbridge toward the mouth of the Miami River. ■

Tequesta people are buried under a bucolic bower shading a centuries-old village site.

Architectural fantasies

As America entered the 1920s, Florida found its first widely known architecture in Mediterranean Revival. Like the fabled sea it is named for, it reflects many cultures: Tuscan, Venetian, Spanish, Andalusian, Moorish, even Roman, while borrowing accents from ancient Greece and Renaissance France and producing bungalows that resemble baby palazzos.

Miami, a city that prided itself on being practically forced upon an inhospitable landscape of swamp and dune, wanted an architecture rooted in imagination. This was, after all, a land brought to Europeans' attention by the conquistadores, seen as romantic figures who granted La Florida a permanent invitation to the fancy-dress ball of historical make-believe.

The signature of Mediterranean Revival was "oldness." Exterior walls were stained to mimic those of Rome. Roof and floor tiles duplicated those in Sicily. For architects, the style was a chance to dream in wood and stucco. The ultimate objective was to seduce through artifice—a millionaire's residence might look like a ruined Spanish monastery. Beams were immersed in saltwater, burned with acid, and scored with chisels. Iron objects were dented, concrete was soaked in bicarbonate of soda. Miami's quest for bogus antiquity wrote the book on painting and plastering techniques still used today. Factories opened to supply designers with "period" furniture, ironwork, tiles, and even leaded glass windows. "Oriental" rugs and "medieval" tapestries were woven. Many chic Miami homes appeared to be furnished with salvage from Spanish convents.

The best of Miami's residential dream merchants created nearly theatrical environments. The interior of a lawyer's office became the suite of a 16th-century Venetian noble, a banker's living room that of a Spanish *ranchero.* The vogue flamed through the Roaring Twenties and guttered out in the Depression, when architects fell under the thrall of moderne and streamline, which seemed to symbolize the new technologies that might deliver America from its economic abyss.

At about the same time that Mediterranean Revival bloomed, the vision of Miami's other indigenous architecture stirred the mind of airplane designer-turned-developer Glenn Curtiss, inventor of the pioneering Curtiss Jennie biplane. Anointed a warrior of the air for piloting what amounted to a box kite with a lawn mower engine from Albany to New York City in 1910, he used his celebrity status to attract investors. The flyer and his architect, Bernhardt Muller, shared a weakness for the Arabic folk tales popularized in English as *The Arabian Nights.* In Hollywood, an Arabian Nights vogue had produced *A Princess of Baghdad* in 1916, *Aladdin and the Wonderful Lamp* in 1917, and *Ali Baba and the 40 Thieves* the following year. Women fainted in 1921 when Rudolph Valentino flashed his dark almond eyes in *The Sheik,* and even male hearts skipped a beat in 1924 when Douglas Fairbanks, Sr., bounded from rooftop to rooftop in *The Thief of Baghdad.* In Russia, the ballet master Sergei Diaghilev created *Scheherazade;* in America his countryman Nikolai Rimsky-Korsakov composed a symphonic suite by the same name. The mass appeal of this international phenomenon was not lost on Curtiss.

What he and Muller envisioned was, in essence, a theme park with permanent residents. They chose a site northwest of Miami that the Seminole Indians called Opatishawockalocka (wooded hummock), removing the tongue-twisting tishawocka part to create the "Arabic-Persian" name Opa-locka. Their headquarters, today Opa-locka's City Hall, looked like the palace of a Saudi king. Every building had to have "romance." A bank was rendered as a ruined Egyptian temple; a gas station was designed with a dome and minarets. Ali Baba Avenue, Sharazad Boulevard, and Aladdin Street were lined with domed, single-story, two-bedroom homes. Buyers came running. Architectural buffs still do, despite Opa-locka's economic anemia and pockets of seediness, to see the relics of a time when unabashed make-believe helped to imbue even the most routine life with a veneer of romantic intrigue. ■

Above: Mediterranean Revival style on Española Way, South Beach. Below left: Traditional details mix with designer's whimsy in this Coral Gables Spanish colonial residence.

Above right: Renaissance Italian lines of Vizcaya. Below: Opa-locka's City Hall is Greater Miami's supreme example of Florida's 20th-century infatuation with fantasy architecture.

Ancient Spanish Monastery

A puzzle solved, this 800-year-old house of worship survived dismantling and an improbable journey across the Atlantic.

BUILT IN THE 12TH CENTURY, THIS IS FAR AND AWAY THE oldest edifice in North America, though it came originally from Spain. After some 700 years as part of a Cistercian monastery, the Cloisters of the Monastery of St. Bernard of Clairvaux fell on hard times and were used as a granary and stable.

Ancient Spanish Monastery

www.SpanishMonastery.com

 32 G6

✉ 16711 W. Dixie Hwy. between N.E. 167th & 171st Sts.

☎ 305/945-1461

💲 $-$$

🕐 Open Mon.–Sat., 9 a.m. to 4:30 p.m.; Sun., 1 p.m.–4:30 p.m.; may be closed for special events

Newspaper mogul William Randolph Hearst purchased the building in 1925 for $500,000, intending it for his California coastal house, Xanadu. He had it dismantled and shipped to New York in 11,000 numbered crates packed with straw. The straw spoiled everything. Customs officials believed it carried germs causing an epidemic of hoof and mouth disease. They uncrated the stones and burned the straw, but got the pieces and boxes hopelessly mixed up. Hearst walked away in disgust. The crates lay in a Brooklyn warehouse for 26 years, until 1952, when new owners had the pieces reassembled here as a tourist attraction at a cost of 1.5 million dollars. A decade later the Episcopal Church acquired the monastery as a house of worship, a museum of early Gothic and Romanesque architecture, a repository of ecclesiastical artifacts, and a place of peace and rest. In the gift shop hangs "La Gracia" by Spanish master painter Julio Romero de Torres.

The monastery is a popular wedding spot so its grounds are often crowded with fancily clad guests on Saturday and Sunday afternoons. ■

Oleta River State Recreation Area

Though surrounded by intensive residential development, most visibly North Miami Beach's posh Bal Harbour community, the park offers an opportunity not merely to retreat from the world for a while, but also to drive, walk, or cycle among mangrove forests and serpentine lagoons. If you stroll, you will encounter wading shore birds, and there is a good chance (especially early and late in the day) of seeing the snout of a porpoise rising from the water. The odds of spotting that strangest of aquatic Florida mammals, the lumbering manatee, are not so high, but these sweet-natured creatures, perched on the brink of extinction, often escape the estuary traffic in the park's quiet coves.

You can rent a bicycle here and cruise the 1.5-mile biking path (looking out for joggers who share it), or rent a canoe or paddleboat and explore the 0.75-mile canoe trail. Locals come to lunch alfresco and read in the shade of picnic-area pavilions, wade into the warm water off the park's 1,200-foot-long sandy beach, and drop fishing lures from a sturdy fishing pier that reaches nearly 100 feet offshore.

It's difficult to imagine, looking at the far skyline of high-rise condos, that 150 years ago this little peninsula teemed with bears, deer, panthers, bobcats, wolves, and alligators, along with the then-plentiful manatees in the surrounding waters. By the 1890s, pineapple and vegetable farms stood here near a village called Ojus. That's all vanished history now. Seven covered picnic pavilions are available on a first-come, first-served basis or may be rented by reservation. When you visit, ask a park ranger for advice on where to find a free copy of Florida's official guide to 145 state parks. You can request a free copy (*tel 850/245-2157*). ■

Oleta River State Recreation Area
www.floridastateparks.org/oletariver
🅰 32 G6
✉ 3400 N.E. 163rd St./Sunny Isles Blvd., E of Biscayne Blvd.
☎ 305/919-1844 (picnic pavilion reservations); 800/326-3521 or www.reserveamerica.com (campsite & cabin reservations)
💲 $

Greynolds Park

Franklin Roosevelt's Civilian Conservation Corps are credited with rendering the site of a rock-mining company (owned by one A.O. Greynolds) into one of Miami's most popular public commons. The company left a pile of junked machinery (including railroad ties and a steam engine) for the CCC boys, who buried it under rock and sand, creating a 40-foot mound still topped by the observation tower they built, and turned the quarries into a lake, where paddle boats can now be rented. A Seminole Indian trading post operated here in the late 1800s, but that has gone now, and what is left is an emporium of outdoor recreation—golf links, a fitness course for joggers, picnic tables, and many places to throw a blanket. The green has a roosting population of wading birds and owls, a rare thing in Greater Miami, attracting bird-watchers to the **Greynolds Park Rookery**. Helmeted mountain bikers speed around the 1.6-mile-long bike path, but it's also a pleasant circuit for leisurely pedaling. There's no admission fee if you walk or cycle in; motorists pay a small sum on weekends. ■

Greynolds Park
🅰 33 G7
✉ 17530 W. Dixie Hwy., N. Miami Beach
☎ 305/945-3425
💲 Free on weekdays and $ on weekends for motorists only

Miami's Russian community

Tatiana Night Club/Restaurant
www.fltatianarestaurant.com

✉ 1710 E. Hallandale Beach Blvd.

☎ 954/454-1222

🕐 Open daily for lunch and evening shows

💲 $$$–$$$$

Sugar Rush
✉ 18090 Collins Ave.

☎ 305/792-4459

💲 $–$$

🕐 Open 5 p.m. to closing (varies, but late)

Chocolada Bakery & Cafe
✉ 1923 Hollywood Blvd.

☎ 954/920-6400

THE SOVIET UNION'S CITIZENS INCLUDED MOSCOW bureaucrats, Siberian shamans, Central Asian Muslims, Buddhist monks, Persian-speaking homemakers, and myriad other groups, and northern Miami's "Russian" community seems to mirror this. South Florida's tennis phenom/fashion model Anna Kournikova is the one best known to Americans but Philip Kirkorov, Russia's top pop singer, a mix of Michael Jackson and the late Freddie Mercury, also lives here much of the year.

Tatiana Night Club/Restaurant, formerly Club Pearl, a lively cabaret with sword swallowers, jugglers and beautiful dancing girls in sequined bikinis, is the Russian community's entertainment focal point. Its meals are delicious, and a metaphor for the homeland: pickled Russian vegetables, meats from Caucasia, caviar from Azerbaijan, Chicken Kiev from the Ukrainian capital, and Siberian *pelmeni* (ravioli). Tatiana serves Russian vodka, Armenian cognac, and Georgian wine.

For a different taste of the Eurasian landmass, visit "the Russian plaza," a beach shopping center filled with Russian-owned bookstores, travel agencies and a café called **Sugar Rush**. If you are new to Russian food, ask the staff to recommend a dish, and be aware that Russian coffee is similar to Turkish coffee.

Drive north on A1A (Collins Avenue) and turn left on Hollywood Boulevard to find **Chocolada Bakery & Café,** another popular Russian hangout. Live music nightly. ∎

The Russian community's preeminent night out: dinner, dancing, and unique cabaret acts at Tatiana Night Club/ Restaurant

Opa-locka

IN A WAY THIS IMPROBABLE PHENOMENON OF MOORISH make-believe is a sad memorial to the wonderfully fanciful visions of Glenn Curtiss (see p. 66), who hoped to take his place as the supreme caliph of Florida entrepreneurs. He aspired to live among the rich, but the city for which he is best known is very poor—an economic ghetto populated mostly by African-American families and recent Caribbean and Latin American immigrants. But what a place it is, the fantasyland Curtiss christened the "Baghdad of Dade County."

Due north of Miami International Airport and due west of I-95 Interchange 13, its domes, minarets, crenelations, pointed horseshoe arches, and crescent motifs rise above uninspired buildings put up since the city's optimistic start 70 years ago.

If nothing else, visit the **Opa-locka City Hall,** where Curtiss based his operatic production under blue and white domes, since repainted mauve and gold—the rest of the building is also now a shade of gold. In this imitation mosque-palace (designated a Thematic Resource on the National Register of Historic Places), architect Bernhardt Muller sketched hundreds of renderings of what was hoped would be the "most beautiful city on the East

Coast," planted with poinciana, bamboo, eucalyptus, and more than 2,500 coconut palms. Appropriately, the building maintains a special shelf for its collection of books telling the tales of *The Arabian Nights.*

Another must-see is the **Hurt Building,** a smaller fantasy of arches, domes, and minarets. After being gutted by fire, the city's train station was rebuilt in 2002 as a beautiful Moorish edifice.

While Muller's notions still fascinate and charm, the September **Arabian Nights Festival** is unfortunately no longer held, due to economic setbacks in this city. For the same reason, crime of all kinds is rampant. It is best to visit the city during the day. ■

No calls to prayer came from these mini-minarets, which decorate Opa-locka's Hurt Building, a warren of offices.

Opa-locka
◪ 33 E6

City Hall
✉ 777 Sharazad Blvd. at Ali Baba Ave.
☎ 305/688-4611
⊕ Closed Sat.–Sun.

Hurt Building
◪ 33 E6
✉ 490 Opa-locka Blvd.

Let it ride!

At about the same time Curtiss and Muller were dreaming up Opa-locka (see p. 71), an unassuming tract on Miami's northwest fringe caught their eye. On it, in 1925, they built Hialeah Park, whose centerpiece is another Curtiss creation on the National Register of Historic Places, a decorative old-style thoroughbred horse racing track sprawling across nearly 230 acres. Its last meet was held in 2001.

Miami Jai-Alai hosts live matches six days a week.

The highest caliber of horse racing in South Florida is at Gulfstream Park Racing & Casino, a "racino" *(901 S. Federal Highway, Hallandale Beach, tel 954/454-7000, www.gulfstreampark.com).* Because Gulfstream is on the Broward side of the border with Miami-Dade, visitors can already play the slot machines, and they can play poker as well as bet on simulcast races at other venues. When Hialeah Park closed, Gulfstream became the region's premier racing attraction. Opened in 1939, it was rebuilt in 2004 to house the slots and showcase a beautiful new track. Its annual Florida Derby is a $1 million precursor to the Kentucky Derby.

In recent years, the gambling situation in Miami-Dade has been highly fluid, with voters in January 2008 passing a referendum to allow slot machines at the county's jai-alai *fronton* and dog and horse tracks; neighboring Broward County and the Seminole Tribe, which has reservations in Broward, legalized the slots in 2005. The vote means the owners of Flagler Dog Track, Calder Race Course, and Miami Jai-Alai will be allowed to install up to 2,000 slot machines each.

During 2008, the owners of Flagler Dogs & Poker *(401 N.W. 38th Ct., tel 305/649-3000, www.flaglerdogs.com)* plan to spend at least $80 million on renovations, including a casino for slots and an outdoor amphitheater. Up to this point the facility, which is located 10 minutes west of Downtown Miami, has offered daily greyhound races and high-stakes poker with no-limit cash games.

Miami Jai-Alai (see p. 48), located in an industrial area outside the city, also may add slots. Currently visitors can play poker and bet on simulcast parimutuel sports shown on big-screen TVs throughout the Crystal Card Room. Calder Race Course *(21001 N.W. 27th Ave., tel 305/625-1311, www.calderracecourse .com),* located near Miami Dolphins Stadium 20 minutes northwest of Miami, presents horse races from January to April but does not offer poker and slots. That could change.

Greater Miami gambling is dominated by the Seminole Hard Rock Hotel & Casino *(1 Seminole Way, Hollywood, tel 866/502-7529, www.seminolehardrockhollywood.com),* which has more than 2,500 Las Vegas-style slots and other games, plus 50 poker tables. In 2008 it expects to add the table games blackjack and baccarat. The massive complex, whose hotel has 481 guest rooms and 86 suites as well as a large entertainment district with live concerts, bars, and shops, is set on the Seminole tribe's Hollywood reservation about 20 minutes north of Miami. Since its opening in 2004, the Seminole Hard Rock has had a giant impact on both locals and tourists looking to socialize. In 2006, the tribe, in poverty a decade ago, bought the Hard Rock empire for $965 million.

Half an hour west of downtown Miami, Miccosukee Resort & Gaming *(500 S.W. 177th Ave., tel 877/242-6464, www.miccosukee.com),* is best known for its 1200-seat high-stakes bingo hall. The casino also has more than 1700 video pull tabs and a room featuring 58 poker tables. The tribally owned complex includes 302 hotel rooms and a golf course for those taking a break from gambling. ∎

Above left: Video poker at the Seminole Hark Rock Casino. Above right: The Seminole tribe recently purchased the entire Hard Rock chain. Below: Racing at Gulfstream Park

More places to visit in North Miami

AMELIA EARHART PARK

Hialeah's Amelia Earhart Park is a family-oriented playground featuring five lakes stocked with fish for anglers, a country store, horseshoe pits, an island for kids to play on, and a Florida-style barn with farm animals for children to pet (and ponies to ride). Chic it certainly is not, but pleasant and friendly it is.

🅜 32 D5 ✉ 401 E. 65th St., Hialeah Park ☎ 305/685-8389 💲 $ Sat.–Sun (free Mon–Tues.)

MIAMI SPRINGS

Miami's recent past is dominated by the schemes of entrepreneurs whose names appear often on street signs: Flagler, Brickell, Tuttle, and, of course, Curtiss, who has both a drive and a parkway named in his honor. But save for a group of historically conscious homeowners of the pueblo revival-style homes Curtiss built in Miami Springs, most residents have no idea that their little community abutting Miami International Airport's north fence sprang from an early 20th-century aviator's imagination.

The pueblo style of red-tiled roofs, thick adobe walls, and wide shade porches had been sweeping the country like a wildfire. To Glenn Curtiss, the validity lay in the vogue, and so the curtain rose on Miami Springs—the Santa Fe of the subtropics.

Miami Springs is best toured with a car and a camera, as almost all of its faux-mission homes are private. But it is pure Miami. Start downtown at the Curtiss Parkway, which runs diagonally between Okeechobee Rd. and N.W. 36th St. and bisects the Miami Springs Golf Course. The adobe bungalows near the parkway are really stucco over wood and tar paper, and the roof support beams that protrude from them don't support anything—but the look is appealingly genuine.

Consider stopping downtown on the parkway at **Miami Springs Pharmacy** (tel 305/888-5259), housed in a handsome pueblo revival building. Inside is a small historical exhibit, along with a curious pharmacological archive. Just up the street is the Fairhavens Retirement Home, originally Curtiss's Country Club Hotel, another pueblo revival gem. There are a few cafés along here, convenient places to

pause to consider whether you would be more in your element living in a home that makes you feel like an 18th-century Spanish colonial.

🅜 32 C4

SHERWOOD FOREST HOUSE

Another private residence worth viewing is the Tudor-style Sherwood Forest House. This is a monument to the broken dreams of a developer named D.C. Clarke, who, in 1925, intended to build Miami's most beautiful subdivision. The raw land was already gorgeously landscaped with subtropical plants—but the collapse of real estate prices dragged him down, leaving only this handsome, half-timbered home to suggest what might have been.

🅜 33 F4 ✉ 301 N.E. 86th St. at N.E. 3rd Ave.

THE PLAYGROUND THEATRE

Among the last great art deco edifices built in South Florida is The Playground Theatre. This is one of the few surviving Paramount Pictures showplaces that were once the studio's exclusive outlets, and were built in most major American cities. Paramount commissioned Miami architect Harold Steward to design it in the late 1930s, when the nation's deco vogue was entering its twilight years, but the war postponed its completion until 1946.

Now it is a performing arts center, where various local troupes delight audiences, especially young children. You can tour parts of the interior, but the exterior is what evokes the bygone era of America's great cinema palaces.

🅜 33 F5 ✉ 9806 N.E. 2nd Ave. at N.E. 98th St., Miami Shores ☎ 305/751-9550 💲 $

VILLA PAULA

The neoclassic old Cuban consulate, a 1920s columned dowager known as Villa Paula, was once among the most sumptuous estates north of Brickell Avenue. Now private, it is named for the wife of its first diplomatic resident, a consul from Havana. It is said she died here under suspicious circumstances, and of course that guarantees rumors that the place, which typifies patrician Cuban architecture of that era, is haunted by her ghost.

🅜 33 F4 ✉ 5811 N. Miami Ave. at N.E. 58th St. ■

Two well-dressed ladies stroll Miami's Haitian quarter.

Little Haiti

This enclave of an estimated 34,000 Haitian immigrants, 3 miles north of Miami's Central Business District, was once Lemon City, a mercantile district surrounded by citrus orchards. Today the neighborhood is a hodgepodge of shoestring merchandising, as much a response to the needs of residents trying to survive here as it is a bid to attract tourists, who, owing to Little Haiti's overblown reputation for crime (and proximity to the 1980s race riots in Liberty City and Overtown several miles south), tend to pass it by.

Lying east of I-95, Little Haiti runs to just a few blocks inland from Biscayne Bay. Its main boulevard is N.E. Second Avenue, and the enclave extends (roughly) from the Miami Design District around N.E. 36th Street to the vicinity of the El Portal neighborhood around N.E. 85th Street. It is a fascinating area: Haitian *compas* rhythms drumming from storefronts; hand-lettered signs in French Creole and English; folk art murals; women in wide-brimmed straw hats and pretty cotton smocks; the smoky aroma of pork and garlic roasting in hole-in-the-wall eateries; and old clapboard houses from Lemon City's maritime days, splashed in vivid colors—yellow, blue, green, magenta, flamingo.

If there is ever a musical about life in Little Haiti, one number is likely to take place in a public night school classroom, where Creole is used as a bridge to learning English. There will probably be a scene at a check-cashing outlet, with a lament about the burden of eking out a living in Miami while supporting a family languishing in Port-au-Prince. There will be a dance number in a café, Little Haiti's primary meeting places, and there will no doubt be a forlorn song of loneliness for a loved one who did not survive the desperate Gulf Stream odyssey. Several thousand Haitians risked the crossing in open sailboats to escape the cruelties and deprivations of the despotic regimes in their homeland. ■

New world, old ways: A Haitian voodoo ceremony in Miami mixes music, dance, and religious faith in search of a better life.

Little Haiti's central district

LEAVE YOUR JEWELRY, YOUR EXPENSIVE WRISTWATCH, and your handbag in your hotel room, park your car, and start your exploration of Little Haiti's heart on N.E. 54th Street, between N.E. Second and Miami Avenues. You could spend a day browsing among the kitsch, the food, and the exotica, advertised by illustrated handmade signs that are themselves worth collecting. If you see a record store, sample *compas*, a melodic, hard-driving Caribbean music immensely popular in Little Havana and Little Haiti nightclubs.

Central District

⚠ 33 F4

As you approach N.E. 54th Street's junction with Miami Avenue, look for the **Veye Yo (Watch Them)**. Little Haiti's political center offers evening lectures, typically about Haitian politics and immigrant concerns. (If they're in Creole, someone will translate for you.) Bring your appetite, too, for one of the best

things about Little Haiti is its cuisine, utterly casual but as tasty as any in the Caribbean. There is nothing nouvelle or New World about it; the sizzling fish and pork dishes are authentic recipes from the island of Haiti.

On weekends, the intersection of N.E. 54th Street and N.E. Second Avenue often becomes an

Mass is not in progress, take a look inside at the vivid panels of stained glass. They illustrate the saga of Pierre Toussaint (1746–1803), a pious Haitian who escaped slavery to become consul of Haiti, a spiritual leader, and a candidate for Catholic sainthood. On another wall is a mural portraying the odyssey of Haitian refugees to America. You are welcome to attend Sunday morning and evening masses, lovely assemblies of Little Haiti's folk, who turn out dressed up in their best for services that include African-flavored Caribbean music and song.

MAPOU CULTURAL CENTER

From the Church of Notre Dame d'Haiti, it's only a short walk to the Mapou Cultural Center *(5919 N.E. 2nd Ave., tel 305/757-9922)*. Owner Jan Mapou has created a focal point for Haitians in Miami to keep alive their language, dance, theater, literature, and other arts. You can buy souvenirs, paintings, and books translated from Kreyòl to English and vice versa.

There are also several inviting places to eat, including color-splashed cottages with tables in their backyards. The food at these restaurants is informal, inexpensive, and tasty, and most patrons are locals who eat nearly all their meals here. Creole names make the dishes sound more mysterious than they are: *lambi* is conch, and *griot* is fried pork (see also the menu reader on pp. 263–64). Almost everything else on the menus is familiar—fried fish and chicken, pickled vegetables, and the ubiquitous Caribbeanside dishes of rice, beans, and fried plantains. It's an authentic and delicious way to sample Haitian culture. ∎

NOT JUST "OFF THE BOAT"

Contrary to occasionally misleading media portrayals, Miami's Haitian newcomers are seldom illiterate or unskilled. Like most immigrants, they boast better résumés than countrymen who stay behind, and often represent Haiti's middle and upper classes. Most who come to Miami are actually secondary émigrés, moved south after years in Haitian enclaves in the Northeast, and are usually college-educated and fluent in English. From them Little Haiti draws its business and community leaders, and much of its hope for the future. ∎

open-air food market where you can buy just about anything eaten on the Caribbean isles. Sadly, a long effort to sustain a permanent Caribbean Marketplace at N.E. Second Avenue and N.E. 60th Street has faltered, even though in 1991 its facsimile of Port-au-Prince's century-old Iron Market won an American Institute of Architects' award for its innovative design and striking color scheme. For the time being it stands nearly empty, a casualty of Little Haiti's weak economy.

CHURCH OF NOTRE DAME D'HAITI

Near the marketplace, on N.E. Second Avenue, is the Church of Notre Dame d'Haiti, once the cafeteria of a Catholic girls' school. If the chapel is open and daily

More places to visit in Little Haiti

Haitian prayer flag detail

BUENA VISTA EAST

If you have not had your fill of old architecture by now, walk or drive through Little Haiti's Buena Vista East, another of Miami's older themed neighborhoods. The styles are eclectic, fanciful, and familiar, as most derive from the Mediterranean vogue of the 1920s. What is especially pleasant about the neighborhood is its cadre of homeowners, a racially mixed group of Miamians united in their affection for these little bandboxes, and in their determination to preserve them.

⚠ 33 F4   ✉ Between N.E. 2nd Ave. & Miami Ave.

Botanicas

These aromatic shops supply the pharmacopoeia and accoutrements of voodoo and *Santeria,* religions arising among West Africa's Yoruba peoples and spread to the Caribbean by the slave trade. The shops provide believers with the medicinal herbs, candles, effigies, images, and other paraphernalia required for rituals. If you enter one, be aware that *botanicas* are not curio shops, nor are they intended for tourists. Consider yourself in a religious setting and act accordingly. Resist any impulse to laugh at what you find—crucifixes fashioned from bones, voodoo dolls bristling with stickpins. To many living in Little Haiti, this is sacred stuff. ∎

CHURCHILL'S HIDEAWAY

Not at all Haitian, but set right down in Little Haiti, is an English-style pub named Churchill's Hideaway. (Winnie never drank here, however.) The food and ale are British, but the music at night isn't necessarily so. Churchill's, since the mid-1980s said to be Miami's leading rock 'n' roll venue, attracts music-world luminaries as well as notable Britons, who drop by for a pint and "pub grub," such as bangers and mash or shepherd's pie, and to watch satellite or cable television broadcasts of British soccer and rugby matches.

⚠ 33 F4   ✉ 5501 N.E. 2nd Ave.
☎ 305/757-1807, www.churchillspub.com

RAY'S FARM

Ray's Farm is a genuine piece of the pastoral life in the midst of urban Miami. It has the appearance of a place where routines are not strictly followed; however, on Saturday nights it hosts a restaurant-bistro where musicians pursue the avant-garde. If you are interested, telephone or drop by during the day to ask about plans for the evening. The farm is a popular excursion for local school kids, garden clubs, and college agricultural classes, and a genuine, pleasant vestige of the flower child era.

⚠ 33 F4   ✉ 7630 N.E. 1st Ave.
☎ 305/754-0000   💲 $–$$ ∎

The districts and developments that make up Miami
Beach's social mosaic give this
barrier island a composite per-
sonality whose temperaments
and styles are distinct from
those found in the no-less
diverse city across the bay.

Miami Beach

**Detail of a 1955 Cadillac,
considered a chic ride
among style-conscious
South Beach habitués**

Miami Beach

IF YOU COME TO MIAMI BEACH FOR A WEEK OR TWO, A STAY IN SOUTH Beach will probably deliver the most variety in the allotted time. If you come to stay a while longer, you might find the five communities below, claiming most of the 7 miles of shoreline south of the Dade–Broward County line, worth considering as well. Each has its appeal—Surfside and Sunny Isles attract those more concerned with economy.

SOUTH BEACH

Between 5th and 41st Streets is the district with which Miami Beach is most popularly associated. Here you will find the majority of the island's 800 art deco buildings, most of its youth-and-beauty-oriented playgrounds, and its best known beaches.

SOUTH OF SOUTH BEACH

South of Fifth Street, things have gone through considerable redevelopment in the past couple of years to include new and reno-vated buildings while retaining their hip, bohemian multiracial funkiness.

NORTHERN MIAMI BEACH

North of where the Julia Tuttle Causeway connects the island with Miami is a mélange of residential and commercial development. Trendy these neighborhoods are not, but all face the same warm blue water, most are near lovely beaches, and a few boast some Dade County bests. One of these is the very popular Las Vacas Gordas, an Argentinian steakhouse (933 Normandy Dr., tel 305/867-1717). Not until you reach the older Surfside community do you find architecture as appealing and charming as in SoBe's Art Deco District. Those into serious shopping will want to head to the mall at Bal Harbour.

CROSSING OVER TO THE BEACH

Five causeways connect the island with Miami, each landing you in a distinct neighborhood. In terms of views and en-route attractions, the most interesting is the MacArthur Causeway, which vaults the bay from Downtown Miami and deposits you in South Beach. Glance at lit-tle Watson Island to see two points of interest.

Heading east toward Miami Beach, look left for the small (one-acre) Japanese Garden. You'll also see Jungle Island (1111 Parrot Jungle Trail, tel 305/400-7220, www.jungle island.com, 10 a.m.–6 p.m., $$$$–$$$$$), which in 2003 relocated here from South Miami. Part of it is an aviary, filled with flap-ping, feathered expatriates from the world's jungles. The park, which is home to an array of mammals, primates, reptiles, and fish, also offers daily shows of its denizens. Opposite Jungle Island lies the Miami Children's Museum (980 MacArthur Causeway, tel 305/373-5437, www.miamichildrens museum.org, 10 a.m.–6 p.m., $$$), which opened a new building here in 2003. The 56,500-square-foot facility includes 12 gal-leries, classrooms, a parent/teacher resource center, and a 200-seat auditorium.

PORT OF MIAMI

The two big islands to the south (Dodge Island and Lummus Island) make up the Port of Miami, the world's largest cruise port, where each year the gangways of floating pleasure domes stream with more than three million passengers. (You can visit the port via a sepa-rate causeway that leaves downtown's Biscayne Boulevard near the Bayside Marketplace.) At night the ships are lit up like Las Vegas casinos.

THREE ENCLAVES OF ABUNDANCE

Look left (north) as you head toward Miami Beach and you will notice bridges leading to Palm, Hibiscus, and Star Islands, their ruler-straight shores bristling with sailboat masts and decorated with luxury manses, some owned by celebrities. These are private com-munities that can, if they wish, limit access to residents and guests. The causeway touches land by the Miami Beach Marina (300 Alton Road, tel 305/673-6000)—a parklike public port with 400 berths that can handle vessels up to 250 feet in length. ■

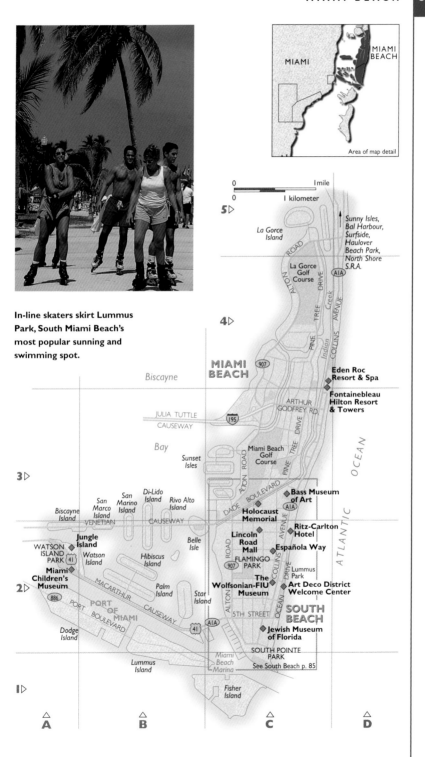

In-line skaters skirt Lummus Park, South Miami Beach's most popular sunning and swimming spot.

MIAMI

MIAMI BEACH

Area of map detail

0   1 mile
0   1 kilometer

5 ▷

La Gorce Island

Sunny Isles, Bal Harbour, Surfside, Haulover Beach Park, North Shore S.R.A.

La Gorce Golf Course

ALTON ROAD

PINE TREE DRIVE

COLLINS AVENUE

Indian Creek

4 ▷

Eden Roc Resort & Spa

Biscayne

MIAMI BEACH 907

ARTHUR GODFREY RD.

Fontainebleau Hilton Resort & Towers

JULIA TUTTLE CAUSEWAY 195

Bay

PINE TREE DRIVE

Sunset Isles

Miami Beach Golf Course

3 ▷

Biscayne Island

San Marco Island

San Marino Island

Di-Lido Island

Rivo Alto Island

VENETIAN   CAUSEWAY

ALTON ROAD

BOULEVARD

DADE

Bass Museum of Art

Holocaust Memorial

A1A

Ritz-Carlton Hotel

Belle Isle

Lincoln Road Mall

Española Way

WATSON ISLAND PARK 41

Jungle Island

Watson Island

Hibiscus Island

FLAMINGO PARK 907

COLLINS AVENUE

OCEAN DRIVE

ATLANTIC

Lummus Park

Miami Children's Museum 886

2 ▷

MACARTHUR   CAUSEWAY

PORT BOULEVARD

Palm Island

Star Island

The Wolfsonian-FIU Museum

Art Deco District Welcome Center

PORT OF MIAMI

41

5TH STREET

A1A

SOUTH BEACH

Dodge Island

Jewish Museum of Florida

Lummus Island

Miami Beach Marina

SOUTH POINTE PARK
See South Beach p. 85

1 ▷

Fisher Island

△   △   △   △
A   B   C   D

OCEAN

South Beach

Though Miami Beach is more than South Beach, the island's longtime image as the American Riviera today indisputably reflects most brightly from here, roughly a 40-block-long stretch beginning on 5th and running north to about 41st Street. Here are the cafés, refurbished streamline and moderne hotels and apartment houses, restaurants, shops, boutiques, museums, beaches, and photogenic habitués commanding the attention of travel magazines.

Known to many as SoBe, it is a remarkable district, exciting to its residents, a sizable percentage of whom are gay men and women. Here, too, is a significant cadre of artists, writers, musicians, and entertainers, many of them full-time residents. It is a walkable, appealing community, blessed with one of the most inviting beaches in South Florida on its Atlantic side.

Ocean Drive is SoBe's most photographed street, a palmy beachfront lined with hotels painted in vibrant colors and trimmed with neon. Ocean Drive between 5th and 14th Streets often appears populated by pretty people for whom leisure is the order of the day. But behind the air of languid indolence affected by many who lounge at Ocean Drive's café tables is a brisk, if volatile, economy spiked most notably by entrepreneurial restaurateurs, hoteliers, retailers, and real estate developers.

On weekend nights, when some 30,000 people stream across the bay for the SoBe nightlife, it's almost impossible to drive. If you do, get your street parking early; there is a small but convenient public parking lot with ten-hour meters at the corner of Tenth and Washington (across the street from the Astor Hotel and the Wolfsonian Foundation). All you need is a roll or two of quarters. Parking enforcement is swift. Don't chance a $20-plus overtime parking citation.

If time is short, visit Ocean Drive for a quick bite at one of its many sidewalk cafés or open-front restaurants, and be sure to cross the street to the Lummus Park beach and put your foot in the water, if only to experience the warmth of the Gulf Stream. It takes less than an hour to walk its ten-block line-up of art deco confections, starting with the 1939 **Bentley Luxury Suites Hotel** at Fifth and Ocean. To say that any Ocean Drive café guarantees a

Lower Ocean Drive's much-photographed row of beachfront hotels and cafés symbolizes SoBe's sybaritic lifestyle.

glimpse of SoBe archetypes would be glib, but an iced tea and sandwich outside the **Colony Hotel** *(736 Ocean Dr., tel 305/673-0088)* carries the likelihood of observing one of the willowy women and hollow-cheeked men from the fashion ads, here at their self-conscious leisure. The **News Café** *(8th St., tel 305/538-6397; see p. 249)* has been described as a watering hole for the simply fabulous, so much so that its tables are often taken by tourists searching for famous faces. But the News is also an excellent eatery, one of SoBe's best. Between Eighth and Ninth is **Larios on the Beach** *(tel 305/532-9577; see p. 248)*, a color-splashed Cuban restaurant owned by Miami singer Gloria Estefan. Another Cuban-style bistro, **Mango's Tropical Café** *(tel 305/673-4422; see p. 249)*, at Ocean and Ninth, throbs at night with Caribbean music and overflows with singles seeking salsa dance partners.

Come evening, SoBe's youth-oriented club scene commences. Doormen will only admit the prettiest and trendiest, and even if you are granted entry, what you often find within is a lot of empty attitude, self-conscious posturing, deafening music requiring you to

read lips, and haphazard (and overpriced) bar service. That said, SoBe does have some places where the elegance is real, among them **Escopazzo** *(1311 Washington Ave., tel 305/674-9450; see p. 247)*.

If you must subject yourself to the club scene's cruel social Darwinism, do it a short walk away at **Mynt** *(1921 Collins Avenue, tel 786/276-6132)*, considered one of the more adult party-till-dawn clubs. Jazz and spirits are served with equal élan at **Jazid** *(1342 Washington Avenue, tel 305/673-9372)*, a friendly bar cherished by locals and tourists alike. With live music every night, this is one of the cooler, and more relaxed, places on South Beach for unwinding. For understated swank, the bar at the pretty streamline-style **Hotel Astor** *(956 Washington Ave., at 10th St., tel 305/531-8081; see p. 246)* is hard to top in this part of town.

Before it was Miami Beach, it was Ocean Beach, where Miamians came first by boat and later by drawbridge to picnic in the cooling trade winds and swim in the warm Gulf Stream current. The beaches that run some 16 miles from the Dade County line to the tip of Miami Beach gave birth to the notion of this as Eastern America's Costa del Sol.

From 5th to 15th Streets, South Beach's wide Atlantic strand is a public recreation area called **Lummus Park,** an expanse of white

A rap-style aerobics class at the annual Sports & Fitness Festival in Lummus Park

sand running to a gentle surf and a bottom that slants away slowly, permitting you to wade safely into the sea that welcomed Christopher Columbus to the New World.

Near Ocean Drive, Lummus has comfortable benches where you can watch pick-up volleyball games, listen to the rustle of palm fronds above, or relax under a thatched hut. The park has a concrete walkway—popular with in-line skaters—running most of its length. There's little in the way of organized beach activity, but call park headquarters for information on events *(tel 305/673-7730)*.

SOUTH POINTE PARK

Its name implies the park's location at the island's southern tip, at the bottom of Washington Avenue. The district below Fifth Street has recently begun to share in the revival just north, but this 17-acre, family-oriented park nonetheless offers a pleasant getaway place. It has a nice swimming beach, grassy walkways, and an observation tower affording a good vantage point for watching passing cruise ships. There are a playground for kids, picnic pavilions, and charcoal grills, and a 150-foot-long pier frequented by anglers juts out into the ship channel. On Friday nights the amphitheater hosts free concerts and a crafts bazaar. During the week, when

Lummus Park's beach can be crowded, South Pointe's can be quieter. On weekends, however, you are likely to find it overrun by extended families on outings.

On the way to or from the park, walk west to the Miami Beach Marina and see some of the most incredible yachts and megayachts you can imagine. You can also find fishing and diving charters here. ■

Why the sea is so blue here

In colder climes, where lower-temperature seawater holds more dissolved oxygen and carbon dioxide, nutrients give rise to dense blooms of tiny plants (phytoplankton) that feed microscopic animals (zooplankton). This rich soup, the foundation of the ocean food chain, often makes chilly waters elsewhere appear murky. South Florida's warm currents hold far lower concentrations of dissolved gases, making them inhospitable to plankton. The absence of suspended matter leaves nothing to filter out the intense blue light that results when sunlight falls on a crystalline sea. ■

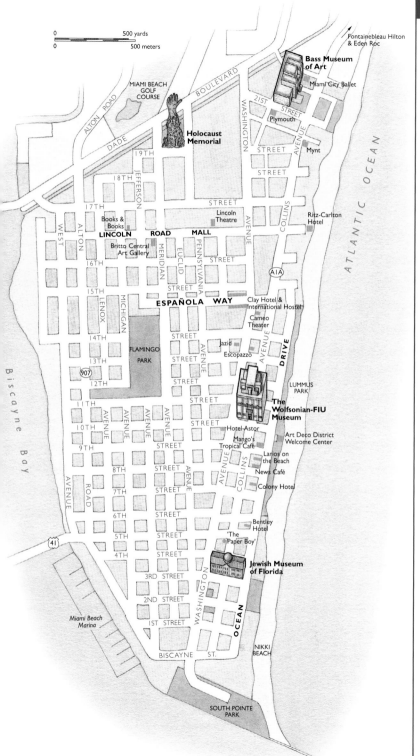

0
500 yards
0
500 meters

Fontainebleau Hilton & Eden Roc

MIAMI BEACH GOLF COURSE

ALTON ROAD

DADE BOULEVARD

Bass Museum of Art

Miami City Ballet

21ST STREET

WASHINGTON

Plymouth

Holocaust Memorial

19TH

Mynt

STREET

JEFFERSON

18TH

STREET

17TH

Books & Books

Lincoln Theatre

Ritz-Carlton Hotel

WEST

ALTON

LINCOLN ROAD MALL

COLLINS

AVENUE

Britto Central Art Gallery

16TH

MERIDIAN

EUCLID

PENNSYLVANIA

STREET

15TH

LENOX

MICHIGAN

ESPAÑOLA WAY

A1A

Clay Hotel & International Hostel

Cameo Theater

14TH

STREET

Jazid

DRIVE

FLAMINGO PARK

13TH

AVENUE

STREET

Escopazzo

907

12TH

STREET

LUMMUS PARK

11TH

STREET

The Wolfsonian-FIU Museum

Biscayne Bay

10TH

AVENUE

STREET

Hotel Astor

Art Deco District Welcome Center

9TH

STREET

Mango's Tropical Café

8TH

AVENUE

STREET

Larios on the Beach

COLLINS

News Café

7TH

STREET

Colony Hotel

AVENUE

ROAD

6TH

STREET

5TH

STREET

Bentley Hotel

41

4TH

STREET

'The Paper Boy'

3RD STREET

Jewish Museum of Florida

WASHINGTON

2ND STREET

ATLANTIC OCEAN

OCEAN

1ST STREET

Miami Beach Marina

BISCAYNE ST.

NIKKI BEACH

SOUTH POINTE PARK

Art Deco District walk

If it were not for the Miami Design Preservation League, a group committed to saving Greater Miami's architectural treasures, there would be no Art Deco District (officially, the Miami Beach Art Deco National Historic District), nor as many surviving examples.

One way to see some of its outstanding expressions is to go to the Art Deco Welcome Center *(1001 Ocean Dr., tel 305/672-2014, www.mdpl.org)* on Tuesday, Wednesday, Fri-day, Saturday, or Sunday at 10:30 a.m., or on Thursday at 6:30 p.m., when league volunteers lead 90-minute walking tours *($$$$–$$$$$)*. Take the tour on your own any day of the week by renting an iPod at the center between 9:30 a.m. and 5 p.m., which guides you along the route *($$$$)*, or using your cellphone *($$$)*. You can also find the buildings on your own as the historical district—running from 6th to 23rd streets— encompasses some 800 structures.

A good place to begin is toward the southern end of Ocean Drive, between Sixth and Seventh Streets, and head north. Among the handsomest buildings here is the **Park Central Hotel ❶** *(630 Ocean Dr.)*, completed in 1937. Its terrazzo floors and front steps, vast lobby, and etched glass details recall the luxurious backdrops of pre-World War II Hollywood musicals—no coincidence, as

the vogue drew inspiration from films of that era.

Venture into the gorgeous lobby of the little **Colony Hotel ❷** *(736 Ocean Dr.)*, which has a fireplace faced with green Vitrolite and a Ramon Chatov mural romanticizing South American rural life. Nor should you bypass the lovely terrazzo floor, molded ceiling treatments, and beautiful light fixtures in the lobby of the **Waldorf Towers Hotel ❸**, farther along Ocean Drive at No. 860.

In the next block at No. 940, the **Break-water Hotel's ❹** 1939 facade mimics a Central American Maya temple. At night, neon lights on its concrete spire spell BREAK-WATER in vivid blue. It shares a swimming pool with the adjoining Mediterranean Revival **Edison Hotel,** which opened in 1935. At this point you will have reached the **Art Deco Welcome Center ❺**, where you can pick up maps and get informa-tion. Walk around it; the back side mimics the bridge of an ocean liner. Cubism inspired the 1937 **Victor Hotel ❻** *(1144 Ocean Dr.)*. Purists appreciate

> ⓐ See also area map p. 85
> ➤ Park Central Hotel, 630 Ocean Dr.
> ↔ 2 miles
> ⏱ 1–2 hours
> ➤ The Hotel
>
> **NOT TO BE MISSED**
> - Park Central Hotel
> - Miami Beach Main Post Office
> - Astor Hotel
> - The Hotel

the three-story **Leslie Hotel** ⑦ *(1244 Ocean Dr.)* for its classic simplicity.

The **Carlyle** *(1250 Ocean Dr.)* went up in 1941, its architect using the wide lot to stretch the deco style horizontally. Side by side in the 1400-block are two of the most exuberant expressions of it you will find on the Beach: the **Crescent Hotel** ⑧, built in 1932, and the **McAlpin Hotel** next door, completed in 1940. Continue to the junction with 15th Street and turn left. On the other side of Collins Avenue is the three-story **Haddon Hall** ⑨ *(1500 Collins Ave.)*, the beach's finest streamline building.

Walk south on Collins and turn right onto 13th Street. Opposite, at No. 1300 on Washington Avenue, is the **Miami Beach Main Post Office** ⑩, a wonderful and rare example of deco federal, which opened in 1939. Details inside the spacious circular rotunda include a beautiful historical mural. Turn left and continue down Washington Avenue. Another streamline beauty, the **Astor Hotel** ⑪ *(956 Washington Ave., at 10th)*, is more restrained. Take Tenth Street back onto Collins Avenue. The nautical moderne design of the 1938 **Essex House** ⑫ *(1001 Collins Ave.)* epitomizes art deco's intense infatuation with ocean travel on the great moderne ships of that age.

Continue south down Collins for a look at beautiful **The Hotel** ⑬ *(801 Collins Ave.)*. With its metal spire and neon, this is one of the finest expressions of art deco spirit on the island. It recently reopened as a small luxury inn. ■

Art deco hotels, Ocean Drive, South Beach

Española Way

ARCHITECT ROBERT TAYLOR CALLED HIS BLOCK-LONG, 1925 Mediterranean Revival complex "a haven for artists and rogues." If so, they were genteel bohemians, for this fanciful Alhambra of gas lamp-lighted private alleys and courts, artists' studios, arched portals, and narrow streets is nothing if not elegant.

Española Way

Ⓜ 81 C2

THE SOUTH BEACH LOCAL

The South Beach Local, operated by Miami-Dade Transit, is a bi-directional circular service to the entire South Beach area (*Mon.–Sat, 7:45 a.m.–1 a.m., Sun. 10 a.m.–1 a.m. For a map, visit www.miamibeachfl .gov/NEWCITY/ sobe_local.asp*). ■

You will find the awnings and balconies of Taylor's Spanish Village between Washington and Drexel Avenues, sandwiched between 14th and 15th Streets. Remarkably, his intent still rules here—the upper floor lofts are indeed occupied by artists. Below, on the sidewalk level, are cafés, interesting shops and boutiques, and several fine art galleries.

The Miami Beach Preservation League occasionally organizes 45-minute Saturday afternoon tours of the area, usually departing at 2 p.m. from the 1925 **Clay Hotel and International Hostel** (*1438 Washington Ave., tel 305/534-2988; see p. 247*). South Beach's only hostel and one of the coolest in the world, this is where Al Capone ran his infamous gambling ring and Desi Arnaz created the rumba craze. In recent years, Don Johnson, Sylvester

Stallone, and Elton John have shot films and videos here. To explore this area, start with a look at the Clay's appealing lobby—found at 406 Española Way—then just roam.

When its curtain rose for the first time in 1938, the nearby **Cameo Theater** (*1445 Washington Ave., tel 305/532-2667, www.cameomiami .com*) screened foreign films. The building's curved facade, with sculptured moldings framing a wall of glass brick, is pure modernism. Lately it has been used as a dance club and rock music hall, attracting a young and determinedly hip crowd.

You can reach Española Way on the South Beach Local (see sidebar). Stops along the route include the Holocaust Memorial (see p. 95), the Art Deco District Welcome Center (see p. 86), and the Jewish Museum (see p. 94). ■

Lincoln Road Mall

ITS HISTORY IS A CLASSIC TALE OF MIAMI BEACH'S ENTRE-
preneurial beginnings: a dirt road through a mangrove swamp transformed by a visionary developer into a chic promenade that is now
occupied by more than 300 restaurants, cafés, art galleries, specialty
stores, clothing boutiques, and studio-galleries.

When Carl Fisher, who established
himself as the creator of the Indi-
anapolis Speedway, announced
plans to create the "Fifth Avenue of
the South," Miami Beach had no
commercial district. Residents had
to make the long drive across the
old drawbridge to shop in
Downtown Miami department
stores. The site Fisher chose for his
new shopping mecca had the dis-
advantage of being below sea level.
Undaunted, he had it built up with
sand dredged from Biscayne Bay,
widened and paved the road, and
named it for his hero, Abraham
Lincoln. He replaced the coconut
palms (which sometimes dropped
fruit on the unsuspecting) with
royal palms. He sold space to pres-
tigious tenants like Saks Fifth
Avenue, Bonwit Teller, Packard,
and Chrysler, and Lincoln Road
soon acquired a reputation for
being posh.

It still is, on the whole, its bazaar
reaching from Alton Road to the
Atlantic shoreline. (The pedestrian
mall stretches between Washington
and Lenox Avenues.) Leave your car
at the 17th Street parking lot and
stroll. If you see a crowd gathered in
front of the **Regal South Beach
18** *(1100 Lincoln Rd., tel 305/674-
6766)*, a giant glass-walled theater,
then it's movie time. The nationally
touring, 90-member **New World
Symphony,** an orchestral company
devoted to training musicians aged
21 to 30, occupies the striking
Lincoln Theatre *(555 Lincoln
Rd.)*, opened in 1936 by Wometco as
a movie theater. Between performances the building is usually
locked, but its facade is pleasing to
behold all the same.

For a more cerebral adventure,
visit **Books & Books** *(933 Lincoln
Rd., tel 305/532-3222)*. This very
popular bookstore hosts talks by
authors, has book signings nearly
every evening, and also houses an

inviting café well worth a visit, the
Russian Bear.

To embrace the visual arts,
visit **Britto Central Art
Gallery**. The joyous work of
Romero Britto, Brazil's contemporary pop artist, has been shown
everywhere from the White House
to Absolut Vodka bottles.

A small antiques fair sets up
on Saturdays, and a farmers' fruit
and vegetable market opens on
Sunday mornings. ∎

Lincoln Road Mall
⚠ 81 C2

**Britto Central Art
Gallery**
www.britto.com
✉ 818 Lincoln Rd.
☎ 305/531-8821

**New World
Symphony**
www.nws.org
☎ 305/673-3331
(box office)

**Café society on
Lincoln Road,
where the only
traffic is on foot**

Art deco

The style takes its name from the 1925 Paris Exposition Internationale des Arts Décoratifs et Industriels Modernes, an exhibition of works embodying machine-age modernity. A stellar group of American designers, architects, and industrialists were soon applying modernism adornments to automobiles (like the Chrysler Airflow, which flopped), airplanes (like the DC-3, which flew), and even kitchen appliances.

The New York Central's sleek Manhattan-to-Chicago express train, christened the 20th-Century Limited, seemed the embodiment of the national faith in progress. Designers described their windswept creations as moderne, streamline, skyscraper, and "Jazz Age," a term coined by F. Scott Fitzgerald. Meanwhile "arts déco" remained a French term, used most often in reference to low-relief geometrical designs: parallel straight lines, zigzags, chevrons, and stylized floral motifs.

Ironically, it was the Depression that gave the deco vogue its strongest push. Bank failures, bread lines, and factory closures had shaken Americans' faith in institutions. They wanted architecture, and public architecture in particular—office buildings, post offices, railroad stations—to be uplifting and encouraging. That was the challenge given to architect Howard Cheney, commissioned to build Miami Beach's new post office at 1300 Washington Avenue in the late 1930s. He succeeded brilliantly.

But what accounted for deco's extraordinary popularity here? Some say its air of ease appealed to Miami's hard-working, winter-weary vacationers. Others suppose that the style's classic foundations appealed to former Europeans who accounted for many of the Beach's visitors and residents, while its thoroughly American look reminded them that they were far from the horrors of European fascism.

Art deco has an assertive handsomeness that many associate with verve and confidence. The theatricality of even the smallest hotels, like the "sea-going" Essex *(1001 Collins Ave.)* and the "Maya" Breakwater *(940 Ocean Dr.)*, each topped with a spire advertising itself in neon, exudes an appealing, amusing air of youthful jauntiness. In 1940, as Franklin Roosevelt's social engineering seemed to be turning things around, architect Anton Skislewicz adopted the heroic pylons of the future-worshipping temples of the decade's world's fairs for his posh Plymouth resort hotel *(336 21st St.)*. Did it matter that you were not a star if you could live in an apartment tower like Robert Collins's Helen Mar overlooking Lake Pancoast—as chic as anything in Hollywood—on an ocean far bluer and warmer than the chill Pacific that sweeps California's coast?

ART DECO STYLE

Bands of windows encourage circulation

Flat roof broken by ve projections

Cantilevered eyebrows for shade and symmetry

Corner windows provide softening to the geometry

Tropical, pastel colors exude the atmosphere of the beach

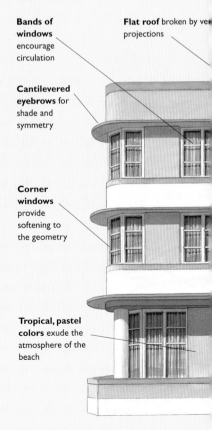

For all its make-believe, art deco was nonetheless practical. Given South Florida's wood-rotting dampness and paint-peeling sunlight, its use of concrete, smooth-faced stone, and metal as exterior architectural coverings enabled art deco buildings to better withstand subtropical weather. Its elements of the Arts Décoratifs—accents created with colored terra-cotta, rose mirrors, stainless steel, plate glass, Bakelite, Vitrolite, glazes, aluminum, and tubular steel—were durable as well. Miami's builders had a rich palette from which to choose, and they used it to build a thousand priceless expressions of the style. ■

Above right: Marine bas-relief, Marlin Hotel

Terrazzo

Composed of stone chips set in mortar and polished, terrazzo was used by most of the architects who worked here in art deco styles to create patterned floors and stairways. (Elsewhere, the effect is occasionally emulated using linoleum inlays.) Architectural historians believe the district holds the world's richest collection of this decorative art. ■

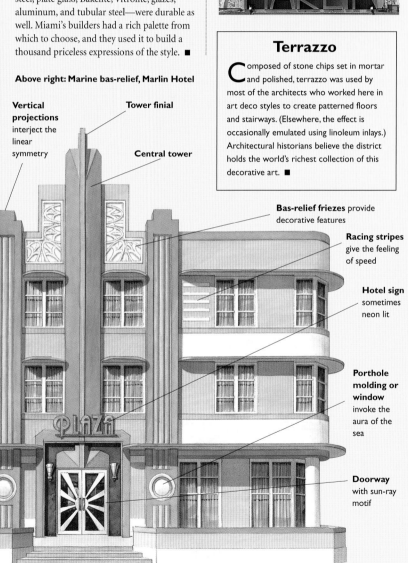

Vertical projections interject the linear symmetry

Tower finial

Central tower

Bas-relief friezes provide decorative features

Racing stripes give the feeling of speed

Hotel sign sometimes neon lit

Porthole molding or window invoke the aura of the sea

Doorway with sun-ray motif

Above: The Spanish-Moorish Wolfsonian

The Wolfsonian-FIU Museum

The Wolfsonian
www.wolfsonian.fiu.edu
- 81 C2
- Washington Ave. & 10th St.
- 305/531-1001
- Closed Wed.
- $–$$

MANY PEOPLE FIND THIS UNUSUAL MUSEUM INEXPRESS-ibly fascinating because its intriguing themes are difficult to explain. Officially, the Wolfsonian examines the "decorative and propaganda arts" and "material culture," which is about as revealing as saying that *War and Peace* is a book about Russia. The museum occupies an imposing seven-story, Spanish-Moorish-style former storage company building, and holds more than 70,000 objects, predominantly from North America and Europe, that "reflect the cultural, political, and technological changes that swept across the world in the century preceding the Second World War."

Mitchell Wolfson, Jr., heir to the Wometco Theater chain fortune, spent years amassing this trove of furniture, paintings, sculptures, architectural models, posters, books, glass, ceramics, metal works, and ephemera—a fever chart of the modern psyche, tracing its swings between mankind's beauty and beast natures. The exhibits are startling and eclectic: Jazz Age kitchen appliances so stream-line they're heroic; a flattering bronze bust of Mussolini; a pinball machine exhorting American kids to kill Axis warlords; and a hand-tooled Braille version of Hitler's *Mein Kampf.* The 52,000-square-foot building was built in 1927 to store the possessions of Miami Beach's patrician set during the low season. Inside, all is now modern, with humidity and temperature carefully controlled to preserve thousands of rare volumes and fragile documents. The bookstore is elegantly stocked with a variety of books, museum publications, and various items selected for their out-standing design. ■

Dudley Vaill Talcott's 1929 aluminum "Wrestler"

Bass Museum of Art

**Bass Museum
of Art**
www.BassMuseum.org

🅰 81 C3

✉ 2121 Park Ave.

☎ 305/673-7530

🕐 Closed Mon.

💲 $$

LIKE THE WOLFSONIAN'S UNUSUAL BUILDING, THE MAYA-themed structure housing the European art collection of the Bass family (the museum's benefactors) was originally devoted to another use, in this case to serve as the Miami Beach Library and Art Center. It is built of keystone—the same rough, mottled gray rock, created by eons of coral-building, that underlies much of South Florida.

The Bass is the only repository of fine art on the island, and its holdings include some old masters and an interesting array of ecclesiastical artifacts said to be the finest of its kind in southeast Florida. Don't expect to see internationally renowned paintings. However, you will find interesting works by Peter Paul Rubens, Albrecht Dürer, and Henri Toulouse-Lautrec, among other important artists. Particularly unusual and rare are the pair of huge Flemish tapestries dating from the 1500s.

This thoughtfully curated institution makes smart use of its limited but attractive spaces, mounting changing exhibitions supplemented by screenings of related films and documentaries in its auditorium. The Bass sits on a plot of land donated to Miami Beach long ago by city father John Collins (honoree of Collins Avenue). Collins' architect grandson Russell Pancoast designed the building, completed in 1930.

Take a close look at the trio of deeply cut keystone bas-reliefs above the museum's portals, all by Gustav Bohland, one of a locally prominent group of architects whose works often reflected the fantasy vogues of Florida's prosperous early-century boom years. The center relief is most interesting, depicting a stylized pelican against a beautifully rendered art deco background of palm, mangrove forest, and ocean. Look closely, too, at the exterior wall of the building, and in the keystone and you will see fossils of ancient sea creatures. ∎

Botticelli and Ghirlandaio's "The Coronation of the Virgin with Saints" (1492), one of the Bass Museum's prized works of ecclesiastical art.

Jewish Museum of Florida

Jewish Museum of Florida
www.jewishmuseum.com

81 C2

301 and 311 Washington Ave., at 3rd St.

305/672-5044

10 a.m.–5 p.m.; closed Mon. & Jewish holidays

$$

THE JEWISH MUSEUM OF FLORIDA IS A REMARKABLE archive devoted to the multifaceted story of Florida's Jewish population, whose saga traces back more than 240 years. The museum occupies two reincarnated deco buildings. The main museum, dating from 1936, was originally an Orthodox synagogue for Miami Beach's first Jewish congregation, Beth Jacob, and was rededicated to its present station in 1995. (Its slanted floor, which improved acoustics and enabled rabbis to be better heard, remains.) Eighty stained-glass windows bathe its interior in sanguine light.

A menorah flames with sunlight inside Miami Beach's first Orthodox congregation, now a museum.

alligator in Jacksonville, 1916," and "Miss Florida, Mena Williams, in Tallahassee, 1885"); heirlooms such as a set of Passover china from the mid-19th century; poignant documents like the Cuban passport of Elisa Gerkes, who immigrated from Poland to Havana in 1917 as a child; and Florida zaniness like the seashell-covered dress Fannie Moss made for a Purim party in 1916.

Other remembrances might make you sad. Old photographs of Miami Beach's "Gentiles Only" hotel signs are especially ironic, given that Miami Beach later became the largest and most vibrant Jewish community in the American Southeast. Be sure to watch the three historical videos. ∎

The second restored synagogue, built in 1928–29, was the original (and quickly outgrown) home of Congregation Beth Jacob. The former sanctuary now houses a second exhibit venue where public programs are held. Both buildings were placed on the National Register of Historic Places in 1980.

The museum's permanent, core exhibit, **"MOSAIC: Jewish Life in Florida,"** is the centerpiece of its cultural documentary. Intriguing revelations include the little-known saga of Jewish people in Cuba, a life that came apart when Castro-style communism came to power there. You don't have to be Jewish or understand Jewish traditions to be charmed by the museum's personal approach, which includes family photographs (for example, baby "Felix Glickstein on a stuffed

Become a part of history

The Jewish Museum of Florida continually collects material of the Jewish experience in Florida to pass on to future generations. From this, the museum produces exhibitions that change three times a year. Florida Jewish residents who would like to have their family heirlooms, artifacts, and/or photographs documented and preserved at the museum should contact the registrar.

305/672-5044, ext. 15 ∎

Holocaust Memorial

Holocaust
Memorial
www.holocaustmmb.org
🅰 81 C3
✉ 1933–45 Meridian
Ave., between 19th
St. & Dade Blvd.
☎ 305/538-1663
🕐 9 a.m.–9 p.m.

MIAMI BEACH, WHICH HAS ONE OF AMERICA'S LARGEST enclaves of Holocaust survivors, has a memorial to the six million Jews who perished in Europe during the Nazis' reign of terror. Dedicated in 1990 in a ceremony that featured Nobel Prize laureate Elie Wiesel, the memorial is laden with symbolism—every element represents an emotional, historical, or philosophical aspect of the Holocaust—and bears the triple burden of memorializing victims, solacing survivors, and ensuring that successive generations do not forget what happened.

Victims' names etch the memorial's interior.

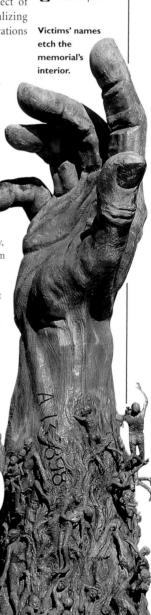

Begun in the mid-1980s near the junction of Dade Boulevard and Meridian Avenue, it's constructed mostly of rose-hued Jerusalem stone and surrounded by a wide reflecting pool. The memorial's most striking aspect from afar is its great bronze hand reaching 42 feet above the water toward the sky. As you draw closer, details conceived by the memorial's architect and sculptor, Kenneth Treister, assert themselves to create an interpretive monument. A trio of panels forming part of a semicircular black granite wall are chiseled with an overview of events from Hitler's ascent to power in 1933 to his suicide amid the ruin of Berlin a dozen years later.

By tracing these events you are drawn to an enclosed, shrinelike space leading into a confining tunnel with walls bearing the names of death camps—Auschwitz and Dachau, Bergen-Belsen, and others. Its ceiling presses lower as you advance. The intent, said Treister, is to symbolize the victims' sense of a diminished self—the replacement of one's name with a tattooed serial number, the loss of possessions, loved ones, freedom, country, and, finally, of life itself. From this grim enclosure you emerge into open air and a circular plaza where the great bronze hand grasps at the sky. Look closely and you see that its forearm is wrapped in a frieze of nearly 100 tormented people clustered in family groups. Examine the hand and you see on it a tattooed number, which on real skin was a mottle of blue ink. Venture farther and you come to the memorial wall of victims' names, intended to create a link between the living and those who have vanished. These names are added as they are submitted by those who remember and honor them. ■

Miami's Jewish heritage

Miami has the second largest Jewish community in America after New York, created by a curious interplay of social forces and historical twists. Jews came to Florida for reasons similar to those drawing other Americans south: clement weather and a chance to establish themselves in a young, still-forming economy. A few settled in 19th-century Key West, finding commercial opportunities in the island city's booming maritime salvage trade; others found refuge in Cuba from European pogroms, later establishing a close-knit community in Miami.

Among the first Jews to arrive were merchants already established in the Northeast, who saw Henry Flagler's and his rivals' railroad building on the Florida Gulf Coast as a sign of an economy poised to expand. By 1912 Miami had a sufficiently large Jewish enclave to establish the city's first synagogue, Beth David (originally B'nai Zion).

The migration from the Northeast that established Miami Beach's reputation as a Jewish retirement community peaked in the years between the world wars. The giddy upward spiral of real estate prices attracted many, while a growing economy created jobs for the educated and opportunities for the learned. Underlying everything else was Miami's aura as a "tropical" city with a healthy climate.

Bitter winter weather elsewhere in the East guaranteed Miami's tourist trade, and as part of the general population who boarded trains for Miami came Jews from the vast New York–New Jersey metropolis, and from Chicago's urban sprawl. They established a tradition of winter sojourns, sparking Miami Beach's building boom in small residential hotels. In 1927 the Reform Temple Israel, one of the most handsome in the country, opened here, followed in 1929 by Congregation Beth Jacob, Miami Beach's

first synagogue, now home to the Jewish Museum of Florida (see p. 94).

(see p. 94)

Along with the flowering came anti-Semitism: restrictive covenants forbidding Jewish folk from renting hotel rooms or buying homes in certain areas (struck down by the Supreme Court in the 1950s). There were restaurant signs reading "No Dogs, No Blacks, No Jews." Upper-crust social enclaves such as the Nautilus Club made it known that Jews need not apply. But they might as well have tried to stop the Gulf Stream from flowing to Florida; Jewish families came by the thousands, checking into Miami Beach's new art deco hotels. With no small irony, a synagogue was eventually built on what had been the Nautilus Club's polo field.

Miami's conversion into a military training center during World War II brought thousands of enlisted men and officer candidates from all around the country. Soldiers (including many who were not Jewish) found

themselves invited into Jewish homes on holy days, and the memories of this unexpected community brought thousands back after the war to settle here and raise their families.

Meanwhile, Miami Beach's popularity as a winter resort continued to grow, and in the 1950s Jewish families began to venture away to neighborhoods in Miami and up the coast. In a little-known historical footnote, following Fidel Castro's ascent to power, some 10,000 members of Cuba's Jewish community made the bitter decision to leave their island, most settling in Miami and Miami Beach.

At the start of the 21st century, Miami's Jewish community now shares Greater Miami with Cubans and other Caribbean immigrants. Generations pass, yet still beneath the sun hats of the Jewish elderly who slowly make their way among Miami's increasingly multicultural populace, there is a deep awareness of having escaped a past many did not, of a long and improbable odyssey to a safe place in the sun, and a determination to remember and give thanks. ■

Jewish wedding group at the Eden Roc Resort, on North Miami Beach

Resorts & towers

Fontainebleau
www.fontainebleau.com

🅼 81 C3

✉ 4441 Collins Ave.,
between 44th &
45th Sts.

☎ 305/538-2000
or 800/548-8886

**Sunrise over the
infinity pool at
the Ritz-Carlton,
South Beach**

STANDING OUT FROM THE REST OF THE 1950s AND 1960s high-rise hotels that line Collins Avenue north of 23rd Street in central Miami Beach, are the eye-catching Fontainebleau and Eden Roc. These resort-era icons created and define a style of American architecture that resists description in the standard lexicon of most critics. Vying for attention with these long-time stars is the glitzy new Ritz-Carlton Hotel, a mile or so to the south.

FONTAINEBLEAU RESORT & TOWERS

Its curves and candy-swirl rooms have been photographed by some of America's most visually acerbic documentarians. Writers have struggled to explain what it represents. (A decadent culture in decline? A time in America whose passing ought to be mourned? The Cheops of Kitsch?) Built in 1954 and recently renovated and expanded, the Fountainbleau is still going strong. Pricey, well run, and well maintained, this grande dame of hotels still impresses people as an icon of a confident, unapologetic postwar America. Others say the twin-towered, 17-story, 920-room, 20-acre behemoth is just a big hotel prone to decorative excess. It is probably all of these—splashy, splendid, and utterly unapologetic, the creation of developer Ben Novak and architect Morris Lapidus, who began his career designing department store interiors. Despite much critical bashing he has been dubbed the Architect of the American Dream.

As you approach the Fontainebleau, you pass "middle" Miami Beach's golf courses and upscale manses lining the Indian Creek waterway across Collins Avenue, along which yachts and colorful sailboats dock. If you cannot find street parking, use the hotel's garage and wander for a while, starting in the lobby with Lapidus's signature, oddly shaped decorative elements he called "woggles." The visual interest lies in these areas, where the vogue in

retro American culture is attracting a younger crowd to a hotel traditionally associated with older vacationers. The faux-tropical lagoon is featured in the opening scene of the 1964 James Bond movie *Goldfinger,* in which Sean Connery surveys the fun and says, "Now, this is the life."

EDEN ROC RENAISSANCE BEACH RESORT & SPA

Another Morris Lapidus creation, a contemporary and rival of the adjoining Fontainebleau, the 18-story Eden Roc has perennially had to suffer the notion that it is somehow less popular, less successful, and less everything than its flamboyant Collins Avenue neighbor. The Roc's swoopy curves will forever testify to its mid-century vintage; however, its bright color scheme, a result of a multimillion-dollar makeover aimed at attracting a new generation of loyals, gives it an appeal that goes far beyond mere flamboyant. At the Fontainebleau, Lapidus's cut-out ceiling holes and squiggly columns grab your attention; inside the Eden Roc it is the Caribbean palette you notice immediately upon entering the hotel's ballroom-size lobby. Through-out the 349-room resort you will encounter exuberant splashes, streaks, and explosions of color.

THE RITZ-CARLTON

The venerable Ritz-Carlton chain now boasts three hotels in Miami, though none of them are as stylish as the one at 1 Lincoln Road in South Beach. This impressive 375-room resort debuted after massive renovations to the DiLido, a hotel created by Lapidus. But instead of de rigueur art deco, it was designed in the art moderne style with clean lines and minimal decoration. It features a black terrazzo floor, a "bubble wall" in the lobby and aluminum railings along staircases. ■

Eden Roc
www.boldnewedenroc.com
🅰 81 C4
✉ 4525 Collins Ave., between 44th & 45th Sts.
☎ 305/531-0000

The Ritz-Carlton
www.ritzcarlton.com/resort /south_beach/
🅰 81 C2
✉ 1 Lincoln Rd.
☎ 786/276-4000

More places to visit in Miami Beach

BAL HARBOUR
A 250-acre enclave of affluence, Bal Harbour is largely reserved for its residents. Sample the lifestyles here by browsing the Bal Harbour Shops *(9700 Collins Ave.)*, a gleaming, upscale mall built on the initially unpromising site of a World War II army barracks, and dominated today by international fashion and jewelery,

At Haulover Beach: a warning to some, a come-on to others

Other architectural tours

The Miami Design Preservation League offers special excursions to unique neighborhoods such as Surfside. There are bus tours focusing on interior detailing, and sub-genres of art deco, including Tropical Deco, a whimsical nod to the gorgeous streamline ocean liners like the long-gone *Bremen*. Some tours take you inside apartment buildings and private homes; others visit the district's hidden world of lushly planted private tropical gardens. For special tour descriptions and schedules, visit the website at www.mdpl.org. ∎

---

including Hermes, Prada, Louis Vuitton, and Tiffany and Co. In addition to all the designer labels typically associated with wealth, you can enjoy the restaurants where the shoppers who have been buying them pretend not to be showing off their purchases.

🅰 81 D5 ☎ 305/866-0311, www.balharbour shops.com 🕐 Mon.–Sat. 10 a.m.–9 p.m.; Sun. noon–6 p.m. (Neiman Marcus & Saks Fifth Avenue close at 7 p.m. on Sun.); see website for restaurant hours

HAULOVER BEACH PARK
It costs nothing to enjoy the secluded soft sand, warm water, and downcoast views of South Miami Beach at Haulover Beach Park, just north of Bal Harbour. The vegetation hides apartment buildings inland, creating a sense of escape. You can rent kayaks to paddle up the nearby Oleta River.

Since 1991, nude sunbathing has been permitted at the north end of the park. (People behave quite decorously, although it sometimes attracts indiscreet gawkers.)

🅰 81 D5 ✉ 10800 Collins Ave.
☎ 305/947-3525

NORTH SHORE STATE RECREATION AREA
Located near Surfside between 79th and 87th Streets, the North Shore State Recreation Area is a bucolic, 40-acre preserve of dunes and native sea grape. Boardwalks lead to changing rooms, picnic tables, barbecue pits, and bike paths. Lifeguards watch over those who swim.

🅰 81 D5 ☎ 305/993-2032

SURFSIDE & SUNNY ISLES
In the old-fashioned neighborhood of Surfside is the **Harding Townsite Historic District,** home to the late great Yiddish scribe Isaac Bashevis Singer, who learned of his 1978 Nobel Prize for literature over breakfast at the now-shuttered Sheldon's Drugstore.

A look of the past also lingers pleasantly in Sunny Isles Beach, whose vintage beachfront hotels are favored by older, long-time regulars (see p. 70 on Miami's Russian community).

🅰 81 D5 ∎

With their shell-strewn beaches, lush parks, and resort communities, these two barrier islands are located only a few minutes from Downtown Miami via the Rickenbacker Causeway, and yet they are a world away.

Key Biscayne & Virginia Key

Red mangrove trees, Key Biscayne

Key Biscayne's bucolic southern reach, once a hideout of pirates and smugglers

Key Biscayne & Virginia Key

THE VIEW OF MIAMI'S SKYLINE FROM THE RICKENBACKER CAUSEWAY IS ONE of the best possible, although you probably won't enjoy it too much until you are off the bridge and safe on Virginia Key, where a left turn off the pavement brings you a view of the city across the water. Better yet are the Keys' long reach into Biscayne Bay, which in spite of the development along its shores remains a remarkably fertile cradle of wildlife. Venturing seaward via the causeway will cost you $1.50 (return trip included).

The span is named for its original builder, America's leading World War I flying ace, Eddie Rickenbacker, a race-car champion who went to war as Gen. John Pershing's personal driver, took up aerial combat, and returned a national hero with 26 victories. He brought his aviation expertise to Miami, founded Florida Airways Corporation in 1926, and soon after launched Eastern Airlines, which for some 60 years thereafter was one of America's major carriers. He charged a toll as well, and then, as now, most considered it a bargain price for access to Greater Miami's best beaches and premier oceanside parks.

However, the road leading north from the causeway boulevard onto Virginia Key is uninviting. Few signs indicate where you are, creating the impression that you are trespassing on government or private property. When you reach Virginia Key, you will notice lengthy

Lifeguards

It might look like an easy way to earn a living, but in fact Miami-Dade County Park lifeguards have to be trained in cardio-pulmonary resuscitation, advanced lifesaving and first aid techniques, underwater search and recovery, and scuba diving. Some are certified emergency technicians and paramedics, and all are on watch for environmental hazards and marine perils. Ask them about dangers specific to your beach—riptides, sudden drop-offs, strong offshore currents, stinging jellyfish—and follow their advice. ■

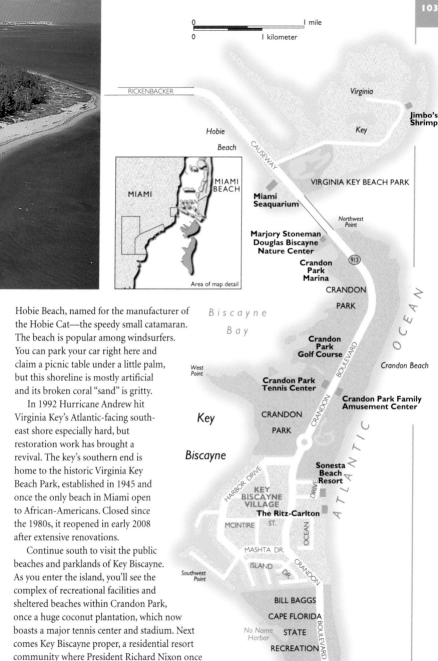

0 | 1 mile
0 | 1 kilometer

RICKENBACKER

Virginia

Jimbo's
Shrimp

Hobie

Key

Beach

CAUSEWAY

VIRGINIA KEY BEACH PARK

MIAMI
BEACH

MIAMI

Miami
Seaquarium

Northwest
Point

913

Marjory Stoneman
Douglas Biscayne
Nature Center

Crandon
Park
Marina

Area of map detail

CRANDON

PARK

O
C
E
A
N

Hobie Beach, named for the manufacturer of
the Hobie Cat—the speedy small catamaran.
The beach is popular among windsurfers.
You can park your car right here and
claim a picnic table under a little palm,
but this shoreline is mostly artificial
and its broken coral "sand" is gritty.

In 1992 Hurricane Andrew hit
Virginia Key's Atlantic-facing southeast shore especially hard, but
restoration work has brought a
revival. The key's southern end is
home to the historic Virginia Key
Beach Park, established in 1945 and
once the only beach in Miami open
to African-Americans. Closed since
the 1980s, it reopened in early 2008
after extensive renovations.

Continue south to visit the public
beaches and parklands of Key Biscayne.
As you enter the island, you'll see the
complex of recreational facilities and
sheltered beaches within Crandon Park,
once a huge coconut plantation, which now
boasts a major tennis center and stadium. Next
comes Key Biscayne proper, a residential resort
community where President Richard Nixon once
took his leisure. Finally, at the island's rustic southernmost tip you'll enter the dune-laden shores and
low thickets of 415-acre Bill Baggs Cape Florida
State Recreation Park, the most remote Greater
Miami retreat reachable by land. ■

Biscayne
Bay

West
Point

Key

Biscayne

HARBOR DRIVE

KEY
BISCAYNE
VILLAGE

MCINTIRE   ST.

MASHTA DR.

ISLAND   DR.

Southwest
Point

Crandon
Park
Golf Course

BOULEVARD

Crandon Beach

Crandon Park
Tennis Center

Crandon Park Family
Amusement Center

CRANDON

PARK

CRANDON

Sonesta
Beach
Resort

The Ritz-Carlton

OCEAN   DRIVE

A
T
L
A
N
T
I
C

BILL BAGGS

CAPE FLORIDA

No Name
Harbor

STATE

RECREATION

PARK

CRANDON   BOULEVARD

Cape
Florida

Cape Florida
Lighthouse

Biscayne Bay

Marjory Stoneman Douglas Biscayne Nature Center

www.biscaynenature
      center.org

🅰 Map p. 103

✉ 6769 Crandon Blvd.,
   in Crandon Park
   on Key Biscayne

☎ 305/361-6767

💲 Parking ($); park
   is free

THE FIRST EUROPEANS TO VISIT THESE ISLES WERE Spaniards commanded by Juan Ponce de León, whose ships replenished their drinking water nearby in 1513. By the 1700s, the resident Tequesta Indians had been wiped out by Old World diseases. Seagoing bandits encamped here until routed by the U.S. Navy in the 1820s. Turtle hunters and sponge fisherman worked the bay through the rest of the century, while farmers had limited success growing pineapples, key limes, tomatoes, and grapefruit amid native mahogany that was logged off, down to the last tree, by the early 1900s. A disastrous hurricane ended agriculture in 1906, leaving the offshore hummocks to serve as getaways for Miami's yachting set and, during Prohibition, hideaways for smugglers of Cuban rum.

Following World War II, as development spread to the Keys, some voiced concern that the bay's coral reefs (the only living coral communities in the continental United States), its sea creatures and birds, and the shoreline vegetation essential to their survival were threatened. Things got so out of hand that a bayside garbage dump grew to 150 feet, earning it the dubious distinction of being the highest point in Dade County. Few realized that the bay was an ecosystem whose grandeur belied a fragile constitution. Few noticed the thinning of its 175 bird species, particularly cormorants and pelicans. One of those who did was Marjory Stoneman Douglas.

She devoted her life as a journalist and writer to campaigning

Palatial residences on sheltered man-made islands in Biscayne Bay are priced in the millions.

to preserve the wetland wilderness west of town. She ran up her battle flag in 1947 by publishing *The Everglades: River of Grass,* a book warning of damage done by development and ill-conceived flood control projects. It rallied conservationists to the 'glades' defense and made her its best known advocate. When she died in 1998, aged 108, newspapers canonized her the patron saint of the Florida Everglades.

The scope of Douglas's concerns, however, extended beyond the wetland plain. Northern Biscayne Bay was, in her words, "one of the most important collections of natural habitats in the country." That is why the **Marjory Stoneman Douglas Biscayne Nature Center** at **Crandon Park** bears her name. Open daily (the causeway becomes Crandon Boulevard when it reaches Key Biscayne), it briefs visitors on the bay's natural world. One of its popular offerings is the Seagrass Adventure, a naturalist-guided walk along Key Biscayne's Atlantic shore. Participants drag nets through shallow beds of sea grass capturing a Noah's Ark manifest of sea creatures: shrimp, crabs, sea cucumbers, even sea horses, which are examined and returned to the water.

Next door is **Crandon Park Marina,** a port for fishing boats and scuba outfitters *(tel 305/361-1281).* Down the road is 18-hole par-72 **Crandon Golf Key Biscayne** *(6700 Crandon Blvd., tel 305/361-9129, www.crandongolf.net, $$$$$ green fee).* Seven saltwater lakes, many sand traps, mangrove thickets, a dogleg par-5 over-water hole, and another flanked by water create sufficient difficulty to rate it among Florida's top public courses and make it a stop on the Senior PGA Tour. One of its tees is the largest in the

world. Top-seeded professionals also come to the 27-court **Crandon Park Tennis Center's** 7,500-seat stadium.

Crandon's main attraction is a 2-mile-long beach consistently rated among America's top ten *(tel 305/361-5421).* The sand is soft, the water calm, the improvements many (winding promenade, picnic areas, and ample parking). The beach is what's called a lagoon-style or low-surf impact beach, with a shoreline sloping from wading depth to about 12 feet, depending on the tide. Thirteen lifeguard stations watch over you. You can take a turn on a restored 1949 carousel at the **Crandon Family Amusement Center.** There's an old-fashioned roller rink here too, along with other vintage rides. ■

In Biscayne Bay, the greatest natural depth is 13 feet; ship channels have been dug to accommodate cruise ships.

A boardwalk to Key Biscayne's southernmost Atlantic beach reduces foot traffic over fragile sea grasses and foliage.

Bill Baggs Cape Florida State Recreation Park
www.floridastateparks.org/
capeflorida

⚑ Map p. 103

✉ 1200 S. Crandon Blvd.

☎ 305/361-5811

§ $–$$

Cape Florida Lighthouse

⚑ Map p. 103

🕐 Guided tours Thurs.–Mon., 10 a.m. & 1 p.m. Arrive 30 min. early to climb to the top of the beacon; tours are limited to the first ten people (over age 8).

Bill Baggs Cape Florida State Recreation Park

NO ONE KNOWS HOW MANY SHIPS LIE IN THE SHALLOWS off the Cape of Florida, the name Ponce de León gave to the southern reach of 4-mile-long Key Biscayne. Low, sandy, and serene, it gives no hint of the offshore perils responsible for hundreds of maritime casualties: submerged reefs and sandbars, swift currents, shifting winds, sudden squalls, and hurricanes. When Florida became a U.S. Territory in 1821, among the first orders of business was to put up a lighthouse here. Its oil lamp was lighted in 1825, and though mariners argued that the faintness of the beacon made it likely they'd run aground trying to find it, the lighthouse signaled the beginning of South Florida's transition from a contested and dangerous frontier.

The whitewashed, 95-foot brick tower moves in and out of view above the trees as you approach the park, named for a *Miami Herald* newspaperman who led the campaign to have the cape designated a state preserve. Its entrance is all the more appealing for being such an abrupt departure from Key Biscayne's condo culture to what appears as a barely tamed if gentle wilderness—what its caretakers refer to as the "Real Florida." State policy is to manage Florida's public preserves so that they appear, to the greatest practical extent possible, as they did to the first Europeans who saw them. Today, nicely weathered wooden boardwalks insinuate themselves through vegetation to beaches stretching over a mile, and a nature walk that winds through the tall scrub.

Because the main road through the park to the lighthouse and the island's southern terminus is closer to the Atlantic side than to the Biscayne Bay shore, it's easy to

inadvertently turn your back on the bucolic thickets between the parking lots and the bayside seawall that protects the low-lying spit from storm surges. A pedestrian/bicycle nature trail loops through this forest. Starting at the park's northernmost parking area, it winds west and follows the seawall south, looping around to end near a parking area and fishing pier a short distance from the beacon. It's a pleasant stroll, requiring less than 30 minutes to complete the circuit. It was probably pleasant during the summer of 1836 as well, though it may also have been lethal. The Second Seminole War—an uprising against settlers' encroachments and forced relocation to Western reservations—was in its second year. Key Biscayne had become an enclave for settlers who abandoned mainland homesteads. The Seminoles struck like commandos, arriving by canoe and besieging the lighthouse, which they attempted to torch, killing one of its two caretakers. Re-lighted in 1842, and shut down by Confederates during the Civil War until 1866, it is still in service, warning sailors away from the watery graveyard offshore.

The beach ends by the old brick pillar. To the east, beyond a low surf of slappy waves, lies Africa; to the south, the mostly uninhabited mangrove islands of Biscayne National Park appear as dark, low shapes on the horizon. Like Crandon Park's shore 2 miles north, this strand occupies a nearly permanent place among America's top-rated beaches in tourist polls. Some people snorkel offshore under the gaze of lifeguards, scuba divers surface and submerge farther out, and families gather for cookouts in the shade of 18 covered picnic pavilions. If you don't feel like roughing it, try the park's Lighthouse Café, a casual eatery with outdoor tables. It adjoins a well-run concession where you can rent bikes, in-line skates, paddleboats, kayaks, and sailboards, buy film and sunscreen, and browse through a selection of Florida's ubiquitous souvenir item—the T-shirt.

If you arrive under sail, you can drop anchor in **No Name Harbor,** where overnight mooring is available, and pay a visit to the lighthouse. ∎

Cape Florida Lighthouse, a lifesaving beacon since 1825, has survived war, fire, and hurricanes.

Hobie Beach to Key Biscayne

THOUGH HOBIE BEACH IS NEITHER SECLUDED NOR particularly pretty, its convenience makes it a popular family destination and draws hundreds to its picnic tables. One result is that the stretch of land between the Rickenbacker Causeway and Key Biscayne's residential midsection is a bazaar of rental conveyances. Look around and you'll find concessionaires eager to rent you a bicycle, a windsurfer or sailboard, a Jet Ski, and, up the road at the Key Biscayne Marina, even a sailboat large enough to sleep an entourage of friends on an overnight excursion to the islands within Biscayne National Park boundaries a few miles south.

Left: Rental windsurfers await customers on Hobie Beach, a popular training spot for beginners.

Steady breezes make Hobie Beach an excellent place to windsurf. No one says this wonderful pastime is easy to learn or easy to pursue. The nice part of windsurfing is that it isn't dangerous, and even if you fall over (which you will, often) you always have something buoyant to grab on to. If you have a neoprene wet suit or vest, bring it.

The sea bottom here is a maritime cemetery, and its warm shallow waters make wreck diving comfortable and safe. On Key Biscayne, wreck dives are a main entrée on the day-trip menu of Divers Paradise, scuba outfitters doing business out of the Crandon Marina (*4000 Crandon Blvd., tel 305/361-DIVE, www.keydivers.com*).

Biscayne Bay, whose barrier islands block Atlantic surges, is ideal for would-be mariners. Take a sailing lesson: During a one-hour introductory sail you'll be at the tiller immediately. A great school, for able-bodied and disabled participants, is Shake-A-Leg Miami, which operates out of Coconut Grove just across Biscayne Bay. It teaches basic sailing skills and fundamentals, including boat dynamics, boat safety, tacking and jibing, and reading the weather and the environment. Individual instruction is available with reservations and is tailored to the specific needs and schedules of participants (*2620 South Bayshore Dr., tel 305/858-5550, www.shakealegmiami.org*). ■

Key Biscayne
Map p. 103

Right: A fisherman at Crandon Park Marina on Key Biscayne tends to a net. The mounted catch advertises charter fishing trips.

More places to visit on Virginia Key

JIMBO'S SHRIMP

Fisherman are among the island's hardest-working people. And among them, no one puts in a longer day than those who mine Florida waters for *Crago vulgaris,* the edible variety of the backward-swimming marine decopods called shrimp. Shrimpers are to South Florida what truffle hunters are to France; among the most distinguished in Miami's shrimper society is James Luznar—a.k.a. Jimbo—for more than half a century the proprietor of Jimbo's Shrimp, hidden on an overgrown mangrove channel on Virginia Key.

Begun as a trawler base for off-loading catches, Jimbo's evolved into a beer joint with a *bocce* ball court and a salmon smokehouse, where fillets are smoked to perfection for restaurants and anyone who finds their way here. Though it may appear to be a squatter's camp, as you'll see, this is a picturesque back-water. Scenes for many movies and television series have been filmed here, including some climactic ones for the Jack Nicholson film *Blood and Wine,* and even a documentary about Jimbo's. Buy a piece of salmon, along with a beer to cut its oily aftertaste, sit down outside at the picnic table, and enjoy the conversation with Jim and his weathered cronies. If Jimbo challenges you to a game of bocce, don't play for high stakes, for he rarely loses.
🅰 Map p. 103   ✉ Duck Lake Road
☎ 305/361-7026, www.jimbosplace.com

MIAMI SEAQUARIUM

There is no recorded instance of a killer whale attacking a person, and there are even tales of the black and white carnivores saving people from drowning, but those acts of mercy are also undocumented. Either way, when the resident orcas blast up from the Seaquarium's huge salt-water pools at the behest of young trainers, arc through the air with a ponderous grace, and belly-flop back into their blue world, you realize immediately that they are awesome, powerful, and extremely intelligent. They are the stars of this long-standing attraction, along with a supporting cast of performing sea lions and porpoises, and a group of manatees. The 38-acre complex includes some interesting marine life exhibits, including a coral reef habitat.

During Miami's hot and muggy low season, consider taking in an evening show.
🅰 Map p. 103   ✉ 4400 Rickenbacker Causeway   ☎ 305/361-5705, www.miamiseaquarium.com 🅢 $$$$

A porpoise leaps at the Miami Seaquarium

VIRGINIA KEY BEACH PARK

Miami is one of the most diverse cities in the United States, so it's hard to comprehend that just 45 years ago racial segregation was enforced here. Virginia Key Beach opened in 1945 as Miami's only beach "for the exclusive use of Negroes." By the early 1960s blacks were allowed to visit any beach in Miami and in the 1980s the so-called "Colored Beach" closed.

For decades, few residents and tourists speeding over the Rickenbacker Causeway to Key Biscayne realized that Virginia Key was a cultural treasure trove. In 2002, it was added to the National Register of Historic Places, an honor befitting the one place where African-Americans could swim, sunbathe, barbecue, and play games during a turbulent era.

In early 2008 Virginia Key Beach reopened. In addition to relaxing under the sun, people of all races can snack on historic treats at the restored concession stand. They also can ride a replica of the park's mini-train and stroll the boardwalk to one of the country's oldest surviving coastal mangrove communities.
🅰 Map p. 103   ✉ 4020 Virginia Beach Drive, Miami 33149 ☎ 305/960-4600, www.virginia keybeachpark.net ■

In 1873 pioneers attracted by the offer of free farmland settled along Biscayne Bay, in an encampment called Jack's Bight, and applied for a post office charter under the name of Coconut Grove, creating Miami's first suburb.

Coconut Grove & beyond

Ballroom at the restored Charles Deering Estate

Coconut Grove & beyond

RURAL SOMNOLENCE CHARACTERIZED LIFE HERE UNTIL THE ARRIVAL OF Flagler's trains in Miami, which brought winter tourists in numbers. (Until the tracks were laid, winter visitors arrived via Key West, whose deepwater harbor was more accessible to passenger ships, and then took shallow-draft, top-sail schooners north to Miami.) Typically, many who came to vacation came back to live. Their homes were often built by a community of Bahamian craftsmen who brought shipbuilding and carpentry skills, along with their families, from the British islands.

An English couple, Charles and Isabella Peacock, opened the Grove's first hotel, the Bay View House, in 1884. By the mid-1890s Cocoanut Grove (as it was first known) had a yacht club, setting a tone of affluent leisure that still characterizes the community, while at the same time acquiring a curious cosmopolitan cross section of people: Northern industrialists, expatriate European nobles, displaced Southerners seeking to reestablish themselves after losing everything in the defeat of the Confederacy, and a community of Bahamian fishermen, who, along with their home-building countrymen, established a Little Bahama district they named Kebo.

Cocoanut Grove lost its "a" in the new century, but retained the small village character that set it apart, then and now, from the mercantile style of central Miami. That distinction endures, perhaps the main reason the Grove's residents, if asked where they live, will say Coconut Grove rather than Miami—even though the Grove was incorporated into Greater Miami in 1923. Its boundaries are indistinct, but its visual trademarks include large, handsome old coral rock homes set back from Brickell Avenue on sweeping lawns; lush overgrowth that gives residential side streets an air of landscaped seclusion; and luxury condominiums in the shape of Maya temples overlooking forests of sailboat masts at Dinner Key Marina, where the last Pan Am Clipper flying boats took to the air for South America.

The most scenic route of entry from Downtown Miami is via either Brickell or South Miami Avenues south from downtown, past the entrance to the Rickenbacker Causeway, where the two streets merge to form South Bayshore. The route takes you along a curving, palm-lined boulevard with

sudden flashes of blue—views across sweeping park lawns to Biscayne Bay. The high-rises to the inland side of Bayshore comprise some of Miami's most sought-after accommodations: architecturally distinguished condominium homes whose quality of design set standards for luxury cooperative homeowning across America.

If you tour Coconut Grove by car you will inevitably find your way to its busy central shopping district, now dominated by a three-level, court-yard-style complex

of shops, cafés, boutiques, and bistros known as the CocoWalk. The spectrum of quality is broad, from kitsch to collectible, with haute couture the rule in the Grove's other shopping center, the upscale Streets of Mayfair. CocoWalk restaurants reflect Greater Miami's diversity, their menus offering Caribbean, Cuban, and Central and South American fare, as well as mainstream French and Italian cuisine.

At the end of the day, it's the Grove's mixture of leisure and garden-variety languor that is most appealing. This attracted moneyed Northerners to build mansions along

Brickell Avenue at the turn of the last century, none more moneyed and lavish and entranced with the possibilities of South Florida living than industrialist James Deering. His estate and gardens here are the ultimate expression of the desire for an exotic tropical escape that has drawn millions to Florida since the the Peacocks first set out their china and silverware and lit candles for hotel guests. ■

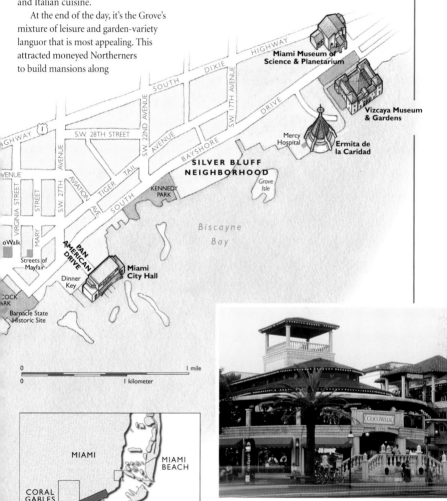

Despite CocoWalk's 200,000 square feet of shops, restaurants, and theaters, Coconut Grove retains a small-town ambience.

Vizcaya Museum & Gardens

**Vizcaya Museum
& Gardens**
www.vizcayamuseum.org
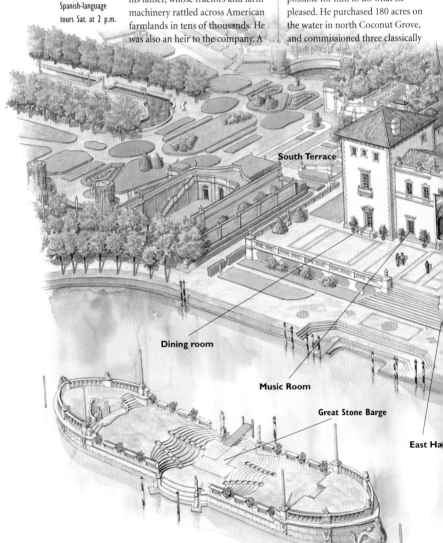 Map p. 113
✉ 3251 S. Miami Ave.
☎ 305/250-9133
🕒 9:30 a.m.–4:30
p.m.
💲 $$–$$$. Audiotaped
garden tours for the
visually impaired;
Spanish-language
tours Sat. at 2 p.m.

ONCE A SOLITARY MAN'S PRIVATE RETREAT, VIZCAYA OPENS
its gates to around 185,000 people every year. In 1994 it hosted receptions for the 34 heads of state attending the Summit of the Americas,
rivaling in opulence the national palaces of all. Yet it remains a
personal place, a fantasy unlike any other, save perhaps William
Randolph Hearst's Enchanted Hill at San Simeon in California.

James Deering was a retired vice
president of the International
Harvester Company founded by
his father, whose tractors and farm
machinery rattled across American
farmlands in tens of thousands. He
was also an heir to the company. A
bachelor immersed in a consuming
fascination with the European
Renaissance, James's wealth made it
possible for him to do what he
pleased. He purchased 180 acres on
the water in north Coconut Grove,
and commissioned three classically

South Terrace

Dining room

Music Room

Great Stone Barge

East Ha

trained architects to build a Renaissance Italian villa and formal garden such as he'd seen on his European odysseys, along with a functioning Northern Italian-style village to house his employees. He wanted the villa to appear as if it had been here since the 16th century, occupied by successive generations of an Italian noble family. For its name he chose a Basque word describing the site, which gently inclined to overlook Biscayne Bay from a low rise: Vizcaya ("an elevated place").

Construction began in 1914, and when it was completed two years later, in time for Deering to celebrate Christmas there, his guests were astonished at what an army of 1,000 workers—ten percent of Miami's population then—had built. Deering led them through a three-story palace of 34 rooms filled with treasures ranging from the 15th century through the 19th—furniture, tapestries, rugs, wall panels, ceilings, mantels, door cases, wrought iron, sculptures, and paintings. The villa's sturdy reinforced concrete skeleton was hidden behind painted stucco and limestone. Outside, cut from mangrove and hardwood jungle, was a terraced 10-acre garden mixing the styles of 16th- and 17th-century Italian hillside estates with those of 17th-century France, a serene place of dripping fountains, with a reflecting pool and statuary walks that would not be fully completed until 1921. Offshore, flanked by two piers (one a yacht landing, the other a tea house), was an ornately carved

Recognizing the beauty of the surrounding native forest, Vizcaya's creator limited his formal gardens to ten acres—one-eighth of his estate.

Courtyard

Entrance

Sitting Room

Living Room

The Music Room, where concerts for guests sometimes ended without host James Deering, whose fragile health often forced him to retire early.

island, called the Great Stone Barge, recalling the coronation gondolas of Venetian princes. Maintaining all this was a staff of domestic workers living in second-floor chambers and in the Italian village, which included a farm with livestock. A concealed private telephone system permitted the mogul and his majordomos to orchestrate his elaborate world of nearly real make-believe.

Deering's health, however, was poor, often leaving him so weary that he rarely attended the suppers served to guests on Vizcaya's gold-trimmed china. His beloved barony was barely completed when he died in 1925, leaving a few staff members to look after it for his heirs. A violent hurricane hit Miami the following year, devastating the city and badly damaging the villa and its gardens. Over time the deteriorating

estate became too much for Deering's inheritors, who sold off all but 28 acres. In 1952 they gave it to Dade County in exchange for one million dollars in revenue bonds, and made the county a gift of the villa's art and furnishings. Succeeding decades brought extensive restoration work, including a glass enclosure to seal off the villa's open court so that the house and its contents could be preserved by a climate and humidity control system. Hurricaines Katrina and Wilma in 2005 devastated Vizcaya, though recovery has been remarkable.

EXPLORING VIZCAYA

The best way to explore this great house and its gardens, a national historic landmark, is in the company of a guide. There's so much to know about the place, and Vizcaya's guides know it all, imparting not only the information but also the spirit that created it in a brisk 45-minute tour. If you prefer to wander on your own, get a copy of the booklet entitled "Museum and Gardens Guide & Map," which has floor plans, a suggested tour route, and detailed descriptions. Among the highlights to seek out are:

The **Entrance Hall,** whose wallpaper panels were printed from wood blocks and hand colored in Paris in 1814.

The **Reception Room**'s tinted plaster ceiling, from a Venetian palace.

The **Living Room**'s 16th-century fireplace, 2,000-year-old Roman marble tripod, and an extremely rare 15th-century Spanish carpet, one of only a few known to exist.

In the **East Hall,** a 15th-century Italian coffered ceiling of terra-cotta heraldic tiles.

Painted wall and ceiling panels in the **Music Room,** with decorations from the Milanese palace of a noble Italian family, the Borromeos, whose son Carlo,

a priest, is a Catholic saint.

Two 16th-century tapestries in the **Dining Room,** once belonging to poets Robert and Elizabeth Barrett Browning, that depict the life of Hermes, messenger of the Roman gods. The marble table in the room is Roman, from the first century A.D.

In the **Tea Room,** gates of bronze and wrought iron opening into the courtyard, another treasure that was originally part of a Venetian palace.

The **Butler's Pantry,** considered state of the art in 1916, where Vizcaya's formal china and crystal are displayed.

The **Manin Room,** decorated in the style of 19th-century Austria.

The **Pantaloon Room,** reflecting the cheerful bucolic styles of 18th-century Venice.

The Vizcaya Café, a modern amenity with little of the Villa's opulence, is nevertheless a pleasant place to rest after climbing stairways and walking in gardens. The gift shop sells Italian crafts including ceramics, jewelry, and tapestries. On occasion the garden is open for moonlight tours, from 6 p.m. ■

Ermita de la Caridad

AMONG THOSE WHO BOUGHT LAND FROM DEERING'S heirs is Miami's Catholic Diocese. Just south of the estate entrance, near Mercy Hospital, you'll find one of the city's more affecting monuments to the "loss" of Cuba—a point of view that even after nearly 50 years keeps Miami's displaced Cubans ready to return to the island at a moment's notice to demand the return of confiscated property.

Ermita de la Caridad

🅰 Map p. 113
✉ 3609 S. Miami Ave.
☎ 305/854-2404

They were the force behind this 90-foot-high conical shrine, called Ermita de la Caridad (Hermitage of Charity). It is intended to resemble a beacon, and is designed so that those who attend daily Mass here face Cuba—to most parishioners a world stolen from them and held hostage 290 miles beyond the south-

ern horizon. A mural above the shrine's circular base depicts Cuba's ever-turbulent history. The shrine occupies a pretty, serene piece of Deering's former hideaway, and looks out on a typically beguiling stretch of Biscayne Bay, making it a lovely spot to leave your car for a while and take a meditative break. ■

Deering Estate

**Deering Estate
at Cutler**

www.deeringestate.org

🗺 134 C3

✉ 16701 S.W. 72nd
Ave.

☎ 305/235-1668

🕑 10 a.m.–5 p.m.;
last entry 4 p.m.

💲 $$. Additional fee
for some tours

**The brother of
Vizcaya's builder
carved his own
retreat into
Biscayne Bay's
shoreline.**

IN 1913, CHARLES DEERING BOUGHT 420 ACRES ON BISCAYNE
Bay, south of Coconut Grove (then called Cutler). While brother
James enjoyed the opulent Vizcaya (see pp. 114–17), Charles set
about developing his own winter retreat. The property includes two
of Cutler's oldest structures—a homestead and a cottage-style inn,
rare examples of South Florida's early frame vernacular architecture.

A collector like his brother, Charles
built a Mediterranean Revival home
of coral rock here, filled it with
paintings, tapestries, antiques, rare
books, and wine, and christened it
Stone House. He dug a boat
basin enabling him to sail the
family yacht nearly to the front
door. In the 1980s the property was
sold to the State of Florida and
Miami-Dade County.

The park was ruined by
Hurricane Andrew in 1992, but
after much restoration reopened,
displaying not only its antique
homes but also a fossil pit of animal
bones and teeth from mammoths,
dog-size horses, tapirs, jaguars,
sloths, and bison dating from
50,000 years ago. Of greater interest
perhaps are the remains of Paleo-
Indians, the earliest known people
of North America, believed to have
arrived here about 10,000 years ago.
Tequesta traces found at the site
date from the time of Christ.

When you grow weary of
moneyed manors, take a stroll in
the 150-acre stand of pine rockland
forest, a relic of ancient Florida,
and one of the last of these primor-
dial ecosystems growing in the
continental United States. This
unusual glade is surrounded by
rare native orchids, bromeliads,
ferns, live oaks, gumbo limbos,
and pigeon plums, as well as about
35 other tree species. The estate
also includes 130 acres of bayside
mangrove and salt marsh, and
the offshore mangrove island of
Chicken Key, which you can
visit on a canoe tour (advance
reservations required). Recent ren-
ovations include restoring period
furnishings and artwork to Stone
House, building a canoe launch
house, expanding a boardwalk
through the shoreline mangroves,
and extending the nature trails. ■

Children enjoy the "Newton's Notions" exhibit at the Miami Museum of Science & Planetarium

Miami Museum of Science & Planetarium

MIAMI PARENTS SEEKING TO INTRODUCE THEIR CHILDREN to the world of the new take them to the Miami Museum of Science & Planetarium, a double bill of natural history and cosmic mystery situated near Vizcaya, just south of the Rickenbacker Causeway entrance.

National traveling exhibits that change every three months start with the basics—gravity, light, sound—and work up from low- to high-tech. The orientation is toward the young; adults without kids in tow might find it shallow. But there's still much of interest for everyone here. The planetarium features daily classic star shows in its 65-foot-high dome, where you can recline in the dark and watch the constellations move and the universe evolve. On the first Friday of the month the star chamber puts on a laser light show of space travel fantasies popular with youngsters. Come Friday night, weather permitting, the museum hosts free telescopic viewing. (Call first to find out what the celestial target is, as it changes regularly.)

One of the museum's permanent exhibits is Smithsonian Expeditions: Exploring Latin America and the Caribbean, in which children discover rare treasures just like Indiana Jones. A second permanent exhibit is Newton's Notions: Force, Motion & You.

To its credit, the museum also focuses attention on South Florida's natural world, keeping a menagerie of creatures on display at its small wildlife center. In addition, the **Falcon Batchelor Bird of Prey Center** houses and rehabilitates injured eagles, ospreys, hawks, owls, and falcons that have been rescued from the wild. ■

Miami Museum of Science & Planetarium
www.miamisci.org
🗺 Map p. 113
✉ 3280 S. Miami Ave.
☎ 305/646-4200
💲 $$$–$$$$

Around Coconut Grove

FANS OF COCOWALK BAZAAR AT VIRGINIA STREET CLAIM their multilevel carnival of food, drink, and fashion is the Grove's true center. So do those whose fortunes depend upon the continued success of the Streets of Mayfair mall (between Mary and Virginia Streets). Ask directions to the heart of the Grove, and a knowledgeable guide will direct you down South Bayshore to its roundabout union with Main Highway (which, southbound, soon becomes the Ingraham Highway). Coconut Grove's central district is the area around Main Highway and Grand Avenue, a dense concentration of restaurants, shops, and small businesses that's easy to explore on foot.

Away from the Grove's retail hub, however, you may find it more practical to explore by car, taking in sights as they slide by, and stopping when your interest is piqued.

Visit the **Silver Bluff Neighborhood** along South Bayshore Drive, where the blocks numbered from 1600 through 2100 hold architecturally distinctive residences designed in the decade following World War I.

Look for the limestone outcropping—a spur of the Atlantic coastal ridge once trod by the creatures whose bones lie within the Deering Estate (see p. 118). A short distance south, at 2484 S. Bayshore, is a handsome Mediterranean Revival manse built in 1923, now owned by the Coral Reef Yacht Club.

Search out the cottages built during the 19th-century flowering of Coconut Grove's Bahamian community, which survive along **Charles Avenue** (*between S.W. 37th Ave. and Main Hwy.*). They can be identified by their long, narrow design, with rooms opening off a side hall running from front to back.

Make your way to one of the Grove's most splendid architectural antiques, the stone mission-style **Plymouth Congregational Church** near Main Highway (*3400 Devon Rd., tel 305/444-6521, www.plymouthmiami.com*). It is the handiwork of a Spanish mason, finished in 1917 when the California-inspired vogue was sweeping the country. Note the church door, hard-carved from walnut planks laid upon oak, taken from a 17th-century monastery in the Pyrenees. Its 11-acre grounds include a rectory, completed in 1926, and Dade County's first public schoolhouse, a one-roomer built in 1887 with wood salvaged from shipwrecks. It was moved here in 1970 from its original site near the Peacock Inn (which did not survive).

It's easy to miss, but you should try to visit **The Barnacle State Historic State Park,** a five-acre patch of native Florida hardwood (*3485 Main Hwy., tel 305/442-*

Left: Coconut Grove's Plymouth Congregational Church mimics California's 18th-century Spanish colonial churches.

6866, *www.floridastateparks.org/ TheBarnacle, Fri.–Mon., $, guided tours at 10:00 a.m., 11:30 a.m., 1:00 p.m. & 2:30 p.m.)* surrounding the beautifully crafted 1891 home of pioneer and master boatbuilder Ralph Middleton Munroe. Many of Miami's residential architects consider it a shrine to thoughtful design. Commodore Munroe, whose grandfather manufactured America's first lead pencils, anchored the house against hurricanes by sinking a termite-proofed, pine log foundation deep into the earth, and gave it extra strength by using stout beams salvaged from shipwrecks and bolted to the foundation. Your appreciation of his skill will increase when you learn that the two-story house was originally a bungalow, until Munroe jacked it up in 1908 and added a level beneath it. Note the unusual roof structure, whose skylights are opened by ropes and pulleys to boost circulation and vent warm air; it reminded the Biscayne Bay Yacht Club founder of a barnacle attached to a hull.

Diagonally across the street is another of the Grove's notable attractions. The Spanish-flavored building opposite the Barnacle started out in 1927 as a movie theater, but in the 1950s thespian-minded folk converted it to the **Coconut Grove Playhouse** *(3500 Main Hwy.).* They demonstrated its high standards in 1956 by mounting the premier performance of Samuel Beckett's *Waiting for Godot.* The struggling theater closed in April 2006 due to sizeable debts. While revitalization is being debated, its fate is uncertain. ∎

Above: Ladies choosing their bonnets at an Easter Hat party in Coconut Grove.

Pan American Drive
& Miami City Hall

ONE OF THE MOST ROMANTIC ERAS IN AMERICAN AIR travel came to an end in Coconut Grove on August 9, 1945, when the last scheduled Pan American Airways System "clipper"—a four-engine Boeing 314—taxied away from Dinner Key Marina and took to the air. Few had expected the big Boeing flying boats to become obsolete so quickly. Pan Am's first B314, the *Honolulu Clipper,* had been delivered to the airline barely seven years earlier, in January 1939; its 12th and last, the *Capetown Clipper,* was only four years old.

But in the 46 months of America's involvement in World War II, the global battlefield had seen change accelerated as never before, and when it was over, places that once seemed so remote, from Brazil to Burma, now had airfields that opened them up to visits by more economical land planes. The high season of the "flying boat" was over.

But what an era it was—and it began here, on September 15, 1930, when Pan Am moved its operations from its 36th Street base (today's Miami International Airport) to inaugurate its flying boat service to South America. There was something about the clippers that enthralled people—their luxury, certainly, but also the implicit romantic possibilities of faraway places. Pan Am's first Coconut Grove headquarters was a two-story houseboat, but

founder Juan Trippe, determined to build a global airline second to none in service, luxury, and panache, commissioned the New York architectural firm of Delano & Aldrich, designers of New York's elegant La Guardia Marine Air Terminal, to create another art deco masterpiece at Dinner Key. The champagne corks popped on May 27, 1934, and reporters rushed to declare it the "most beautiful marine air transport base in the world," and it was. Miamians who love it and come here to relax on a bench overlooking the marina's armada of sailboats and cruisers still think it is, though the cheers and the roar of the clippers have been replaced by the quiet, steady clinking of ropes against hollow aluminum masts.

Though today you turn off South Bayshore Drive and follow

Miami City Hall

- Map p. 113
- 3500 Pan American Dr.
- 305/250-5300
- Closed Sat.–Sun.

Pan American Drive to the terminal (which has served as Miami City Hall since 1954), Dinner Key, as its name suggests, was once an island. In 1917, Navy engineers filled in the channel separating it from the shore to create a seaplane base.

Park at the bottom of the circular drive and walk across the lawn to the historical marker and its account of Dinner Key's past. Look across the channel at the hangars, now a boatyard, that housed the clippers and admire the terminal building's horizontal lines. The row of globes that once framed Pan American World Airways now flank Miami City Hall.

Enter City Hall's lobby, once an airy waiting room, and see a floor mosaic of the globe. From 2001–2003 the building went through an extensive renovation that transferred the old terminal from lackluster administrative offices back to aviation's pioneering days of the 1920s and 1930s. Today you'll see a ceiling with canvases of the zodiac signs (recreated from originals that were damaged when sound-absorbing tiles were added after City Hall moved in). And at the far end of the room stands the dais on which city council meetings are held. Behind it hangs the original Pan Am clock.

Behind the building, sit on the promenade and listen to the palms rustle beside the shimmering blue water in the channel opening out to the Caribbean, where the first clippers journeyed from Key West to Havana, flying without radios but with carrier pigeons ready to fly away for help in case of a ditching. Think about all that, and this place takes on a peculiar and wholly pleasant timelessness. ■

A Sikorsky flying boat is towed behind Pan American Airways' new marine air terminal in the mid-1930s. Today, the art deco diva (opposite) performs civic duty.

Main Highway to Old Cutler Road

Old Cutler Road

134 D4

IF YOU HAVE THE TIME, YOU WILL FIND THE DRIVE SOUTH from Vizcaya memorable for its subtropical sights: residential neighborhoods sunk in vines and overflowing with bougainvillea; mangrove channels reaching inland like crooked fingers, hiding little marinas and waterside houses; wonderfully exuberant arboretums such as the Fairchild Tropical Botanic Garden; and beautifully designed bayside public parks such as Matheson Hammock, where you can picnic by Biscayne Bay in the shade of a palm tree, swim, or beachcomb along the northern reach of Biscayne National Park.

Although it's hard to get lost if you stay close to the bay shore, taking along a road map will alert you to turnoffs and let you better plan your exploration. From Vizcaya, take South Bayshore Drive

Serpentine channels leading to Biscayne Bay reach into the gardens of Matheson Hammock Park south of Miami.

south to central Coconut Grove, where it enters a kind of roundabout of streets and turns into Main Highway.

Near Coconut Grove's southern boundary, beside a lagoon at 4013 Douglas Road, is a home built in the 1870s to emulate an Indonesian retreat. Known as the **Kampong,** the inspiration of the brother of early Coconut Grove hotelier

Charles Peacock, it eventually passed into the hands of David Fairchild, founder of the Fairchild Tropical Botanic Garden, who landscaped the home with exotic flora. Today, the Kampong functions as a tropical plant research site. Although it's private, on occasion the compound is open for special events (*tel 305/445-8076*).

Continue down Ingraham Highway until it merges with Le Jeune Road, along the way passing by lovely secluded residential neighborhoods. Turn off onto any street and you'll find houses that epitomize an ideal image of South Florida living, many of them hidden behind overgrown walls.

Ingraham becomes Old Cutler Road, which leads on to **Matheson Hammock Park** (see p. 137) and the **Fairchild Tropical Botanic Garden** (see p. 136). Just south, Old Cutler comes to a T-junction at Red Road (also Fla. 959).

This is a good place to begin your return. Turn right (north) onto Red Road, and let it take you back 5 miles into the heart of Coral Gables, where the incomparable **Biltmore Hotel** (see p. 129) rises above the City Beautiful, its lion-colored spire a twin of the Giralda, the minaret-turned-bell tower of the Cathedral of Seville. ∎

Coral Gables began in 1921 in a family citrus grove, when George E. Merrick borrowed the name of his parents' rustic and craggy coral rock home for his new subdivision of Mediterranean Revival houses.

Coral Gables

Orchids, Fairchild Tropical Botanic Garden

Coral Gables

MIAMI'S LAND BOOM WAS RUNNING AT FULL THROTTLE IN THE 1920s, AND in five years George Merrick's Coral Gables claimed 10,000 acres. He opened the Biltmore Hotel, a resort as luxurious as any in America, its great Spanish-Moorish tower and buildings rising grandly above Anastasia Avenue like a king's palace, its pool the largest in the continental United States. A towered building with a 40-foot arch was put up at the city's Douglas Road entrance, making it clear to visitors that they were entering a special place.

Merrick called his creation the City Beautiful, and it was: with broad streets connecting broad plazas, public amenities such as the gorgeous Venetian Pool on De Soto Boulevard, and a fantasy of waterfalls and grottoes. Those who bought homes here became zealous apostles, keeping their lawns manicured, trees trimmed, and sidewalks swept clean, while urging friends to join them. It was a vision of utopia, it was real, and it lasted, surviving the collapse of the Florida land boom right up to the present day.

Merrick would be proud. The trees he planted now arch over his boulevards like great arbors, shading downtown sidewalks in sun-dappled coolness. The turret-topped Colonnade building, site of Merrick's offices, still stands, now part of a stately hotel. The Venetian Pool is as grand as it was the day it opened, and Coral Gables' houses are still every bit as desirable as then, sought after by buyers who make up the affluent core of the city's 42,000 residents. Its corporate residents include over 140 of the biggest and most important businesses and financial institutions in South Florida. The 260-acre University of Miami's Coral Gables campus counts nearly 15,500 students and a faculty of 1,500, and has an unusually rich repository of fine art and antiquities at its Lowe Art Museum (see p. 132).

Coral Gables' 12 square miles are bounded on the east by Douglas Road (S.W. 37th Ave.) and on the west by Red Road (S.W. 57th Ave.). Its northern boundary line is the Tamiami Trail (S.W. 8th St.), and its southern frontier traces Sunset Avenue (S.W. 72nd St.) and Old Cutler Road, putting Coral Gables' southeast corner close to Biscayne Bay and its shoreline tropical gardens.

Coral Gables' streets are legendary for being confusing, so much so that they are able to hide something as big as the Biltmore! You will probably get lost here, so your only hope is to use a map. If you're passing through during weekday work hours, stop by the Chamber of Commerce building (360 Greco Ave., tel 305/446-1657). It stocks an array of brochures, including the city's official map. Another excellent source of where-to-go, what-to-see information and advice is the staff at the city's Department of Historic Preservation, who occupy a small office in City Hall (see p. 131) during weekday business hours. Ask about architectural brochures and booklets that may be in stock (tel 305/460-5216).

While you're in the area, be sure to drop by one of Greater Miami's best-rated bookstores, Books & Books (265 Aragon Ave. & Salzedo St., tel 305/442-4408, www.booksandbooks.com), whose rooms and rooms of ceiling-high bookshelves hold about 5,000 titles. Like its namesake sister store in Miami Beach (not to mention its Bal Harbour and Grand Cayman siblings), this booklover's paradise, set in a 1927 Mediterranean Revival building, has a full program of authors' appearances, book signings, lectures, and a very good rare book department.

Mediterranean Revival architecture dominates Coral Gables, but other exotics bloomed here, too. Sloped tile roofs distinguish the Chinese Village on Riviera Drive at Menendez Avenue. The rural residences of 17th-century Dutch South African colonials are re-created at Maya Street and Le Jeune Road. Antique French urbanity is revived on Hardee Avenue at Maggiore Street, and the tastes of Normandy dress up Le Jeune Road at Vizcaya Avenue. Italian village life is the theme on Altara Avenue at Monserrate Street, and on Santa Maria Street, houses in the Colonial Village celebrate Miami's Yankee heritage. ■

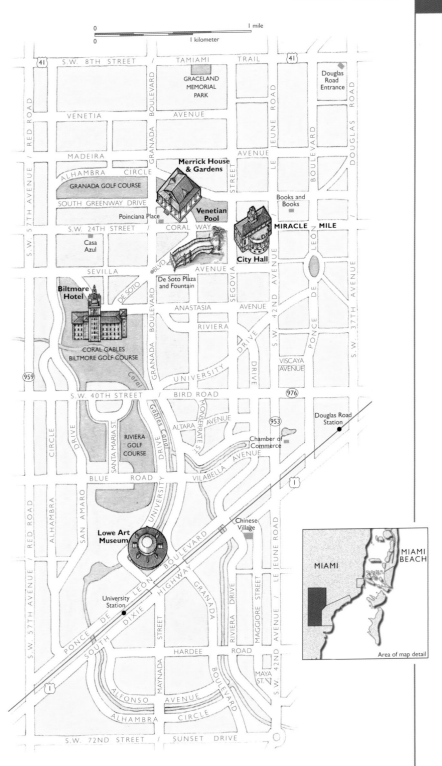

0   1 mile

0   1 kilometer

S.W. 8TH STREET / TAMIAMI TRAIL

GRACELAND MEMORIAL PARK

Douglas Road Entrance

VENETIA AVENUE

MADEIRA

ALHAMBRA CIRCLE

GRANADA GOLF COURSE

SOUTH GREENWAY DRIVE

Merrick House & Gardens

Books and Books

Poinciana Place

Venetian Pool

S.W. 24TH STREET   CORAL WAY

MIRACLE MILE

City Hall

Casa Azul

SEVILLA

De Soto Plaza and Fountain

Biltmore Hotel

ANASTASIA AVENUE

RIVIERA AVENUE

CORAL GABLES BILTMORE GOLF COURSE

VISCAYA AVENUE

UNIVERSITY DRIVE

S.W. 40TH STREET / BIRD ROAD

ALTARA AVENUE

Douglas Road Station

RIVIERA GOLF COURSE

Chamber of Commerce

VILABELLA AVENUE

BLUE ROAD

Chinese Village

Lowe Art Museum

University Station

MIAMI

MIAMI BEACH

Area of map detail

HARDEE ROAD

MAYA ST.

ALFONSO AVENUE

ALHAMBRA CIRCLE

S.W. 72ND STREET / SUNSET DRIVE

RED ROAD

S.W. 57TH AVENUE

GRANADA BOULEVARD

LE JEUNE ROAD

DOUGLAS ROAD

PONCE DE LEON

S.W. 42ND AVENUE

S.W. 37TH AVENUE

PONCE DE LEON BOULEVARD

SOUTH DIXIE HIGHWAY

SANTA MARIA ST.

SAN AMARO

CIRCLE

DRIVE

SEGOVIA STREET

MONSERRATE ST.

MAGGIORE STREET

MAYNADA STREET

RIVIERA DRIVE

From this once-rural coral rock family home came the name for George Merrick's dream city.

Merrick House & Gardens

THE 19TH CENTURY WAS COMING TO AN END, AND Solomon Merrick, a New England Congregational minister-turned-Florida homesteader, wanted his family to have a proper residence. Their avocado and citrus orchards were flourishing, and there was money to do it right.

Merrick House & Gardens

- Map p. 127
- 907 Coral Way, between Toledo St. & Granada Blvd.
- 305/460-5361
- Open Weds. & Sun. only, 1 p.m.–4p.m.; tours at 1 p.m., 2 p.m. & 3 p.m.; or by appointment
- $

Solomon's wife, Althea, sketched the design: a slanted tiled roof with prominent gables topping columns and walls of termite-resistant Dade County pine and keystone, the coral rock underlying this part of the county. She circled the house with a veranda and added classical details to entrances and windows. Construction continued until 1906, and when it was completed, they called it Coral Gables. It was the start of one of America's first planned communities.

Today the house the Merricks built is a community shrine, used for meetings, lectures, and receptions. The building, not its few furnishings, is the reason to visit. Some of the Merricks' original fruit trees still grow in the garden. You can wander about the house and grounds on your own, or join a guided tour. ■

Castles in Spain

Since his childhood, George Merrick intended to be a writer, living an artist's life among the Iberian castles he had seen in picture books. Called home from college to manage the family's 3,000-acre tract of citrus and pineland following his father's death, he married Eunice Peacock. They created a salon of artists, and dreamed of creating a city that would have the sophistication and beauty of the European places that fired their imaginations. ■

Biltmore Hotel

GEORGE MERRICK GOT HIS SPANISH CASTLE IN 1926 WHEN he opened the Biltmore. He rejected perfectly good U.S.-made "Spanish" roof tiles, importing thousands from Spain because they were authentic, and paid the same wonderfully stubborn attention to details throughout, determined that his hotel would rival anything in Europe. When you enter its vast lobby you sense the intensity of his ambition—a room measuring 8,500 square feet, ceilings 45 feet high, massive stone columns. The detail is also in keeping: tropical songbirds in an ornate cage, bellmen quietly moving luggage, telephones muted, and everyone in the lobby behaving just a little bit better because of it all.

Biltmore Hotel
www.BiltmoreHotel.com
 Map p. 127
✉ 1200 Anastasia Ave.
☎ 305/445-1926 or
   800/915-1926

His castle soon faltered, however, as a result of a brutal hurricane, the collapse of Florida's land boom, the 1929 market crash, and the Depression. When Miami went to war in 1941, the Army moved in, turning suites where Bing Crosby, Judy Garland, and the Duke and Duchess of Windsor had stayed into wards for the wounded. The Biltmore remained a military hospital until the 1960s, barely escaping demolition. It was added to the National Register of Historic Places, then gobbled up millions in renovation money before re-opening in 1992. Two years later it hosted the presidents and prime ministers attending the Summit of the Americas, acquitting itself impeccably and announcing to the world that life truly can begin at 70.

You don't have to be a guest to experience some of its finer points. On Sundays, brunch is served in the central Courtyard Café, a sumptuous affair with roving flamenco guitarists and fountains doing what fountains do best. You must see the pool; at 22,000 square feet it's big enough to host a canoe race. Better yet, drop by the ground-level fitness center to check the menu of non-guest packages, which include access to the water. Green fees for the 18-hole, par-71, championship golf course are competitive with local public courses. You can park by the tennis courts and enter via the pool area and the fitness center. There are fine restaurants and lounges and an excellent cigar shop.

At night the Biltmore's 18-story tower is softly illuminated, rising above Coral Gables' neighborhoods like a benevolent feudal castle. Looking at it, you wonder who builds such places. The answer is, no one anymore. ∎

The Biltmore's central spire, modeled after Seville's Giralda Tower, reflects its builder's lifelong fascination with Spanish antiquity.

Venetian Pool

Venetian Pool
www.venetianpool.com

Map p. 127

2701 De Soto Blvd.,
between Almeria
& Sevilla Aves.
at Toledo St.

305/460-5356

No children under
age 3

$$

THERE ARE SWIMMING POOLS, AND THEN THERE ARE swimming pools. This is one of the latter, the prettiest public splash-o-rama in South Florida. It began as an ugly duckling: a hole in the ground left by stonemasons quarrying limestone for Coral Gables' construction.

Artist and designer Denman Fink and architect Phineas Paist, who built much of the city, had a choice: either fill it up or find a use for it. The creative pair concocted a Venetian fantasy of diving platforms, waterfalls, cave grottoes, street lamps faithfully modeled on those in the fabled City of Canals, an observation tower, and an island connected to the pool deck by a graceful arch-bridge. It opened in 1924, and everything is still lovely, including the pool's tilework and the vine-draped Italianate loggia.

During the 1920s, the Venetian Pool was used as a showcase for beauty pageants and fancy parties. There's a nice selection of vintage photos here to prove it. Until 1986, the unfiltered pool was drained nightly, then refilled with 800,000 gallons of fresh artesian well water. These days, the water is recycled through a natural filtration system.

Though you will hear it said about nearly every pool in Greater Miami, the incomparable water ballerina Esther Williams really *did* perform here, as did Hollywood's archetypal Tarzan, Johnny Weissmuller (a champion swimmer and high diver). A swim here will be unlike any other you've ever had. ∎

City Hall

George Merrick wanted a civic headquarters worthy of his vision of what the City Beautiful would become, and was willing to invest $200,000—a lavish expenditure in 1928—to achieve it. Viewed from any angle, the semicircular City Hall, with its triple-tiered, Spanish-Renaissance clock and bell tower, and imposing array of columns, is impressive. It ought to be; it's on the National Register of Historic Places. The gray blocks in its walls are of oolitic limestone, quarried locally from ancient coral reefs marooned above sea level eons ago. From ground-breaking to ribbon-cutting, the building took four months to complete, a remarkable achievement. ■

Miracle Mile

Some say the real miracle along this retail stretch of Coral Way, between 37th and 42nd Avenues, is that it has survived so long. The arrival of national chains has some worried that the one-of-a-kind Coral Gable originals that make many of these storefronts unique are on their way out.

Coral Gables' architecture is indeed pleasing to the eye—the fundamental beauty of the City Beautiful. There are splendid examples along Coral Way, including **De Soto Plaza and Fountain,** where Sevilla Avenue and De Soto and Granada Boulevards come together. Merrick designed 14 of these water plazas, and this one, circled by traffic in a European-style roundabout, is among the most handsome.

Casa Azul, a private home at 1254 Coral Way *(between Madrid St. & Columbus Blvd.),* owes its name to a roof of azure glazed tiles. The architect, H. George Fink, was so esteemed in Spain for his well-publicized use of Spanish designs in Coral Gables that King Alfonso XIII summoned him to an audience and made him Don Jorge.

Poinciana Place *(937 Coral Way, between Toledo St. & Granada Blvd.)* was George and Eunice

Merrick's first home, put up before Merrick commenced building his city. This is the kind of house the area's citrus-growing elite lived in before Coral Gables turned everyone into pretend Mediterraneans.

The **Merrick House** *(832 S. Greenway Dr. at Castile Ave.),* not to be confused with Merrick's boyhood home (see p. 128), is now a private museum. Merrick decided he needed a bigger house to impress prospective home buyers. His cousin Don H. George designed a rock and stucco Alhambra for him, sprawling over one square city block, secluded behind a wall with a distinctive covered gate. ■

An abandoned quarry in central Coral Gables became Greater Miami's most fanciful swimming pool.

City Hall

⬛ Map p. 127

✉ 405 Biltmore Way at Le Jeune Rd.

☎ 305/446-6800

🕐 Closed Sat.–Sun.

Right: The De Soto Plaza and Fountain is the centerpiece of a circular intersection in the City Beautiful.

Lowe Art Museum

Lowe Art Museum
www.lowemuseum.org

Map p. 127

1301 Stanford Dr. on the University of Miami Campus, off US 1/S. Dixie Hwy.

305/284-3535

Closed Mon.

$–$$

TUCKED AWAY ON THE CAMPUS OF THE UNIVERSITY OF Miami is South Florida's first art museum, known most for its collections of Renaissance, baroque, American, Native American, pre-Columbian, and Asian art, any one of which would do a museum proud. You could spend a day here and not see everything on show, but you will take away the memories of Picassos you have seen only in art books, and African masks, textiles, and beadwork so rare they cannot be sold, but only loaned to other museums.

"Le Neveu de Rameau" (1974) by Frank Stella dominates one of the gallery walls in Florida's oldest and leading fine art treasury. The nearby lifelike statue is by Duane Hanson.

There is jade from ancient Japan, Ecuadorian and Colombian antiquities, and cloth woven in the American Southwest by Navajo, Pueblo, and Rio Grande people before Europeans arrived. You might not be able to recall what it was about the abstracts by Frank Stella, or what the girl in the Lichtenstein painting said—there's just too much to take in—but the gauzy rainbows of Bierstadt, the sanguine Yankee palette of Rembrandt Peale, Tintoretto's gently smiling Renaissance faces gazing from out of time, John Sloan's gritty early 20th-century working men, Claude Monet's blues, and Paul Gauguin's deep earth tones you will not forget.

Lying under glass are the Lowe's Egyptian antiquities—those almond-eyed gods clutching their staffs and snakes, half-smiling as if amused by the cosmic joke of once ruling an ancient kingdom and then ending up in Coral Gables.

Buy an exhibition catalog from the superb bookstore and take it home with you. ∎

Miamians call it South Dade and consider Homestead and Florida City its provincial capitals. Others call these century-old farming plains the Redlands, the name arising from their rich, red-hued soil.

South Miami

Zebra, Miami Metrozoo

South Miami

DESPITE SPREADING RESIDENTIAL AND COMMERCIAL DEVELOPMENT—
mini-malls especially popped up overnight like mushrooms in a yard—much of South
Dade remains what Miami once was: rural Southern "pick-up" country where everything
from avocados to zinnias thrives in the fertile, fragrant soil, and the pace is slower, particularly in the miles of agricultural flatland running west to the great Everglades wilderness.

Most people drive through on their way to the
Everglades, Biscayne National Park, or the
Keys, letting the flat fields and fruit stands
flash by, their windows rolled up, the air con-
ditioner on high. That's a shame, because one
of the things people say about this rural inter-
lude between urban Miami and the cluttered
Upper Keys is that it smells so nice—of

blossoms, standing fresh water, even the pleasantly clean oily smell of a wooden barrel of
nails in an old hardware store.

Inevitably, this has been noticed by urban-
ites seeking a change. Farmhouses left to rot a
generation ago are being jacked up and set
back down on new foundations under new
roofs, turned into weekend rural getaways.

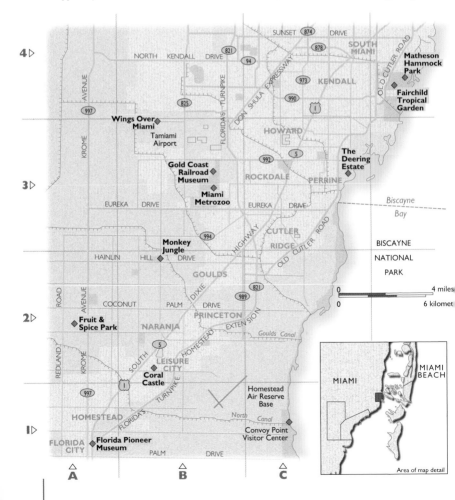

A placid lake, surrounded by the flowered jungles of Fairchild Tropical Botanic Garden, reflects the broken light of a stormy sky.

Agriculture—strawberries, turnips, citrus, onions, tomatoes, squash, herbs, avocados, and a score of other mainstays—sets the tone of South Dade. Orchids thrive in its irrepressible fertility, the result of nutrient-rich topsoil, abundant water, and a hothouse sun. Specialty organic farms supply Greater Miami's restaurants and gourmet kitchens.

You can speed down from the Greater Miami area on US 1, the South Dixie Highway, but unless you're on a tight schedule you should take the slower, more scenic path along the Atlantic shore: South Bayshore Drive to Main Highway, through Coconut Grove, continuing south on Ingraham Highway, and then picking up Old Cutler Road, famous for its lush ficus canopy and exclusive gated communities. The advantage is aesthetic: The route is prettier, more relaxing, and reveals more of South Florida's subtropical nature and the way it affects how people live and work. It also takes you to one of Greater Miami's finest and prettiest oceanside public greens, Matheson Hammock Park, and the Fairchild Tropical Botanic Garden, a splendid preserve where the prima donnas of the world's most exotic flora are fussed over, groomed, and dressed up for daily performances.

Marking the southern fringe of hurricane-battered South Dade, Homestead suffers as the butt of jokes, maligned for homeliness and a lack of sophistication. It's not much to look at, nor are fine dining and nightlife among its strengths. As its name implies, its first settlers were mostly farmers who planted avocados, oranges, lemons, and limes. Railroad workers employed by Henry Flagler made Homestead their South Florida base, and filled up its cottage community, buying their food in farmers' markets and living a rural village life. Florida City fares little better, its humble avenues built paycheck by paycheck and not through grand schemes like George Merrick's Coral Gables.

In 1992 Hurricane Andrew delivered a catastrophic blow to both cities, leaving them strewn with the wreckage of shattered houses and stripping natural foliage down to a white-boned nakedness. Recovery has been slow, but most of the damage is nearly erased.

With a good map in hand, it's worthwhile setting out to explore this wide-open rural grid of streets and avenues, some with numbers, some with names, many sharing both. You'll discover an out-of-the-way corner of the Real Florida stretching east–west from Biscayne Bay to the Everglades. ■

Fairchild Tropical Botanic Garden

Fairchild Tropical Botanic Garden
www.fairchildgarden.org

🅰 134 D4

✉ 10901 Old Cutler Rd.

☎ 305/667-1651

💲 $$–$$$$

A floating bouquet fills a quiet pool along one of Fairchild's nature trails.

SOUTH FLORIDA IS THE ONLY REGION IN THE CONTINENTAL United States where tropical and subtropical plants can survive the year. For that reason, southeast of Coral Gables on Biscayne Bay you'll find the largest American tropical botanical garden outside of Hawaii, an exquisite 83-acre greenery in its seventh decade as one of the world's leading centers for botanical research. You can ponder life beside eleven lakes and lily pools in this palmy oasis of orchids, ferns, and flowering trees. It also lets you explore South Florida's ancient environments, such as a pristine mangrove preserve and a hardwood hammock, the Florida of the Tequesta people. Children are entranced by the vine-draped, tunnel-like limestone pergola, and hidden passages through rain forest canopies shading all in green-tinted light.

The design of the garden creates magic. It opened in 1938 and is named in honor of Dr. David Fairchild, a globe-trotting botanist and writer whose adventures in far-off places earned him a reputation as a plant explorer, the Indiana Jones of orchids. His memoir, *The World Was My Garden*, is to some botanists what *The Compleat Angler* is to flycasters.

A United Nations of ferns, plants, and orchids grows round the lakes here: Australia's fire tree, Brazil's birthwort, South Africa's Pride of the Cape, the passion flower of Nicaragua and Venezuela, Vietnam's herald's trumpet, and Burma and Thailand's shower of orchids. Their exotic names fill a book—the African baobab tree, the Malay Glorybower, the ylang-ylang tree *(Cananga odorata)*, whose plain flowers produce an oil used in Chanel No. 5 perfume. The variety is overwhelming, a strong argument for joining a guided walking tour along the garden's many theme paths, though you're welcome to wander on your own. Narrated tram tours run hourly, weekdays 10 a.m–3 p.m., and to 4 p.m. on weekends. ∎

Matheson Hammock Park

THE DRIVEWAY INTO DADE COUNTY'S OLDEST PARK SUGGESTS you have arrived at some billionaire's secluded Biscayne Bay hideaway, with its well-tended lawns and spiffy marina. It is, in fact, the legacy of a wealthy man, Commodore W.J. Matheson, a manufacturer of dyes and chemicals, once the owner of Key Biscayne, whose will bequeathed the first 100 of the park's 520 acres to the county in 1930. (Commodore was not a military rank but an approbation often bestowed back then on prominent members of the sailing set, usually founders and presidents of yacht clubs.)

Around 400,000 visitors a year make Matheson's gift one of Greater Miami's most popular outdoor recreation spots, not surprising given its design—a man-made swimming lagoon (the Atoll Pool) refreshed by the tides, a handsome coral rock restaurant building, picnic pavilions and cooking grills, and a Biscayne Bay panorama. There are nature trails for exploring the park's mangrove swamp, a piece of primeval Florida that accounts for much of the acreage.

Before you park, reconnoiter by car. Take the turn-off to the marina and yacht club and continue past the boat ramp south along the shore to parking lot 5, situated beside a lovely wading beach with sandbar shallows, making it especially safe for children and non-swimmers. It is also a popular destination for guided naturalist tours focusing on shallow-water sea life. The north fork of the entrance road continues past the marina and ends beside the swimming lagoon, where you'll find a lifeguard on duty, a snack bar, and restrooms. There's an asphalt walk around the lagoon's sandy beach and park benches facing Biscayne Bay.

Ask a park ranger for a map that shows paths through the woods and bicycle trails. If the lagoon is crowded, try the wading beach by parking lot 5, often a quieter place. ∎

At leisure in the shade of rustling palms at Matheson Hammock, one of Greater Miami's favorite family oriented parks on Biscayne Bay

Matheson Hammock Park

🅰 134 D4

✉ 9610 Old Cutler Rd., between Campana Ave. & Journey's End Rd.

☎ 305/665-5475

💲 $

A reading chair
is part of Coral
Castle, a Latvian
immigrant's
peculiar
monument to
a lost love.

Coral Castle

Call him obsessed, call him neurotic, call him whatever you please, but no one calls Ed Leedskalnin a 97-pound weakling. A slender Latvian immigrant who stood 5 feet tall, Leedskalnin spent 28 years, beginning in 1923, building his bizarre Coral Castle (once called Rock Gate Park). He often worked at night so no one could see how he moved and lifted the massive blocks of oolite, including a nine-ton gate, that make up and furnish (rather uncomfortably) his strange home. Three of his original ten acres are open to the public. It's said he built it as a monument to a lost Latvian love, a 16-year-old girl named Agnes Scuffs who broke their engagement and, reputedly, Ed's heart as well.

That's not quite the whole story, and this place isn't quite a castle either. It's missing a roof, and is more of a courtyard filled with coral chairs, a banquet table in the shape of Florida, odd sculptures, a sundial, and a rock "telescope" fixed on the North Star. Coral Castle may have failed to win back Ed's girl, but it did establish him as the undisputed king of Florida kitsch. ∎

Coral Castle
www.coralcastle.com
🗺 134 B2
✉ 28655 S. Dixie
Hwy./US 1,
Homestead
☎ 305/248-6345
💲 $$

Monkey Jungle

Monkey Jungle
www.monkeyjungle.com
🗺 134 B2
✉ W of US 1 at
14805 S.W. 216th
St./Hainlin Mill Dr.
near S.W. 147th St.
☎ 305/235-1611
💲 $$$$–$$$$$

You can see just as many monkeys at nearby Metrozoo (see p. 140)—but you will not get as close to them there as you can here. In this 30-acre garden of botanically correct Amazonian jungle, you, not the primates, are caged. They run free (or think they do), swinging from limb to limb and screeching wildly. The simian family is extended here, from baboons, chimpanzees, orangutans, and macaques to small, lesser known species, whose eyes seem to register constant surprise. If you have young children along, odds are they will enjoy this place. ∎

An aviation buff peers up at a World War II-era Navy torpedo bomber. Its folding wings conserved space aboard aircraft carriers.

Wings Over Miami

Among aviation buffs, Miami enjoys mythical status for attending the birth of Pan American World Airways, one reason champion aerobatics pilot Kermit Weeks founded an air museum at the old Kendall-Tamiami Airport in southwest Miami. Now a museum called Wings Over Miami, it has assembled an impressive fleet of vintage aircraft, many in flying condition, including some of the burly warbirds that turned the tide in World War II. ■

Wings Over Miami
www.wingsovermiami.com
🗺 134 B3
✉ 14710 S.W. 128th St. Take the Florida Turnpike to S.W. 120th St., go W to S.W. 127th Ave.
☎ 305/233-5197
💲 $$

Shops at Sunset Place

Shopping in vibrant Greater Miami takes on an entertainment atmosphere in the Shops at Sunset Place. Between jaunts to Ann Taylor Loft, Armani Exchange, Barnes & Noble, the Disney Store, and dozens of other stores, visitors can watch giant creatures at an IMAX theater or catch the newest Hollywood films at a multiplex. Best of all is GameWorks, a joint venture of SEGA and Universal Studios, where visitors can eat, drink, and play in a restaurant and bar pulsating with more than 200 games and interactive attractions. The frenetic locale stays open late, until 2:00 a.m. on weekends.

Other restaurants here include Cheeseburger in Paradise, Coco Pazzo Cafe, Dan Marino's Town Tavern, and Johnny Rockets. ■

Shops at Sunset Place
🗺 134 C4
✉ 5701 Sunset Drive
☎ 305/663-4222

Miami Metrozoo

Miami Metrozoo

www.miamimetrozoo.com

 134 B3

✉ 12400 S.W. 152nd St. Approx. 1 mile W of Florida Turnpike Extension exit 16 (Eureka Drive/S.W. 184th St.), 3 miles W of US 1/S. Dixie Hwy. via S.W. 152nd St.

☎ 305/251-0400

$ $$–$$$

THIS IS NOT ONE OF THOSE OLD-FASHIONED BLEAK CONCRETE animal prisons that make you want to set the inmates loose. Its 290 acres of jungle, grassland, and forest make up what is considered one of America's finest wild animal parks, and its only subtropical one, home to 800 species of rare and exotic creatures that roam free.

There are no cages, no bars; you walk among animals, seldom seen except on TV, on well-marked protected footpaths, or ride above the herds in air-conditioned monorail trolleys. Rare white Bengal tigers recline regally on the "ruins" of a 13th-century Cambodian temple modeled on Angkor Wat, and silverback gorillas peer out from a tropical jungle, while reticulated giraffes, along with zebras, gazelles, and ostriches roam a Serengeti-like African plain.

In another habitat, the black rhinoceros and the African elephant, whose wild populations have been decimated by poaching, scuff the sunburned veldt as barrel-bodied warthogs run back and forth on spindly legs.

There is a new wildlife carousel and also a petting zoo for kids. Not for petting are a pair of Komodo dragons, 10-foot-long, 300-pound carnivorous lizards from Indonesia. In the Asian River Life exhibit you walk in the mist of tropical waterfalls, surrounded by otters, clouded leopards, water monitors, and primitive muntjac deer. Half a world apart in terms of habitat, kangaroos, wallabies, and koalas inhabit the zoo's Australian Outback. Times are posted for animal feedings, which tend to reveal intriguing if less charming aspects of the creatures' personalities. ∎

Gold Coast Railroad Museum

WE KNOW WHERE ALL THE FLOWERS WENT, BUT WHERE did the great locomotives and plush sleeping cars of railroading's golden era go? Gone to scrapyards every one, mostly. But fate has saved a few. You will find 30 of them at this retired World War II naval air station next to the Miami Metrozoo, including a 1949 *Silver Crescent* dome car and the most history-laden piece of rolling stock that ever traveled the nation's steel roads: the magnificent *Ferdinand Magellan*, a 1928 Pullman sleeping car redesigned in 1942 for President Franklin Roosevelt.

Gold Coast Railroad Museum
www.goldcoast-railroad.org
🄰 134 B3
✉ 12450 S.W. 152nd St.
☎ 305/253-0063 or 888/608-7246
💲 $–$$

FDR was content to travel by regular Pullman, but the war was on and his security detail feared Nazi assassins, so the *Magellan* was purchased and fitted with armor plate and 3-inch-thick bullet-resistant glass. Its dining-cum-conference room was enlarged and an observation lounge added, along with escape hatches and features permitting Roosevelt, semi-disabled by polio, to move about more easily. When the work was done, the car's weight had increased from 160,000 pounds to 285,000. At nearly 143 tons, it was the heaviest American passenger railcar ever used, and it is the only one designated a national historic landmark.

Roosevelt and Winston Churchill huddled over its solid mahogany conference table in the war's darkest days. It secretly spirited Roosevelt away to Miami for his January 1943 flight to the Casablanca Conference aboard Pan Am's *Dixie Clipper.* (FDR and aide Harry Hopkins were the only passengers, booked as Mr. Smith and Mr. Jones.) The President traveled some 50,000 miles aboard the *Magellan,* at a preferred speed of 35 mph, including his final journey to Warm Springs, Georgia, on the last full day of his life. Harry Truman, who used the Pullman for his trademark whistle-stop campaigns, logged 28,000 miles, setting the throttle at 80 mph. (The famous 1948 photograph of a victorious Harry displaying an incorrect newspaper headline declaring "Dewey Defeats Truman"

shows him aboard the *Magellan.*) Dwight Eisenhower also made use of it while in office. Future Presidents opted for air travel, but during his 1984 presidential campaign, Ronald Reagan borrowed Truman's bully pulpit for speeches between Dayton and Toledo, Ohio. You're free to mount the platform and give one of your own. A train ride is included in the price of admission. ∎

Armored and outfitted for presidential travel, this customized Pullman is the only national historic landmark on wheels.

Fruit & Spice Park

Fruit & Spice Park
www.fruitandspicepark.org
▲ 134 A2
✉ 24801 S.W. 187th
    Ave./Redland Rd. at
    S.W. 256th St.
☎ 305/247-5727
$ $–$$. Guided tours
    daily at 11:00 a.m.,
    1:30 p.m. &
    3:00 p.m..

**Seed pods dangle
from one of
hundreds of exotic
trees grown for
study by Fruit &
Spice Park
agronomists.**

There is little that will not grow in South Dade's Redlands. Regarding fruit, vegetables, herbs, and spices, South Florida's fecundity has, from the early 1800s, inspired agronomists to experiment, often wildly, and sometimes with edible results.

About 35 miles south of Miami, near Homestead, is a layman-friendly outpost of serious planting and experimentation that is probably the last word on this business—the unusual Fruit & Spice Park, a county park established in 1944 to showcase what South Florida was capable of producing. The 32-acre garden cultivates around 500 varieties of exotic and subtropical fruit, nut, and spice trees, along with

many varieties of herbs. And it works with other plant centers around the world to develop new and better strains. (The carambola, or star fruit, was developed here.) There's even an area devoted to poisonous plants.

Activities and programs include classes and tours of nearby fruit- and vegetable-growing regions, and lectures on gardening and botany. (The Redland Natural Arts Festival takes place every January. The event features craftspeople and artists and draws big crowds to the park.)

The gourmet-style gift shop sells preserves, chutneys, jellies, marinades, spices, seeds, and other exotic ingredients often hard to find, along with regionally oriented cookbooks and culinary guides, and treatises on plant propagation. There's history here, too, in rustic, vintage, coral rock buildings, including a schoolhouse built in 1912, which in the Redlands qualifies it as a pioneer relic.

Unless you really know your fruits and spices, you'll probably enjoy yourself more on a guided tour—there's so much to see here, despite the loss of many plants during the 1992 debacle of Hurricane Andrew. You're not supposed to pick from the trees, but anything on the ground is yours to take. ■

Florida Pioneer Museum

Florida Pioneer Museum
▲ 134 A1
✉ 826 Krome Ave.
    between N.W. 8th
    & 9th Sts.
☎ 305/246-9531
🕐 Open Weds. & Sat.
    afternoons
$ $

This small but informative museum of local pioneer and Indian artifacts is an example of South Dade's frame vernacular architecture—shady veranda, clapboard siding, peaked roof, attic, and dormer windows—built in 1904 to house a Florida East Coast Railroad station

agent, and moved to this site in 1964. This was the nation's last railroad frontier. The old caboose outside is believed to be one of only a few wooden models still in existence. Opening hours can be irregular. It is wise to call ahead to confirm times. ■

B eyond Greater Miami lies the Real Florida: land of the ancient Tequesta, and current home of the Miccosukee and Seminole; the River of Grass; the marshes and plains of Big Cypress country to the north; the islands and reefs of Biscayne Bay to the south.

Excursions from Miami

Heavy-lidded eyes and a fixed smile belie the Everglades alligator's speed and ferocity as a predator.

Excursions from Miami

TO SAY THAT EVERGLADES NATIONAL PARK ENCOMPASSES 1.5 MILLION ACRES, OR even that its shimmering wetlands, in reality a river sometimes only inches deep but always miles wide, are not duplicated anywhere on Earth, does not prepare you for its peculiar wilderness. It is not simply wild, but also alive in a way that other natural places do not always appear to be. This is the only place in the world where alligators and crocodiles exist side by side amid a chorus of birds (more than 300 nesting and migratory species), myriad fish, a painter's palette of butterflies, manatees, and Florida panthers, to cite only a few examples of the wildlife.

If you have a day to spare, you can drive into its outer regions and walk on nature trails and boardwalks, shake hands with the denizens of this primordial soup, and take home indelible impressions of the world as it was before humankind. Despite what some believe is irreparable damage done to the Everglades by agriculture and development and flood-preventing ditches and dikes that diminished the flow of source water into these magnificently placid wetlands, their protected areas still look pristine and are, for many, a captivating remnant of the vanishing Great American Wild.

Less evident, but no less vital, is the hidden wilderness beneath the waves of sheltered Biscayne Bay, in particular the 180,000 acres enclosed by the boundaries of Biscayne National Park (only five percent of which is land). The park represents a line drawn in the sand between the compulsion to develop, and the far more difficult path of balance between the impulse to live comfortably now and the obligation to protect and preserve the natural world for those who will come later. It encloses a vital portion of the only living reef within the continental United States, protecting not only that underwater world but all the ecosystems, from upper Biscayne Bay to the Keys, that depend on the health of this reef.

The Miccosukee depended upon these wilds for their survival, living among the Everglades in traditional thatched-roof wooden dwellings called chickees. For this branch of the Creek Indians, who lived in southern Alabama and Georgia in the 1700s and got their name from their Mikasuki dialect, the balance most difficult to achieve was not ecological but political—finding an accommodation with the Seminole, their Muskogee-speaking Creek cousins. Tensions between them compelled the Miccosukee to move south, an odyssey beginning in the late 18th century and ending in the Everglades. There the tribe of 5,000 found themselves forced to address an even more aggressive people: Spanish and Anglo-American settlers, who demanded their allegiance even as they pushed the Miccosukee from their domains. After the Seminole uprisings—the banner under which the feuding cousins united in resistance to settlement and forced relocation—disease, deportation, and despair diminished their number until the Miccosukee rolls counted only 100 members. They fled deep into the Everglades to live and wait for the future to find them, and to keep their culture alive through devotion to traditional ritual and religion, meanwhile sustaining themselves as they always had, by hunting and fishing.

Here they lived in relative peace until the early years of the 20th century, when the appetite of Florida's land boom—for any land dry or wet—elbowed them from the dinner table on which they depended, even as roads cut into the wetlands brought motorists who gawked at these strange people in their brightly colored garments and wondered how anyone could live this way. Keep this in mind when you drive west on the Tamiami Trail into the Everglades and the Miccosukee Indian Reservation, some 300,000 acres, mostly underwater, running across two counties toward Naples. Today the tribal roll numbers about 650, a determined band of people, utterly American in their striving for community and a dependable way of life that holds the promise of a future of renewal and growth—exactly the ambition of their non-Indian fellow South Floridians—for the Everglades as well as for themselves. ∎

Airplane propeller-driven flatboats offer speedy transport across Everglades wetlands, but only those outside national park boundaries.

Biscayne National Park

Biscayne National Park
www.nps.gov/bisc
🅼 145 D2
✉ 9700 S.W. 328th St., Homestead

Dante Fascell Visitor Center, Convoy Point
🅼 145 D2
☎ 305/230-7275

THIS IS ONE OF THE MOST ACCESSIBLE NATIONAL PARKS AND also among the most remote. Unless you have a boat, the 95 percent of Biscayne National Park that is underwater, and the 40 or so small barrier islands that compose its allotment of land, are beyond reach. You must either comb its beaches and mangrove fringes, or let a concessionaire's boat take you out across the water to the park's secret splendor: the rainbow-colored coral reefs beneath the waves.

Getting to the park from Miami is easy. The most direct route, which is neither scenic nor interesting, is via S. Dixie Highway (US 1), a drive of about an hour from downtown. Take it south for 25 miles, past Cutler Ridge to Goulds (some 15 miles north of Homestead). Watch for a park billboard, which is soon followed by a park sign. Turn left here onto S.W. 137th Avenue (Tallahassee Road) and proceed to S.W. 328th Street (North Canal Drive). Turn left and continue to the end of the road 6 miles ahead. The entrance to Biscayne is on the left. If you go via the Florida Turnpike, follow the Homestead extension south to Campell Drive exit. Turn right from the ramp and continue east to the next intersection (Kingman Road). Turn right and continue to S.W. 328th Street and continue as described above.

If time permits, consider taking a longer, more scenic route along the shore. From Miami, follow S. Bayshore Drive to Main Highway and Coconut Grove, continuing south on Ingraham Highway and then picking up Old Cutler Road. Follow Old Cutler south past the Deering Estate (see p. 118) and Cutler Ridge and the Florida Turnpike west to Allapattah Road, then turn left and follow Allapattah due south to S.W. 328th Street. A left turn, east, toward the sea, brings you to the park's Convoy Point entrance.

By far the most popular excursion here is the **Reef Cruise,** a three-hour voyage from the **Dante Fascell Visitor Center** aboard a glass-bottom boat. Save for a sun hat, sunglasses, and sunscreen—all mandatory items—you need no equipment. (Do bring a camera and binoculars, however.) The trip begins with a park ranger's briefing on the things you will see and their significance. The boat has a viewing chamber running lengthwise, comprised of thick-paned glass ports opening downward. The water's natural tint is green, diminishing slightly the colors of the fish, coral, and other life-forms that pass by below, but the clear water makes for fascinating views. Unless you have snorkeled or dived in tropical waters, this will introduce you to a wholly new world, most of it less than ten feet deep.

Look up and you'll see pelicans skimming the water, their ungainly waddles on land replaced by flight so graceful you have to sigh. Look back down to the sandy plain of waving sea grass blowing in the warm current, stalked by spiny lobsters and crabs. Flashes of color identify some of the 200 species of fish that live in these calm waters, protected by barrier islands from Atlantic surges. Herons and cormorants skim and soar, cocking their heads to peer through surface glare in search of fish.

A highlight of the trip is a close

look at the offshore barrier islands, the northernmost Florida Keys, fringed with mangroves, their interiors dense with tropical hardwood forest dating from prehistory. Beyond, as far out as 7 miles, are the reefs, where some 50 shipwrecks—rusting skeletons lying amid massive brain coral and great mounds of star coral, fish, and sea fans—testify to the peril in these gorgeous shallows.

If your itinerary doesn't permit a half-day on the water, you'll take away an experience that in its way is just as memorable by spending an hour walking the mangrove-tangled shoreline of **Convoy Point,** which is also a lovely place to picnic. Although they are elusive, bald eagles and peregrines do frequent this area, as do manatees, to feed and find cover beneath the dense overhead canopy. When you arrive at the visitor center, check the schedule and ask about guided nature tours, including boat trips to **Elliott Key.** Inquire about canoe tours and rentals, as well as snorkeling and scuba diving excursions; you can also make reservations *(tel 305/230-1100).* ■

The mostly submerged acreage of Biscayne National Park slides by beneath the feet of passengers aboard a glass-bottom boat.

Everglades National Park

Everglades National Park

Punting canoes, built using Seminole Indian designs, through the backwaters of the Everglades

Everglades National Park
www.nps.gov/ever
145 C2
40001 Fla. 9336, Homestead
305/242-7700
$$

THE RIVER OF GRASS IS THE LARGEST REMAINING SUB-tropical wilderness in the continental United States and the third largest national park outside Alaska. It is designated a World Heritage site, an International Biosphere Reserve, and a Wetland of International Significance. Until you venture in and have a look for yourself, you cannot imagine how different it is from anything you've ever encountered—no matter how many photographs you have seen.

Once you decide to explore the Everglades, plan to spend a long day, whether you visit the Shark Valley region west of Miami or venture southwest to Florida City for a more extensive visit to the park's southern half and its Gulf of Florida shore. Either way, you absolutely must wear a sun hat and sunglasses, and plaster on insect repellent. In the Everglades, mosquitoes are a crucial part of the food chain, and without

repellent you will become part of it, too—and extremely uncomfortable as a result. Park weather is mild and pleasant from December through April, but summers are hot and humid, with temperatures and humidity in the 90s and occasional afternoon thunderstorms. Wear loose-fitting, long-sleeved shirts and pants, and bring drinking water and snacks, since these are not widely available. Information on mosquito

tour the road yourself (a two- to three-hour circuit), but if you do, bring water and ask a ranger for tips on social etiquette for meeting the gators. You'll also encounter wading birds and turtles and, across the waters, tree islands called tropical hardwood hammocks and small shrubby ones known as bayheads.

If you forgo the tram ride, take a stroll along the **Bobcat Boardwalk** and **Otter Cave Hammock Trail,** both near the visitor center, which have photogenic views of these little turfs, whose elevation above the water makes them mini-Noah's Arks of resident wildlife.

An alligator greets strollers along the park's Anhinga Trail.

levels in summer is available *(tel 305/242-7700).*

EXPLORING SHARK VALLEY

The Shark Valley entrance and visitor center lie 25 miles west of Miami via S.W. Eighth Street (US 41/Tamiami Trail) on the park's northern border. Beyond the gates is the heart of the great river, whose flow runs imperceptibly from Lake Okeechobee to the Gulf of Mexico, a distance of only 100 miles. The river is so broad, the volume spilled into Florida Bay is enormous.

Park your car and board the open-sided tram for a two-hour narrated tour along a 15-mile loop road, one of the best ways to view park wildlife, including alligators. You can also rent bicycles (state law requires that children 16 and under wear helmets, which can be purchased at the tram office) and

TOURING THE LOWER EVERGLADES

From Miami, take the Florida Turnpike (Fla. 821) south to the Florida City exit. Turn right at the first traffic light onto Palm Drive and follow the signs to the main Visitor Center at the park boundary. Check postings for ranger-led walks at the Royal Palm Visitor Center, 4 miles west, and also for that day's cruises from Flamingo Visitor Center on Florida Bay, 38 miles southwest of the entrance via a scenic and interesting road featuring a

Shark Valley Visitor Center

- 145 C2
- Fla. 9336
- 305/221-8776 (information & reservations), 305/221-8455 (bike rentals)
- Ranger-led walks during winter months only. Tram tours year-round
- $$ per car, $$ per pedestrian/cyclist

world of water and wildlife.

Stop at the **Royal Palm Visitor Center** for a stroll along the **Anhinga Nature Trail** and the **Gumbo Limbo Trail,** both half a mile long. The Anhinga is a boardwalk featuring wildlife and visits a freshwater slough. Gumbo Limbo skirts a saw-grass marsh, hardwood hammocks, and thickets of the red-barked gumbo limbo tree. Guided walks offer insights that untrained eyes frequently miss, so try to join at least one.

Stop again to walk the **Pinelands Trail,** 7 miles down the road, through remnants of the pine forest that once covered most of southeastern Florida. You'll find inviting picnic spots at **Paurotis Pond, Nine Mile Pond,** and **West Lake.** At **Flamingo,** sign

up for a two-hour backcountry boat tour at the marina ticket office near the visitor center *(Nov.–April)*. It takes you into the deep wild, places impossible to reach by land, places impossible to anticipate. Bring your camera and binoculars, and marvel at the thought that this utter perfection was once global. ■

Below: Wildlife of the Everglades

Osprey

Royal palm

trangler fig

Roseate spoonbill

The long–necked Anhinga, seen in characteristic pose drying its wings after diving

Brown pelican

Airplant

Barred owl

Mangrove

Great white heron

Crocodile

ap fern

Coon oysters

Mangrove snapper

Turtle grass

Manatee

Pink shrimp

Loggerhead turtle

Tamiami Trail driving tour

The name Tamiami Trail—US 41—was coined in 1928 to signify its endpoints, Miami and Tampa, but it is the 106-mile Miami–Naples stretch for which it is best known. The opening of the trail took little note of the road's ecological and social consequences. Besides permitting tourists to aim their vehicles into the heart of the Everglades, it impeded the great river's southward flow. To the Miccosukee, clinging to traditional ways by retreating ever farther into the wilderness, the Tamiami was a trail of tears leading to a future when a culture sustained by hunting and fishing would no longer fit into the way of life being forced upon them.

That said, and taking the road simply in terms of the extraordinary landscapes it crosses, the Tamiami is a remarkable sampler of wild Florida. Its eastern miles skirt the northern boundary of Everglades National Park (see pp. 148–51), affording an opportunity to stop at the **Shark Valley Visitor Center** ❶ and walk for a while, and perhaps take the tram tour along the 15-mile loop road that plunges south into the preserve's soggy saw-grass marshes and hardwood hammocks, where alligators lie in the sun.

A few miles west, the 650 members of the Miccosukee tribe maintain the **Miccosukee**

Indian Village ❷, a bridge between old ways and new lifestyles that engage the larger world. Traditional handicraft outlets present a public face, while issues of tribal autonomy and welfare are debated elsewhere by lawyers, state officials, and tribal representatives. Meanwhile, tourists stop at MM (Mile Marker) 25 at the **Miccosukee Restaurant** *(tel 305/223-8380, www.miccosukee.com)* for home-cooked catfish and frog legs served breaded and deep-fried, with a side dish of pumpkin bread.

Continue west to **Big Cypress National Preserve** ❸ *(Ochopee, tel 239/695-1201, www.nps.gov/bicy)*, nearly three-quarters-of-a-million acres of marshland, prairies wet and dry, stands of hardwood, mangrove, pine, and,

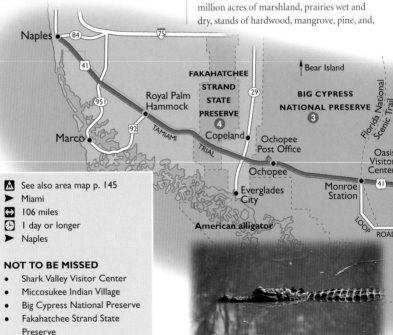

American alligator

See also area map p. 145

► Miami

↔ 106 miles

🕐 1 day or longer

► Naples

NOT TO BE MISSED

- Shark Valley Visitor Center
- Miccosukee Indian Village
- Big Cypress National Preserve
- Fakahatchee Strand State Preserve

Canoeing the Wilderness Waterway

The 100-mile Wilderness Waterway between the Gulf Coast and Flamingo winds through one of the largest uninhabited expanses in the East. Most visitors use canoes or sea kayaks to avoid disturbing the wildlife. The best time to take the week-long journey is mid-December to mid-April; outfitters return you to your starting place. Bed-and-breakfasts offer lodging at either end; in between you camp in Miccosukee-style "chickees." Guides, maps, and lists of outfitters are available at Flamingo Visitor Center *(tel 239/695-2945, www.nps.gov/ever)*. Florida National Parks and Monuments Association *(tel 305/247-1216, www.nps.gov/archive/ever/fnpma)* offers charts of the route, marked by numbered pilings. ■

of course, cypress, the "big" referring not to size but number. Despite logging, cypresses grace about a third of the preserve. The Big Cypress watershed supplies the Everglades, flowing south across the boundary they share. A different kind of wild exists here, explained by the Oasis Visitor Center's 15-minute film. The **Tree Snail Hammock Nature Trail** is designed to introduce you to creatures that live here, including the rare, elusive Florida panther. During winter, rangers lead walks along the path. The 26-mile loop road and two other auto routes are scenic but best suited to high-clearance, four-wheel-drive vehicles. If you've brought a bicycle with you, ask about rides in the Bear Island

area. Picnic tables make this a pleasant place for a driving break. You might share them with hikers trekking the Florida National Scenic Trail, which winds through here.

A side trip 3 miles north on Fla. 29, near Ochopee (population about 200), leads to the **Fakahatchee Strand State Preserve** ❹ *(Copeland, tel 239/695-4593, www.friendsof fakahatchee.org)*. Its elevated walkway angles through an unusually pretty stand of bald cypress, a community of royal palm, and colorful bursts of wild orchid. The group of royals is said to be North America's largest, the **Ochopee post office** America's smallest. Ask the rangers about the scenic drive. ■

Miccosukee totem pole

Tree Snail Hammock Nature Trail

Big Cypress National Preserve

Paolita

997

Miccosukee Restaurant

94 — ❷

Tamiami Canal

826 MIAMI

95

Miccosukee Indian Village

TAMIAMI TRAIL

41

Shark Valley Visitor Center

Tram Tour

START

❶

EVERGLADES NATIONAL PARK

997

0 10 miles

0 20 kilometers

Fort Lauderdale

Fort Lauderdale
still has a lively
beach life,
although the days
of boisterous
student parties
during spring
break belong to
the 1960s.

FORT LAUDERDALE IS REMEMBERED FROM *WHERE THE BOYS Are*, a 1961 Hollywood morality play about thrill-crazed youth on a lust-mad rampage during Fort Lauderdale's annual bacchanal called spring break, when thousands of college students come from afar to crowd its bars and Fort Lauderdale Beach, and act out the verb "to party." They still come here—restrained somewhat by strict public and private policies adopted to save them from themselves—but during the rest of the year, this most unmilitary city defines a kind of living wonderfully free of, say, San Francisco's self-consciousness about being San Francisco, or New York's self-importance, yet achieves a level of comfort and beauty rare among American cities.

Fort Lauderdale
◩ 145 D3

Like Miami, Fort Lauderdale has a history of wild boosterism, with more than 300 miles of canals, channels, and rivers, most dating from the 1920s land boom, served by water taxis with colorful guides. An all-day pass permits unlimited boardings *(www.watertaxi.com)*.

To get to downtown, take I-95 north from Miami to the Broward Boulevard exit, turn toward the Atlantic and follow Broward to one-way N.W. First Avenue. To cruise the city, go right onto N.W. First and go south until it takes you left onto Las Olas Boulevard.

The well-respected **Museum of Art** *(1 East Las Olas Blvd.,*

tel 954/525-5500, www.moafl.org, closed Tues., $$) stands on the corner. If you want to visit it, proceed to the municipal garage by making the first left turn possible onto S.E. Third Avenue, and then making an immediate left on S.E. Second Street. (The garage is on your right at the other end of the block.) Among scholars and art lovers, who find a unique appeal in older works produced during what was once considered the avant-garde movement in Copenhagen, Brussels and Amsterdam, this collection is a treasury. It occupies an Edward Larrabee Barnes building that architectural critics adore, which was expanded in 2001. Its permanent collection is noted for 20th-century American and European masters: Alexander Calder, Salvador Dalí, Henry Moore, Pablo Picasso, Larry Rivers, Andy Warhol, and Frank Stella, among others.

The New River runs through Fort Lauderdale's central district, flanked by a glittery arts and entertainment district, where you can applaud touring Broadway plays by the river at the glassy **Broward Center for the Performing Arts**. If you come here on business, this is a pleasant district in which to book a hotel, not least because of its after-hours clubs featuring music—mostly jazz, blues, rock, and reggae, in that order. There are cafés ideal for a casual dinner on a warm evening, and it's all within walking distance, including the Fort Lauderdale Historical Society (see p. 156).

After dinner, take a stroll along the **Riverwalk,** a mile-long promenade on the river's north bank, which crosses over and continues for another half-mile on the south side. What's particularly nice about this ramble are the tropical

Broward Center for the Performing Arts
www.browardcenter.org
✉ 201 S.W. Fifth Ave.
☎ 954/462-0222

landscaping, interpretive displays that tell you about Fort Lauderdale, and the river overlooks.

ALSO OF INTEREST

At Las Olas and S.E. Sixth Avenue is the city's oldest standing structure, built in 1901, **Stranahan House** *(tel 954/524-4736, www.stranahan house.org, closed Mon.–Tues.)*, which retains its original furnishings.

Handsome Spanish colonial arcades house designer boutiques, jewelers, and several fine art galleries on Las Olas, between 6th and 11th Avenues. The Isles, at the end of Las Olas, is acknowledged as Fort Lauderdale's preeminent address, where finger islands are lined with luxurious manses.

The **Fort Lauderdale Historical Society** *(219 S.W.*

An excursion boat boards sightseers for a cruise of Fort Lauderdale's sheltered inland waterways.

2nd Ave., tel 954/463-4431, www.old fortlauderdale.org, closed Mon.,) relates the melodramatic history of this nevertheless relaxed region.

The **Broward County Main Library** *(100 S. Andrews Ave., tel 954/357-7444, www.broward.org/ library)* is a beautifully designed Marcel Breuer building.

Fort Lauderdale Beach is reached by following Las Olas to its

dead end, where you can take Atlantic Boulevard along the water in either direction and stop according to your tastes. This is a world of beach umbrellas claimed by people with fat paperback novels and slim cell phones, particularly between Las Olas and Sunrise Boulevards.

Bonnet House Museum & Gardens *(900 N. Birch Rd., tel 954/563-5393, closed Mon. & all of Sept., $$$$)*, once the 35-acre winter residence of an artist couple, Frederic and Evelyn Bartlett, is in the beach area. Their aesthetic estate still exhibits the youthful zest for art, beauty, and romance that inspired George Merrick and his bride to create Coral Gables.

The **International Swimming Hall of Fame Museum** *(1 Hall of Fame Dr., tel 954/462-6536, www.ishof.org, $$)* is perhaps the only grand South Florida swimming hole that doesn't claim to have been graced by Johnny and Esther. The museum, which includes an aquatic complex with two 50-meter pools, celebrates the achievements of Weissmuller and Williams, and has a theater that screens their films. The specialty archive is chockablock with trophies won by athletes honored here.

The **Hugh Taylor Birch State Recreation Area** *(3109 E. Sunrise Blvd., tel 954/564-4521, $)* is reputedly the finest natural place away from Fort Lauderdale's shoreline: 180 acres of tropical landscaping etched by a meandering nature trail that is really more of a poet's walk. Let others spike volleyballs, lob horseshoes, paddle canoes, pedal bikes, take Segway tours *(M. Cruz Rentals, tel 954/235-5082)*, or press their noses to glass in the pioneer-oriented **Birch House Museum.** Take your walk, spread out a picnic, and read Marjory Stoneman Douglas's *River of Grass.* ■

Despite overdevelopment and ever-increasing tourism, the Florida Keys, a low-lying archipelago of jungle coral isles arcing southwest from the mainland, retain a wild beauty, making them one of America's most naturally exotic places.

Upper Keys

French angelfish

Upper Keys

THE 126-MILE OVERSEAS HIGHWAY LINKS MORE THAN 40 INHABITED ISLES and is arguably America's most unusual scenic drive, crossing 42 bridges and skimming vividly blue tropical waters—the Gulf of Mexico on one side, the Atlantic on the other. It vaults over coral reefs, saltwater mangrove forests, sea-grass meadows, and flowering jungle hammocks sprawling between idiosyncratic tourist towns, and terminates in raffish Key West, continental America's southernmost city. Starting in Florida City, green roadside signs, known as Mile Markers (MM), provide a countdown from MM 126 to MM 0 at Key West. Sometimes called Mile Zero, Key West marks the end of the road but not of the Keys; they and their vast embroidery of reefs end 70 miles west in the lonely breeze-swept desert islands of the Dry Tortugas.

The Keys were once the domain of the Calusa—sometimes spelled Caloosa—an indigenous tribe. Europeans first laid eyes on their world on Sunday, May 15, 1513. The Europeans were led by Christopher Columbus's ambitious Spanish lieutenant Juan Ponce de León, who was searching for the fabled Fountain of Youth. The expedition's chronicler, Antonio de Herrera, later wrote that "To all this line of islands and rock islets they gave the name of Los Martires (The

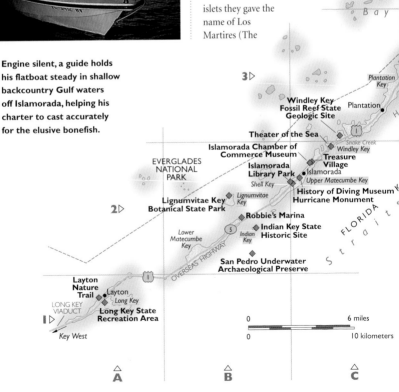

Engine silent, a guide holds his flatboat steady in shallow backcountry Gulf waters off Islamorada, helping his charter to cast accurately for the elusive bonefish.

6▷

Card Sound

Grayvik

997

CARD SOUND BRIDGE

905A

Florida City

Crocodile Lake National Wildlife Refuge

Key Largo

JOHN PENNEKAMP CORAL REEF STATE PARK

1

5

Barnes Sound

905

5▷

Gulfstream Shores

Lake Surprise

Blackwater Sound

HIGHWAY

EVERGLADES NATIONAL PARK

Key Largo Chamber of Commerce

Dagny Johnson Key Largo Hammock Botanical State Park

OVERSEAS

Key Largo

△ F

1. Wild Tamarind Trail
2. Cannon Beach
3. John Pennekamp Coral Reef S.P. Visitor Center
4. Fish House Restaurant & Seafood Market
5. Mangrove Trail
6. Far Beach

Key Largo 2

Largo Sound

3

4

Dolphin Cove

5

6

Newport

5

USS Spiegel Grove

Dolphin Plus

Rock Harbor

1

△ E

orida Keys ild Bird Center

Harry Harris County Park

Tavernier

NATIONAL MARINE SANCTUARY

Florida

TIONAL

of

△ D

Fort Lauderdale

Miami

Key West

Area of map detail

if you see the abbreviation "OS" used in connection with an address, it means the (Atlantic) ocean side of the Overseas Highway; "BS" refers to the (Florida) bay side. ■

Martyrs)." To the Spaniards the islands seemed, as they rose into view, to resemble the prostrate forms of suffering men. "The name remained fitting," wrote de Herrera, "because of the many that have been lost there since."

The conquistadores' interest in the islands waned in the absence of gold, and three centuries passed before the first Anglo-American settlement was staked out at what is today Key West. Another half-century went by before settlers, attracted by federal homestead programs, arrived in the Upper Keys. They built houses of the driftwood and flotsam

heaped on the beaches by a never-ending succession of ships that gutted themselves on the submerged reefs. Before the advent of lighthouses, maritime mishaps were so frequent off the islands that many "wreckers" became wealthy from the salvage trade, an occupation discredited by a few unscrupulous entrepreneurs who set up false lighthouse beacons to lure unfortunate mariners off course.

Most of the Upper Keys' newcomers were stolid farmfolk who, for a time, coaxed harvests of lemons, limes, melons, tomatoes, and pineapple from the meager topsoil and shipped them north by sea. They cheered when Henry Flagler's railroad reached Key West in 1912, believing a link to mainland markets ensured prosperity. But they were quickly edged out by lower-priced produce shipped to Key West from Central and South America. Successive battering by hurricanes administered a coup de grace to the Keys' agricultural hopes.

Restaurant patrons dine by Islamorada's Hawk's Channel. Across the water is part of the Keys' vast mangrove fringe.

The 20th century brought chronic hard times, during which many islanders eked out livings in the fishing trade. Dreams of a strong locally generated economy died hard in the Depression, when islanders, assisted by federal programs, commenced the development of the island's tourist industry.

What has not died, however, is the isles' promise of an escape to peace and recreation. The Upper Keys themselves begin unobtrusively enough when US 1 crosses over the placid channel between Barnes Sound and Blackwater Sound via the 223-foot-long Jewfish Creek Bridge at MM 106, officially becoming the Overseas Highway. The crossing takes only a few seconds by car, but it delivers you into a region unlike any other in North America.

In the Upper Keys especially, the trick is to make a point of pulling off the highway to explore. You'll find anchorages crowded with charter fishing boats rigged for marlin and blue dolphin, scuba diving outfitters eager to show you the reefs—home to over 600 species of fish—and concessionaires keen to rent any kind of water conveyance you desire. Anglers come here to hone their skills against the elusive bonefish and permit, and the feisty tarpon and jack cravalles, the quest for which is regarded by aficionados as being close to meditation. Hidden in foliage beyond roadside kitsch are resorts, many of them funky, a few surpassingly luxurious. People come to sojourn, beachcomb, or wander paths through junglelike thickets of pigeon plum, poisonwood, Jamaica dogwood, satin leaf, and palm. Their curiosity is rewarded by glimpses of such beautiful creatures as the great white heron (rarely seen elsewhere), mangrove cuckoos, roseate spoonbills, and white-crowned pigeons. Diverse possibilities define the Keys, beginning with the longest, hence its Spanish name Cayo Largo (Long Key). ■

Hands uplifted 20 feet underwater at John Pennekamp state park, the nine-foot bronze "Christ of the Deep," a 1961 gift from the Underwater Society of America, blesses those who work or play in the sea.

How the Keys came to be

In primordial times, coral reefs grew atop limestone ridges in these shallow seas. Between 120 to 100 thousand years ago, polar ice caps enlarged and the oceans receded, dropping sea levels by 20 to 30 feet and exposing the top of the reef, which died and became a barren archipelago of fossilized coral or limestone rock. Over the millennia, waves, tides, and storms deposited seaweed, driftwood, and other organic debris, which decayed to form soil. Seeds drifted ashore or were brought in the stomachs of migrating birds. Those that sprouted eventually created the Keys' distinctive junglelike tropical hammocks, virtual samplers of the West Indies' flora from which they derive. ■

Key Largo

IT'S EASY TO OVERLOOK WHAT'S OFFERED BY THIS 30-MILE-long island, as the dive shops, motels, billboards, and short-order outlets facing the roadway can spark an impulse to drive on—or retreat to Miami. But this is friendlier, more interesting country than you might suspect, for the local inhabitants depend upon the goodwill of travelers, and make up with cordiality and humor what their often humble establishments might lack in big city-style sophistication.

Sails hang in slack winds on a Key Largo beach.

Key Largo
159 D4

Key Largo Chamber of Commerce
159 E5
106000 Overseas Hwy., MM 106–9
305/451-1414 or 800/822-1088

If you arrive via US 1 from the direction of the Everglades, you might miss North Key Largo's expanse of virgin hardwood hammock and mangrove. Coming from Miami, it's simple to veer east and take Card Sound Road (Fla. 905) south from Florida City. (If you missed North Key Largo southbound, take Fla. 905 north.) The Card Sound Bridge charges a toll ($1.50), whereas US 1 is free, but the fee is worth the opportunity to experience the Keys as the wilderness they were before settlement began—not to mention the two-time winner of *Miami New Times's* Best Tollbooth. Card Sound Road and US 1 join at Lake Surprise, at which point, if southbound, you are now truly in the Keys.

The end of Eden?

Environmentally, Florida Bay and the Everglades are Siamese twins; if one dies, the other is doomed. Farming and development have drastically reduced the Everglades' area and vitality, agricultural pollution has sickened it, and water diversion to protect adjacent homes and farms from natural flooding has dried up wetlands. The results include once crystalline Florida Bay water clouded by algal blooms, its sea-grass "prairies" killed and turned to mud, and sponge die-offs robbing young shrimp, fish, and lobsters of food. Despite new laws intended to protect the Everglades, its prognosis is uncertain. ■

Take time to find a side road to the Atlantic side of the island for your first view of the only living coral reef found off the continental United States. Eons ago this natural barrier formed the Keys. Scarred by collisions with ships, broken by boat anchors and the dynamite of commercial coral collectors, it is now ailing from effluents dumped into the sea. It faces an uncertain future but continues to protect the islands it created from the grinding action of ocean waves—that's why so few beaches here have fine sand.

CROCODILE LAKE NATIONAL WILDLIFE REFUGE

Had you been one of the uncounted thousands of Spanish fortune-seekers shipwrecked along this coast, and managed to escape being crushed between your ship's hull and the reef that tore it open, your joy at survival might have waned as you swam toward Key Largo's mangrove-tangled shore. For lurking in these pale green shallows were not only the Calusa, a tribe of tall men and women known to enslave castaways, but swarms of crocodiles whose main interest was feeding. The reptiles are still here—as many as 100 winter at the Crocodile Lake National Wildlife Refuge, which lies on the island's dreamily serene backcountry coast. While not open to the public, it is worth taking a look from the observation road.

If you have an extra hour, consider taking Card Sound Road to Upper Key Largo. The two-lane toll road is an interesting alternative to US 1, crossing the hardwood hammock county at Florida's southeastern tip, and vaulting mile-wide Card Sound to Key Largo via a high bridge that gives a brief but unusual panorama.

In the 1950s this tract was slated to be the site of a new city—"an

imitation Mediterranean coastal village." The Nature Conservancy and the federal government bought the land from its bankrupt would-be developers. For now the fragile swampy expanse is undeveloped. There are plans to install an observation platform and a boardwalk through the wetland, and a butterfly meadow was recently developed along Fla. 905.

The refuge's crocodile community is believed to be North America's most populous. Using binoculars, you can observe the exceedingly shy lizards sunning themselves on the banks farthest from the observation road. Resist the impulse to wander down to the water; it is illegal to trespass, puts you in rattlesnake territory, and also destroys the ground-level nests of migratory terns that roost here.

JOHN PENNEKAMP CORAL REEF STATE PARK

Many guidebooks call this mostly underwater preserve the premier natural attraction in the Keys. The 54,000-acre park is 25 miles long, extends 3 miles out into the Atlantic, and, combined with the adjoining Key Largo section of the **Florida Keys National Marine**

Crocodile Lake National Wildlife Refuge
www.fws.gov/southeast/crocodilelake
🗺 159 E6
✉ Follow signs from Card Sound Rd. in North Key Largo to entrance, MM 106
☎ 305/451-4223

Charter fishing boats like these offer visitors an opportunity to fish deeper offshore waters, including the Gulf Stream, for big quarry such as sailfish and marlin.

John Pennekamp Coral Reef State Park

www.pennekamppark.com

🅰 159 E5

✉ Park entrance at MM 102.5 on US 1, Key Largo

☎ 305/451-1202 (information); 305/451-6300 (boat & snorkeling tours & reservations, sea kayak & canoe rentals); 305/451-6322 (scuba tours); 800/326-3521 (camping)

💲 $ per car, $ per person; check website for fees for tours, camping, boat slips, & mooring

Rent a canoe and paddle along the tidal creeks and through the mangrove forests in John Pennekamp Coral Reef State Park.

Sanctuary, protects a 178-square-nautical-mile sweep of coastal water and 2,350 acres of tropical hammock and mangrove forest. Its centerpiece is an undersea coral reef garden of ethereal beauty.

You can't see much of it from shore, however; you must venture seaward. Weather permitting, the park offers daily glass-bottom boat tours (*9:15 a.m., 12:15 p.m., and 3:00 p.m., $$$–$$$$*), snorkeling tours (*9 a.m., noon, and 3:00 p.m., $$$$–$$$$$*), and scuba tours (*9:30 a.m. & 1:30 p.m., $$$$$*). Boat tours depart from the park marina adjoining the visitor center and last about 2.5 hours, mask-and-fin expeditions about 90 minutes.

The pellucid world beneath the sea is spectacularly abundant—a magical garden decorated by gracefully waving sponges, sea fans, whips and plumes, barnacles, 27 species of anemonelike Gorgonians, spiny sea urchins, and 55 varieties of coral, and patrolled by crabs, snails, lobsters, shrimp, worms, mollusks, sea stars, sea cucumbers, sand dollars, and more than 500 species of vividly colored fish.

If you prefer to remain on dry land, you can still have an eyeball-to-eyeball encounter with some of the reef's resident creatures at the visitor center's 30,000-gallon **saltwater aquarium,** a living technicolor kaleidoscope of fish

darting among tentacled anemones, graceful coral, and sponges. Several touch tanks let you reach safely underwater to feel the peculiar textures of these fanciful-looking creatures. Take the time to view at least one of the films shown here continuously, for the more you learn, the more wonderfully mysterious the reef becomes.

There's snorkeling at **Cannon Beach** (behind the visitor center) and the **Far Beach area,** a rocky reef-sheltered lagoon at the terminus of the entrance road from MM 102.5, where tropical fish congregate. (You can rent equipment at the main concession building.) The cannon, anchor, and ballast stones of the Spanish galleon shipwreck scattered on the pale bottom in

shallow water about 130 feet offshore are re-creations, put there by park officials. Spanish galleons often came to grief in storms along this coast, though, and more than one bather has walked out of the water considerably wealthier than when he or she waded in.

Don't leave without strolling two short and easy trails through a living encyclopedia of local flora. A looping footpath that begins and ends near the visitor center parking lot, the **Wild Tamarind Trail,** circles through a hardwood hammock. Hammock is a Southern variation of the word "hummock" and refers to a thickly wooded tract of fertile land that's usually elevated. Save for the footpaths, this is prehistoric Florida—a dense knotted jungle of gumbo limbo, West Indian mahogany, strangler fig, and thatch palm.

Winding away from the Far Beach area, the **Mangrove Trail** follows an elevated boardwalk that provides a close-up look at salt-water forests of red, black, and white mangroves. These trees, perched upon bowed spider-leg trunks, create a virtually impenetrable barrier between sea and shore that are havens for young fish.

Another way to explore this enchanting preserve is by canoe, along a serpentine, 2.5-mile water-way of placid tidal creeks through mangrove forests. The main concessionaire rents canoes and sea kayaks. The trail ends at the Far Beach area, an inviting swimming

Palm trees swept by the sea breeze in John Pennekamp Coral Reef State Park.

BIRDS OF THE KEYS

The 19th-century ornithologist and artist John James Audubon was astonished by the variety of birds in the Keys. Millions of migratory birds such as terns flutter down to roost in spring and fall, joining a permanent population of wading birds including the heron and egret. The Keys also abound with bald eagles, ospreys, barred owls, brown pelicans, and pileated woodpeckers. None, however, surpass the ability of the swallow-tailed kite to perform an aerial ballet on the gentlest of breezes. ■

Dagny Johnson Key Largo Hammock Botanical State Park

Ⓐ 159 E5

☎ 305/451-1202

🕑 Open daily. Tours 10 a.m. Thurs. & Sun.

$ $

spot with showers to wash off the salt when you're finished.

The preserve has 47 campsites with showers, water, and power, half of which can be reserved for a moderate fee.

DAGNY JOHNSON KEY LARGO HAMMOCK BOTANICAL STATE PARK

Time was when the Upper Keys were for the most part a vast bristle of West Indian tropical hardwood fringed by mangrove. Where much of this perfect chaos once rustled softly in the trade winds, you can now park your RV, order up key lime pie or a beer, buy bait, charter a fishing boat, or book a motel room.

Inside the Dagny Johnson Key Largo Hammock Botanical State Park, over 2,000 acres of this ancient scrub endure. The tract, just north of US 1 on Fla. 905 in North Key Largo on the ocean (Atlantic) side of the highway, is the largest remaining stand of hardwood hammock and mangrove wetlands in the Keys—the jungled shoreline that Juan Ponce de León saw as he charted the islands in the early 16th century (see pp. 158–59).

You can easily and enjoyably explore the preserve on your own, guided by the information brochure given out at the park entrance. Points of interest are keyed to num-

bered boulders along the paved trail, which is wheelchair-negotiable. If you visit on a Thursday or a Sunday morning, inquire about ranger-led tours that point out many of the 84 species of protected plants and animals found here, a large number of them rare or endangered, and introduce you to native fruits you can sample.

Did Bogie sleep here?

Maybe he did—Humphrey Bogart was an avid sailor and traveler—but not while making the 1948 film classic *Key Largo* with Lauren Bacall. Except for several scenes which were shot in Key Largo's Caribbean Club bar *(MM 103.5, tel 305/451-4466)*—still serving—the movie was filmed on sound stages in far-off Hollywood. A local enthusiast determined to link the island with Bogie bought the steam-powered work boat that was used in John Huston's film *The African Queen*. When in town, you can see the venerable craft moored at the Key Largo Marina *(MM 99.7)*, by the Holiday Inn. ■

Here, as at Crocodile Lake National Wildlife Refuge (see p. 163), government agencies are buying up adjoining tracts to block encroachment and expand the trail system. This is a battleground of environmentalists and developers: Coming out of a thicket, you're likely to confront the shells of uncompleted and abandoned buildings.

NATURE TOURS

Want to get close and personal with Flipper? Key Largo is the place to learn about dolphins, which are among the most intelligent and playful mammals on the planet. At **Dolphin Cove** and nearby sister facility, **Dolphins Plus,** you can swim with these engaging creatures and spot them on nature tours. Dolphin Cove, set on a 5-acre natural lagoon, has a wide range

of interesting programs.

Most visitors come here for the Dolphin Encounter, an in-water program that includes direct involvement with frisky Atlantic bottlenose dolphins. The adventure starts with a 30-minute ride aboard an Everglades deck boat through the beautiful Keys backcountry, with experts on hand to lecture about all aspects of the creatures, from their anatomy to the behavior and social structure of dolphins in the wild—they live and travel together in "pods"—and how they communicate with humans. Environmental issues and the threats to dolphins play a key part in this educational journey, and there is careful instruction on how to interact responsibly with dolphins when you eventually meet them in the water.

Visitors watch for rare butterflies and birds at Dagny Johnson Key Largo Hammock Botanical State Park

Dolphin Cove
www.dolphinscove.com
✉ MM 101.9 Bay Side
☎ 305/451-4060 or 877/DOL-COVE
💲 $$$–$$$$$

Dolphins Plus
www.dolphinsplus.com
✉ PO Box 2728 Key Largo 33037
☎ 305/451-1993 or 866/860-7946
💲 $$$$$ for swims

A trail near Tavernier enters a hardwod jungle.

You can learn more about dolphins in workshops, and there are opportunities to explore the area on a guided kayak tour, and even go scuba diving.

TAVERNIER

As you drive southbound toward the lower tip of Key Largo you'll come to the land's-end sprawl of Tavernier, a vestige of the Key's original outpost, once over-optimistically named Planter. It's said that Tavernier takes its name from a small nearby island that the Spanish dubbed Cayo Tabona—Horsefly Key.

Tavernier is a laid-back, colorful town, and makes a good base for exploring, with plenty of accommodations and restaurants. The town is bordered by Tavernier Creek and Plantation to the south, offering boaters easy access to

Harry Harris County Park

⛰ 159 D3

✉ MM 93.5, via Burton Dr.

☎ 305/852-7161

Florida Keys Wild Bird Center

www.fkwbc.org

⛰ 159 D3

✉ 93600 Overseas Hwy., MM 93.6 BS, Tavernier

☎ 305/852-4486

💲 Donation

both ocean and bay waters.

The first reference to Tavernier was in a survey done in 1775 by the British Navy. During the 18th century the island was a base for reef hunters in search of booty from shipwrecks. In the 1860s Bahamina farmers from Key West moved in and established Tavernier as a fishing and farming village. The arrival of Flagler's railroad brought a demand for pineapples, coconuts and other fruits that could be grown here. A packing house, from where the produce was once shipped, has been restored near the railroad tracks.

The town proudly claims a historic district of sorts—a neighborhood where wooden, early 20th century buildings survive, and stolidly built 60-year-old Red Cross houses squat in defiance of hurricanes and, to all appearances, artillery shells. After the devastating Labor Day Hurricane of 1935 denuded the Matecumbe Keys (drowning hundreds), the Red Cross built these four-room bunkers of reinforced concrete, with steel window sashes anchored in foot-thick walls. Daunting to an aesthete, the structures symbolize a basic fact about Keys residents then and now: They are in denial of what another great hurricane, which some predict will bring 20-foot tidal surges, will do to an archipelago whose highest point, on Windley Key, is 18 feet.

Harry Harris was a one-time county commissioner and local wheeler-dealer. His influence is emphasized by the name of Tavernier's pleasant public green, the **Harry Harris County Park** on the OS or Atlantic Ocean side of the road, at MM 93.5 via Burton Drive, which angles right and left, sometimes confusingly, en route to the beach. Just follow the signs—you can't get lost here—to a nice little lagoon with a man-made

beach for swimming and a boat launch ramp. You'll probably find softball and basketball games in progress and the air redolent of meat broiling on public charcoal grills.

About a half-mile north of the turn-off to Harry Harris County Park stands the **Florida Keys Wild Bird Center,** opened in 1984 by naturalist Laura Quinn to provide care for injured waterfowl and shore birds. (It's easy to miss; watch for carved wooden birds perched on the bay side of the highway at MM 93.6.) The center's state-licensed rehabilitators work with veterinary clinics to rescue injured and orphaned birds in hope of eventually releasing them back

into the wild. Most injuries involve collisions with vehicles, power lines, and windows. The birds—usually pelicans—arrive choking on half-swallowed baited fish hooks and lures or entangled in monofilament fishing line. Others break their wings after becoming entangled in fishing nets. Permanently disabled creatures are kept in the bayside mangrove wetland here, among the best spots to study herons, cormorants, brown pelicans, broad-wing hawks, terns, and ospreys close up. There's also a short self-guided nature trail winding through the stand of hardwood hammock adjoining the center. ■

A heron and pelicans share the roof of Tavernier's Florida Keys Wild Bird Center.

PIECES OF EIGHT

The fabled Spanish silver coins, minted from the late 1500s to the early 1600s, were also known as reals. Back in those days, a conquistador might earn one a month. Struck by hand, no two are alike, and weight, not size or shape, was the measure. You can buy one in the Keys, but demand a certificate of authenticity. The dealer may ask as much as $2,000. Shop around, and haggle. Remember, this was once pirate country. ■

Protecting Keys bird life

Never leave fishing hooks and line in the wild. If your lure snags in a tree, do everything possible to retrieve it. Never discard hooked bait or fishing line by tossing it into the water. If you hook a bird, don't let it fly away without cutting away any attached line, as it dooms the creature to entangle-

ment and death by starvation. If a bird has swallowed a hook or is badly entangled, bring it to the rehabilitation center or call for a pick up *(tel 305/852-4486)*. When cleaning fish, don't toss unwanted parts into the water, as birds can choke on them if they are larger than their usual prey. ■

Snorkeling & diving in the Keys

The Keys' warm water and reefs attract thousands of scuba and snorkel aficionados annually, a recreation statistically about as safe as swimming.

How to get started

If you have some basic swimming skills, snorkeling is easy. It requires only a mask to see underwater, a snorkel for breathing, and fins for propulsion, all of which can be rented. (Most tours also provide buoyant vests.)

Scuba diving, however, uses sophisticated equipment and requires training by qualified teachers. The best way to learn is to take lessons from a certified member of the Professional Association of Diving Instructors, or PADI, the largest scuba training organization in the world. PADI Dive Center locations are listed on the Web (www.padi.com). The organization develops scuba programs and diver training products, monitors training programs conducted worldwide by over 107,000 professional members in more than 170 countries and territories, maintains diver certification records, and issues the credentials you must present to be allowed on open-ocean dives in the Keys without on-site instruction.

Who can dive?

Just about anyone over the age of 12 in normal good health can learn to dive. (Kids between 12 and 15 receive a Junior Open Water Diver certification, which requires them to dive with a certified adult. At age 15, they can upgrade to a regular Open Water Diver certification.) You'll be asked to complete a routine medical questionnaire to determine if your health requires a consultation with your physician to ensure that it's safe for you to dive. Wearing soft contact lenses poses no problem, but hard lenses should be gas permeable. Many people who take up snorkeling and diving have prescription lenses fitted into their masks.

Typically, an entry-level course begins in a pool and includes four training dives. If you'd rather try out scuba diving before committing to formal instruction, PADI offers a Discover Scuba Diving program lasting only several hours, including a shallow ocean dive supervised by an instructor after a short pool session to familiarize you with your equipment. This will allow you to master some basic techniques, such as learning to adjust your ears to the surrounding pressure so they don't hurt when you descend. A shorter pool dive program is offered in places without natural open-water diving sites.

How long does it take to be certified?

PADI courses are performance based, meaning students progress according to their demonstrated mastery of the required knowledge and skills. A beginner's PADI Open Water Diver course might consist of five or six sessions completed in three to four days, or spread over six weeks.

If you want to wait and see how the Keys look to you before taking a lesson, PADI-certified introductory resort courses can have you exploring the reefs in hours. They don't result in certification, but they do enable you to dive in the afternoon with an instructor following a morning of classroom and pool instruction.

Is it costly?

As a rule of thumb, scuba diving ranks with snow skiing. Dive centers and resorts rent state-of-the-art equipment, so there's no need to buy. Consider purchasing your own mask, snorkel, and fins, however, as they can be uncomfortable if not properly sized.

If you want a lasting record of your exploits, several major companies sell inexpensive one-time-use underwater cameras that produce good shallow-water images when the sun's out (on overcast days you lose color contrast). Some dive shops rent underwater video cameras. ■

A diver off Key Largo swims toward a giant brain coral—some of which attain the size of a small car.

One of Plantation
Key's popular
recreation
beaches

Plantation Key

SOUTHBOUND AGAIN YOU'LL CROSS TINY PLANTATION
Key, whose name commemorates banana- and pineapple-growing
estates that flourished here from the 1880s until World War I,
employing native Bahamians as field workers.

Plantation Key

📖 158 C3

✉ MM 90.5–86

KEY LIMES

Key limes are not
just any lime, but
a Florida hybrid.
Small and round—
a bit smaller than a
golf ball—they are
available all year.
Their thin, mottled,
yellow-green skin
holds juicy flesh that
is high in vitamin C
and tastes powerfully
sweet-tart. Their
most famous associ-
ation is with Key
lime pie—a Graham
cracker crust filled
with yellowish lime
custard and topped
with meringue. ■

There's little evidence of the
plantations today—the island is
densely developed—nor of the
Calusa, who lived here and on
adjoining Windley Key as far back
as 4,000 years ago. Archaeologists
study the refuse heaps they left for
clues to the tribe's lifestyle.

Just offshore is a complex of
reefs teeming with sea creatures,
including the very large but benign
manta ray. The best formations are
Inner and Outer Conch, Davis
Reef, and Crocker Wall—tables,
drop-offs, and coral rises cradling
corridors of white sand. ■

Key enterprises

Early settlers grew limes, bread-
fruit, and pineapples, supplying
most of the eastern United States
until the thin soil's fertility was
exhausted. Next came a shark
factory on Big Pine Key, where
hides were salted and shipped
north for curing into a tawny
leather known as shagreen.
Meanwhile, Key West "wreckers"
grew rich on maritime misfortunes,
and sponge fishermen had a good
run until the sponges were gone.
Cuban cigarmakers set up factories
in Key West, but their products
failed to garner the respect accorded
to Havana stogies. Flagler's railroad
hauled wealthy vacationers south
until the infamous 1935 hurricane
blew it away. Following World
War II, tourists discovered the
Overseas Highway, and shrimpers
found markets for their wriggling
"pink gold." ■

Windley Key

Relaxing on a
coral beach on
Windley Key

CONTINUING SOUTH ACROSS THE SNAKE CREEK DRAWBRIDGE
at MM 86.5 is Windley Key—originally two adjacent isles, now joined
by landfill poured in during the early 20th-century railroad construction era. Extracting the fill stone from here left quarrylike pits
whose walls expose a pretty formation of limestone coral rock laid
down about 125,000 years ago, containing fossils of reef creatures.

Just south of the bridge, look to the
bay side for these holes, now part of
the **Windley Key Fossil Reef
Geological State Park.** The
park (MM 85.5) recalls past times,
when slabs of the beautiful fossil-
rich keystone were quarried for
building facades. Five trails meander past rusting machinery to the
quarries, which amount to a dissec-
tion of the ancient reef.

More accessible to the public in
recent years, Windley Key is closed
only on Tuesdays and Wednesdays.
If you would like to explore the
quarries, you must stop by the
visitor center to purchase tickets
(*305/664-2540, $*). You can also
obtain a brochure at the visitor
center that guides you along the
trails. This detour and the back-
track to Long Key (MM 67.5) are

worthwhile, however, for devotees
of fossils only.

Close by there's a similar quarry,
dug in 1907 by railroad construction crews and filled with seawater
in 1946 to create one of the world's
first marine parks. Daily shows at
the **Theater of the Sea** feature
a troupe of creatures led by performing sea lions and dolphins,
along with other denizens of the
Keys. The shows have a reputation
for enthralling children, and the
theater also offers visitors the
chance to swim for a half-hour in
the company of dolphins, sea lions,
or rays (available by advance reservation only). Among the memorable attractions here are feeding
time in the shark pool and a 300-
gallon aquarium containing a living
reef environment. ■

Windley Key
🗺 158 C2

Visitor information
✉ Key Largo Chamber
of Commerce,
106000 Overseas
Hwy., MM 106–9, BS
☎ 305/451-1414

Theater of the Sea
www.theaterofthesea.com
🗺 158 C2
✉ Islamorada, MM 84.5
☎ 305/664-2431
💲 $$$$–$$$$$;
$$$$$ for swims

Fishing in the Keys

South Florida is perhaps best known for offshore fishing in the deep blue waters of the Gulf Stream, where anglers in heavy harness use stout rods and reels with the diameter of coconuts to catch hard-fighting dolphin (the fish, not the mammal), dorado, sailfish, wahoo, and marlin. The Keys are also one of the world's premier shallow-water, light-tackle, spin, and fly-fishing regions, where world records are set by steely eyed experts, many of them professional fishing guides so steeped in the craft and lore they write books about it.

Most of this arcane adventuring takes place in the shallows and backwaters of the Upper Keys Florida Bay backcountry. In this wilderness of uninhabited islands, lost in watery mangrove jungles and shimmering basins carpeted with gracefully bending sea grass, where the silence is broken only by the occasional startling cries of seabirds, the water is often a mere two or three feet deep. Here, open-sea bravado and brawn take a back seat to stealth and the deft manipulation of delicate tackle in pursuit of elusive inshore fish. The sport is characterized by slow approaches toward instinctively wary fish known for hair-trigger alertness.

Unless you're experienced in this kind of fishing, own your own gear and boat, and know your way around the backcountry, the services of a licensed professional guide are necessary, if for nothing more than to ensure that you don't get hopelessly lost.

Backcountry fishing boats (skiffs) are in essence casting platforms from 16 to 20 feet in length, with broad flat-bottomed hulls that allow them to float in little more than a foot of water. As you approach a fishing ground, your guide will turn off the electric motor and use a long pole to push the boat along. You'll stand at the bow on a raised platform, with a high-angle line of sight into the water.

A good guide's knowledge is vast. He—or she—knows the best times of day to fish for a particular species, weighing that against variables such as weather, tides, and temperatures. Depending on what fish interests you, your guide will pick a destination. In the Florida Bay backcountry the water teems with redfish, snook, pompano, tarpon, black drum, lady-fish, sheepshead, and shark.

If you'd rather fish from shore, a guide is still a valuable adviser for showing you where to cast your line, and how. In springtime, fishing for tarpon with live bait is a popular activity on bridges and along deepwater channels from Key Largo to Key West. (This is an inexpensive way to learn, while enjoying the possibility of hooking a hard-fighting game fish.)

Fishing is permitted in both national parks and the NWR, whose boundaries embrace the Keys. You'll find regulations available for free at the headquarters of each. Biscayne National Park (see pp. 146–47) includes the North Key Largo area; Everglades National Park (see pp. 148–51) covers Key Largo nearly to Marathon; and the Great White Heron National Wildlife Refuge (see p. 198) spans much of the territory between Marathon and Key West.

Check on requirements for state fishing licenses available for periods from three to ten days to five years, all for modest fees. There are fishing supply stores throughout the Keys. One of the finest fly-fishing outfitters in the Keys is the Saltwater Angler in Key West (*243 Front St., tel 305/296-0700, www.saltwaterangler.com*). ∎

Right: Flatboat fishing off Islamorada
Left: Larger boats and heavier tackle are required to land big game fish.

Upper Matecumbe Key

SHAPED LIKE A 5-MILE-LONG GREEN BEAN, RUNNING FROM MM 84 to MM 79, Upper Matecumbe Key was briefly America's leading pineapple-growing center. Limes were grown here, too, although today the fruit used to make key lime pie is grown on the Florida mainland. Cuban competition and the 1935 hurricane quashed the Keys' agricultural industry, and today Upper Matecumbe, whose commercial center is Islamorada, gets by very well by showing visitors a good time.

The town of **Islamorada** (pronounced EYE-la-mor-AH-da) claims to have more resident fishing vessels per square mile than anywhere else in the world, and bills itself as the Sport Fishing Capital of the World. For many years, U.S. presidents and sports celebrities have fished here with great fanfare—and the telephone directory lists over 350 fishing charter operations. Fringed by marinas and fishing boats, its roadside sprawl lined by outfitters, bait suppliers, bistros, cafés, and a charming if sometimes funky variety of shops, Islamorada looks the part.

It is said that Spanish explorers noted the coastline's purplish color, a phenomenon created by the lavender shells of janthina sea snails, and added the name *islas moradas* (purple isles) to their charts. Local historians claim the town's 19th-century founders named it after the sailing ship that brought them there, the schooner *Island Home*. In deference to the Keys' Spanish heritage, it's said, they translated this into Islamorada, giving rise to tales of a name coined by conquistadores, not Methodist farmers. Either way, it's a pretty name.

If you're bound for Key West and just passing through, consider a stop at the **Islamorada Library Park** at MM 81.5 on the bay side,

Many dive shops, like this one on Upper Matecumbe Key, offer day trips on and under the water.

behind the town library. The water's clear and shallow here, although a swift current requires parents to keep an eye on children. Public restrooms, picnic tables, and patches of lawn make this little beachfront oasis a pleasant place to relax.

Near MM 82, look for the red railroad caboose marking the **Islamorada Chamber of Commerce**'s museum and chamber building, where the ill-fated Florida East Coast Railway's depot and worker's encampment stood until Labor Day 1935 (see below). Inside, souvenirs of the laborers' daily life here evoke the Key's early 20th-century isolation. The museum is open daily without charge.

Near MM 83 is the **Florida Keys History of Diving Museum** *(82990 Overseas Hwy., tel. 305/664-9737, www.diving museum.com, $–$$)*, dedicated to artifacts, photographs, books, and oral history about the underwater sport throughout the world as well as in the Keys.

As you journey south you will see the pale coral limestone of the

Florida Keys Memorial, known as the hurricane monument, at the roadside at MM 81.6. The memorial commemorates the Labor Day Hurricane of 1935, the most devastating storm ever known to hit the Keys. In Key West on the evening of Saturday, August 31, 1935, the air was still, hot, and humid. By Monday, September 2, storm warning flags snapped downtown as citizens nailed up shutters and prepared for the worst, and by midnight wind-blown rain were rattling the town's tin roofs. Wires snapped, trees fell, palm fronds cartwheeled—but the storm's full fury bypassed the island, moving north to Islamorada, where it drowned some 500 people, most of them railroad workers aboard a rescue train swept from the tracks by 200 mph gusts and a 20-foot tidal surge. The monument marks the grave of 423 who died in the tempest. Key West resident Ernest Hemingway chartered a boat to carry food and water for survivors. Finding few, he later wrote that in this region there was no autumn, "only a more dangerous summer." ∎

Trained sea lions perform at the Theater of the Sea near Islamorada (see p. 173).

Lignumvitae Key

Many Keys plants, like these on Lignumvitae, are from the Caribbean.

Lignumvitae Key Botanical State Park

www.floridastateparks.org/ lignumvitaekey

🅰 158 B2

✉ Islamorada, MM 78.5

☎ 305/664-2540 or 305/664-9814 (tour reservations)

🕐 Closed Tues. & Wed. Guided walks: 10:00 a.m. & 2:00 p.m.

💲 $

IT IS STILL POSSIBLE TO SEE WHAT THE UPPER KEYS WERE like in their natural state, before agricultural and entrepreneurial ventures cut, quarried, burned, buried, paved, or otherwise rendered them tame. In 1970 the Nature Conservancy and the State of Florida joined forces to buy and preserve 280-acre Lignumvitae Key and nearby Shell Key on the Florida Bay side of the Matecumbes, just south of Islamorada, and historic Indian Key on the Atlantic side.

A true island roughly a mile out of alignment with the Keys' coral spine, **Lignumvitae Key Botanical State Park** lies in shallow mangrove flats outside the sight line of railroad surveyors' transits, and was fortuitously left alone. Early in the 20th century, the hardwood hammock was purchased by Miami pioneer and financier W.J. Matheson (see p. 137), who built a four-

bedroom hideaway of coral rock but left the rest of his retreat unspoiled. (A windmill generated power; fresh water came from a 12,000-gallon cistern filled with rainwater captured by the house's roof.) The result is that Lignumvitae's tropical forests still hold dense stands of the island's blue-flowered namesake tree, whose Latin name means the "wood of life." (The wood of the *lignum vitae,* which can grow for more than 1,000 years, is among the world's hardest, and so dense that when used in boat construction it routinely outlasts bronze and steel.)

The *lignum vitae* share the island with thickets of mahogany, mastic, strangler fig, poisonwood, pigeon plum, and gumbo limbo, and more than 120 native plants. Peaceful it is, but silent it is not, for Lignumvitae's isolation (and now its strict management) makes it a wild bird refuge where you'll see reclusive creatures such as white-crowned pigeons, ospreys, double-crested cormorants, and great white herons.

Don't let the fact that this piece of Eden is accessible only by private or charter boat deter you; if your schedule allows for a two-hour adventure, this is a must. You'll return with a better sense of the natural Keys than most of the 87,000 people who call them home. Tour boat concessions operate out of **Robbie's Marina** at MM 77.5, and you can kayak or canoe from Indian Key Fill at MM 79.5. As only 50 people are permitted on the island at a time, you will need to make reservations.

Because the island's ecosystems are delicate, exploring on your own is forbidden. All visitors tour the island and the old Matheson estate in the company of park rangers, who lead one-hour guided walks.

If you plan to arrive on your own boat, you must still notify a park ranger in advance to reserve tour space and arrange to be met at the dock. There is a charge of $1 per person (children under six are admitted free). Unfortunately, the nature of the island makes access

difficult for people with disabilities. Call ahead for a ranger's advice.

Finally, wear good walking shoes and make sure you're well covered with a proven insect repellent. Lignumvitae Key is a natural subtropical environment at its most pristine: In the Keys, that means swarms of aggressively biting mosquitoes. ∎

Right: A Keys park ranger examines a climbing vine, common in hardwood hammocks.

Robbie's Marina
www.robbies.com
 158 B2
✉ MM 77.5
☎ 305/664-9814 or
305/664-4196
Tour boats generally depart one-half hour before listed tour times; reservations required.

Hurricanes

On average, the Atlantic Basin generates nine tropical storms each year, six of which become hurricanes, two of them intense. Florida's hurricane season begins June 1 and ends on the last day of November. Usually born off the African coast, they are watched by the National Hurricane Center in Miami from the time they start their westward drift, and can no longer strike without detection. If one threatens the Keys, warnings are issued several days in advance. If evacuation is ordered, visitors are given priority to leave first. ∎

Above: A crushed coral footpath on Indian Key recalls earlier times, before 1838, when the Overseas Highway ended the islands' isolation.

Indian Key

ABOUT THREE-QUARTERS OF A MILE SOUTHEAST OF LOWER Matecumbe Key, at the edge of the Gulf Stream, lies another lushly jungled piece of the past, 12-acre Indian Key, named for the Calusa who once lived here. They were replaced by 19th-century Bahamian turtle hunters and fishermen, who themselves retreated in 1831 when an ambitious and wealthy young New Yorker named John Jacob Housman bought the island as a base for his ship salvage business. (Accused of slippery business practices, Housman had been expelled from Key West's community of wreckers.) The location offered opportunity: a supply of fresh water on nearby Matecumbe and reefs with a reputation for disemboweling ships.

**Indian Key
Historic State
Park**
www.floridastateparks.org/
indiankey
⚠ 158 B2
☎ 305/664-4815
🕐 Ranger guided tours
9 a.m. & 1 p.m.
Thurs.–Mon.
💲 $

INDIAN KEY
HISTORIC STATE PARK

Housman turned his rocky isle into a company enterprise, building a general store, a hotel, and a cluster of cottages with cisterns. The shoreline sprouted warehouses, and wharves reached out toward the wrecking grounds like greedy fingers. Housman prospered for a time, then suffered reverses in the wake of renewed accusations of wrecking misbehavior, and was forced to mortgage his island. The outbreak of the Second Seminole War in 1835 evaporated his trade with local Indians, and in 1838 Housman sold out to a physician named Henry Perrine, whose true love was tropical botany. Perrine took over Indian Key flush with cash: He'd talked his way into a government grant of money for the cultivation of useful

Right: A copy of the original stone marks the grave of John Jacob Housman. Hired out as a salvor, he died at sea in 1841, crushed between the hulls of two ships during a salvage effort.

San Pedro Underwater Archaeological Preserve State Park

www.floridastateparks.org/sanpedro

⚠ 158 B2

✉ Islamorada

☎ 305/664-9814
(Robbie's Marina)

tropical plants, particularly agave (for hemp), and also coffee, tea, mangoes, and bananas. He built a nursery on Matecumbe and experimented with plantings until the summer of 1840, when about 100 Indians attacked his village, looted its stores, and set houses afire. Perrine was killed. His family escaped by hiding beneath the floor of their house, and later fled.

With such a somber past, it's not surprising that Indian Key has been uninhabited since the early 1900s. You can still see remnants of Housman's village—there's an observation tower on the island that offers a tree-top reconnoiter—but that's about it. So why visit? Time travel: Indian Key retains its pre-European wildness; visitors are transported back to a perfect semblance of the Calusas' world. The vestiges of Housman's village—foundations and cisterns where archaeologists occasionally dig for artifacts—peek out of the undergrowth along a self-guiding trail.

Hurricanes destroyed Indian Key's boat dock so motorboats no longer have access. But you can paddle there in your own kayak or canoe or rent one from an outfitter along US 1. Floating across the grass flats is a specatacular chance to see manatees, dolphins, sharks, and rays. And anglers can fish for a variety of species, including bonefish, tarpon, and snapper. Near shore you'll likely see wading birds such as the great heron and the snowy egret, and you might get lucky and see a magnificent frigatebird or bald eagle.

Indian Key shares a headquarters with Lignumvitae Key Botanical State Park (see pp. 178–79), where information is available. Once ashore, pick up a free brochure and use its map and historical accounts to guide yourself around the island. Be aware that the island's management plan forbids

both restrooms and picnic facilities—you'll find neither here.

SAN PEDRO UNDERWATER ARCHAEOLOGICAL PRESERVE STATE PARK

In the 1960s, divers probing an area of white sand, turtle grass, and coral 18 feet underwater in Hawk Channel, about a mile south of Indian Key, found ballast stones and cannon identifying the wreck of the *San Pedro*. This 287-ton Dutch merchantman had been sunk by a hurricane along with 20 other vessels, part of the ill-fated 1733 Spanish treasure fleet.

The easily accessible site has been set aside for sport divers as an underwater archaeological preserve, and is a fascinating opportuni-

ty to examine a genuine wreck site. The ship's original guns and timbers have been removed for preservation and study and replaced by reproductions and a period-style anchor, but divers still occasionally find 18th-century coins. For more information (or to find out about snorkeling trips), call Robbie's Marina. If you have a boat equipped with LORAN (radar tracking device), the wreck's coordinates are 4082.1 and 43320.6. Be sure to tie up to mooring buoys at the site to prevent anchor damage to the delicate bottom. ■

Long Key's
dense waterfront
development
conceals interior
parklands
catering
to campers.

Long Key

THE SPANISH NAME FOR LONG KEY WAS CAYO VIVORA—
Rattlesnake Key. There are no rattlesnakes here, however, the isle's
sinuous shape and widespread "boca" (mouth) apparently reminded
some creative conquistador of a rattler in mid-strike. Opinions differ
as to whether this peaceful 965-acre state park affords an excellent
idyll or merely a very good one. If you like the idea of grassy tidal flats
so shallow you can walk hundreds of feet into the Atlantic before the
water rises to your waist, it's excellent, and certainly a safe place for
kids to swim.

Long Key
 158 A1

**Long Key State
Park**
www.floridastateparks.org/
longkey
 158 A1
 MM 67.5
 305/664-4815
 $–$$

**Layton Nature
Trail**
 158 A1
 Long Key, MM 68
 305/664-4815
 $

LONG KEY STATE PARK

Mangroves fringe the shore, providing cover for waterbirds like
heron, and you can rent a canoe to
paddle their channels, or explore
them on a boardwalk that angles
through the wave-lapped jungle,
its wildlife and flora described by
interpretive information boards.
The elevated 1.25-mile footpath is
called the **Golden Orb Trail,**
named for the large red and gold
spiders whose webs can be seen
draped among the limbs like old
lace. This is a popular camping
area year-round. Check at park
headquarters for ranger-led guided
walks and snorkeling, fishing, and
marine ecology activities. If you

enjoy canoeing, paddle the **Long
Key Lakes Canoe Trail.** Come
evening, park personnel present
campfire programs.

Across the highway on the
Florida Bay side, at MM 67.7, the
Layton Nature Trail offers a
half-hour stroll through stands of
tropical hardwood. (If you have old
tennis shoes, bring them.) You'll see
delicate blades of sea grass waving
at you from underwater. There's a
historical marker here noting the
origins of the Long Key Viaduct, a
sinuous old railroad bridge that
begins a short way down the road
and parallels the Overseas Highway
for several miles, and Flagler's long-
gone fishing retreat. ■

The Middle Keys run from tiny Conch Key at MM 65 past Pigeon Key to the southern landfall of Seven Mile Bridge at MM 40, the longest of the Keys' 42 spans, and among the longest bridges anywhere.

Middle Keys

Colorful kites for sale in the Florida Keys

Middle Keys

LONG KEY VIADUCT WAS HENRY FLAGLER'S FAVORITE BRIDGE, AND ITS 180 Romanesque arches were featured on his railroad's travel literature. His trains usually puffed along at a sedate 15 mph, but today motorists speed by much faster, stopping perhaps briefly to snap a picture and walk a stretch of the old Seven Mile Bridge, now reserved for pedestrians only. Those who stay often have a rod and reel with them, or a mask and fins, as these islands offer superb fishing and diving. Some of the best is found within sight of the Sombrero Reef lighthouse, which watches over an extravagantly rich coral kingdom of sea life 25 feet beneath the waves.

The Keys' commercial fishing industry began here in the early 1800s. Over the years the business of hooking fish has resulted in an equally large business of enticing visitors who want to fish. An armada of charter fishing boats crowds the waterfront in Marathon, on Vaca Key, where upstanding bait poles fringe the shore like a willowy canebrake, their captains waiting to take anglers out to fish underwater canyons plunging a thousand feet. Great white herons leisurely wing their way to their namesake wildlife refuge, a vast offshore expanse of water and mangrove reaching south into the Lower Keys.

You can swim with dolphins at the Dolphin Research Center on Grassy Key. Time, or at least the changes wrought in the Keys by time, has been arrested within the 63 acres of the Crane Point Hammock, the last known undisturbed stand of thatch palm, once common in the archipelago and now shrunk to this beleaguered tuft of the past. The islands' odd geology, peculiar wildlife, and

dramatic human pageant are the concern of Marathon's Museum of Natural History of the Florida Keys. A cultural trail from the nearby Florida Keys Children's Museum loops through one of the Keys' oldest conch-style residences and the ruins of a mid-19th-century Bahamian village, whose inhabitants earned their living by producing charcoal. On little Pigeon Key—a 2-mile walk on the old Seven Mile Bridge from Knight's Key—you'll find what must certainly be America's loneliest national historic district. Here the study of Keys history and culture is centered around a restored early-20th-century camp for railroad workers—the people who built the bridges and laid the track. ■

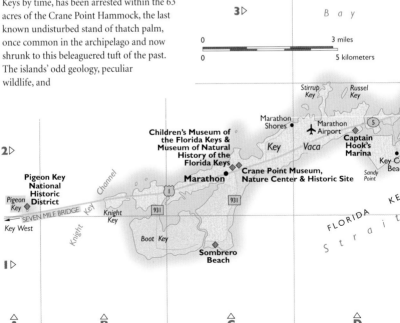

A visitor to Grassy Key enjoys a watery waltz with a resident of the Dolphin Research Center.

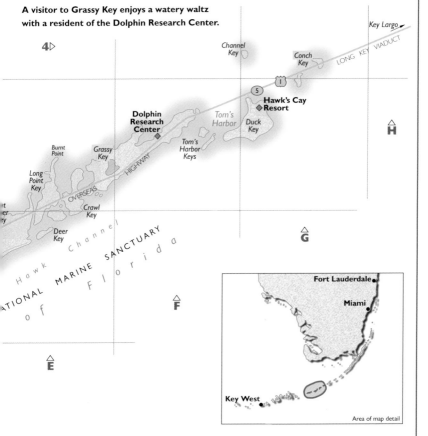

Conch & Duck Keys

Just before you cross Long Key Bridge southbound, turn off the highway onto the ocean side at MM 65.5 for a striking view of Flagler's old arched viaduct. Walk down the embankment to the water to encounter striking photogenic angles on the viaduct's graceful leaps off into the blue infinity. Long Key Bridge makes its landfall on 16-acre Conch Key, home of retirees and fishermen and those who harvest the Florida spiny lobster. You'll see their boxlike snares, known here as "crayfish traps," stacked haphazardly all over the island.

At MM 61, another bridge—the 12th since Key Largo—brings you to Duck Key, site of the sprawling Caribbean-style **Hawks Cay Resort** (tel 305/743-7000; see p. 254), the Middle Keys' most luxurious retreat. The salmon and green West Indies-style hideaway is a 1959 creation of the architect Morris Lapidus, who also designed Miami Beach's opulent Fontainebleau and Eden Roc. The resort caters to those used to being catered to, who want their golf close by, their tennis on clay, and their drinks served poolside. ■

Grassy Key

Few creatures are as fascinating and mysterious as dolphins, whose brains are larger and more complex than ours and, some suspect, might possess intelligence rivaling our own. This accounts for the appeal of Marathon's nonprofit **Dolphin Research Center** at MM 59, home to 19 of the sociable mammals, who may be touched under staff supervision. There's little chance of missing the center; a 30-foot-high statue of a mother and baby dolphin fronts it on the bay side of the road at MM 59. The

24-year-old education and research facility offers programs on dolphin biology and communication, culminating with an opportunity to meet, touch, and "talk" with the creatures. As you approach their pools during narrated presentations, they'll surface, clicking and chattering in a way that seems as if they understand you perfectly. To swim with the animals—the Dolphin Encounter program— reservations (305/289–0002) may be made after the first day of any month for the following month. ■

Key Vaca

The lion's share of 6-mile-long Key Vaca is claimed by the self-proclaimed capital of the Middle Keys, which got its name when Flagler exhorted his railroaders to make a "marathon" effort to finish the line to Key West before his impending demise.

MARATHON
Marathon, whose pace is nowhere near as fast as its name implies, is an extended cluster of unadorned commerce. Just about every guidebook calls it laid-back, which it is, even though there's an airport here with a busy commuter airline

Conch & Duck Keys
 185 G3

Grassy Key
 185 E3

Dolphin Research Center
www.dolphins.org
✉ Grassy Key, MM 59
☎ 305/289-1121
🕐 Open daily
$ $$$–$$$$$

Key Vaca
 184 D2

Marathon visitor information
✉ Greater Marathon Chamber of Commerce, 12222 Overseas Hwy.
☎ 305/743-5417 or 800/262-7284

schedule, along with several resorts and an enthusiastic community of concessionaires eager to rent you a boat, take you scuba diving, or get you out fishing for sailfish.

As you drive through town, stop by the venerable **Captain Hook's Marina,** ocean side at MM 53 *(tel 800/278-4665, www.captainhooks .com),* for a quick immersion in Middle Keys fishing culture. Even if your notion of nirvana doesn't include deep-sea adventures, the tackle shop is an education in man's astonishing ability to produce arcane devices. If you stay on Vaca Key, check the marina's schedule for fishing charters, evening cruises, and "Heart of Darkness" voyages into the Everglades.

Come sunset, people gather wherever the subtropical sun sets. Waterside establishments like the **Island Fish Co.** *(12648 Overseas Hwy., tel 305/743-4191, www.island fishco.com)* advertise their sundown views. Nearby, the old Seven Mile Bridge, now a walkway to Pigeon Key (see p. 189), offers sunsets for free. (Leave your vehicle in the parking area at MM 46.8.) If you time it correctly, you can stroll south over the water, leaving the party atmosphere behind in favor of wave-lapped peacefulness, and enjoy the evening spectacle that elicits cheers and clapping up and down the Keys every sunny evening.

Although it's on the wrong side of the road for sunset worship, **Sombrero Beach,** just south at the end of Sombrero Road at MM 50, is a lovely spot for an evening wade or swim in Hawk Channel. There's deep water here, a well-kept strand, and a verdant little park and playground where you are likely to find locals playing softball.

A family volleyball game at Marathon's Sombrero Beach, one of the biggest public beaches on the Middle Keys' Atlantic side

A bas-relief on the copper door of the Museum of Natural History of the Florida Keys depicts fish swimming among sea fans and coral.

Crane Point Museum, Nature Center & Historic Site

www.cranepoint.net

184 C2

5550 Overseas Hwy., Marathon, MM 50.5

305/743-9100

9 a.m.–5 p.m.; Sun. noon–5 p.m.

$$

A reconstructed native hut and a 19th-century settler's home at the Children's Museum of the Florida Keys on Key Vaca

CRANE POINT MUSEUM, NATURE CENTER & HISTORIC SITE

At MM 50.5, on the bay side of the highway, incongruously surrounded by Marathon's commercial clutter, is one of the Keys' most extraordinary natural places. Many of the islands once resembled this 64-acre virgin thatch palm hammock, the last of its kind in North America.

Walk the quarter-mile loop trail through the forest, a stroll made more meaningful if you have a copy of the self-guided brochure that identifies the red mangrove, palms, and exotic hardwoods bending over you, hiding the creatures whose unseen scuffling and odd cries add a peculiar spookiness. There's much to identify here, including 160 native plants and a menagerie of creatures, some of whom, like the graceful ibis, stand at the brink of extinction. Along the way, look for rare tree snails, and don't miss an unusual pit gouged in the island's coral foundation by rainfall erosion, exposing fossil star and brain corals from the primordial sea that formed the Keys.

Here archaeologists have uncovered a rich cache of pre-Columbian artifacts, including weapons, tools, a dugout canoe, and pottery. The oldest vessels, possibly 5,000 years old, are handsomely displayed at the adjoining **Museum of Natural History of the Florida Keys,** the islands' preeminent archive of ancient things. Among the most popular of the museum's 20 major exhibits (supplemented by a half-dozen changing displays) is one on the many shipwrecks that brought wealth to these once isolated isles. Bronze cannon, gold and silver from the Spanish main, and everyday items commemorate the anonymous fortune-seekers who found only watery graves on the reefs here.

If you're traveling with kids, set them loose at the **Children's Activity Center,** an outdoor facility with touch tanks and a galleon complete with pirate clothes and treasure. It should whip up their enthusiasm for a stroll along the preserve's mile-long indigenous loop trail, which visits the site of a long-gone Bahamian village, and the well-restored **Adderly House Historic Site,** said to be the oldest example of the Keys' quaint gingerbread conch architecture north of Key West. Its rough-textured walls are made of tabby, a mixture of limestone and crushed sea shells. ■

Pigeon Key

BEFORE YOU COMMIT YOURSELF TO THE DRIVE SOUTH across the new Seven Mile Bridge, consider a visit to Pigeon Key, an idyllic and historically unique 5-acre island located 2.2 miles from the northern end of the old Seven Mile Bridge. Like the old Florida East Coast Railroad causeway that casts a shadow line across the little key, Pigeon is listed on the National Register of Historic Places.

The view of Pigeon Key's historic district from the old Seven Mile Bridge includes the bridge foreman's restored house and dock.

PIGEON KEY NATIONAL HISTORIC DISTRICT

From 1908 to the infamous 1935 Labor Day hurricane, the island was a workers' community, home to painters, maintenance crews, and bridge tenders. Children attended a one-room school and all bought staples from the company store. After the storm caused the railroad's demise, the town (whose population once rose above an overcrowded 400) set to work converting the railroad to a two-lane vehicle causeway, which opened in 1938.

Park your car at the visitor center, situated in a vintage red and silver Florida East Coast Railway coach located at the west end of Marathon, just north of the new Seven Mile Bridge near MM 47.

Beginning at 10 a.m., a ferry shuttles visitors 2.2 miles south, near the old Seven Mile Bridge, to Pigeon Key. A walking tour guide accompanies each ferry. (The key's main structure, now the island's administrative headquarters, served as a dormitory for 64 railway workers in the 1920s.) Though the price of admission includes round-trip passage on the ferry, many prefer to stroll south to the island and return aboard the ferry. The restored early 20th-century village includes a small historical museum that documents the half-century struggle to link the Keys by rail, ferry, and auto. Locals, however, come here mainly for day-long getaways on a picnic blanket with a good book. ∎

Pigeon Key National Historic District

🔼 184 A2

✉ MM 47

☎ 305/743-5999

🕐 Shuttle operates daily

💲 $$ (includes shuttle)

Seven Mile Bridge

A drawbridge once occasioned impromptu get-togethers between the Middle and Lower Keys; the new roadway arcs over sea-going traffic.

TO BE PRECISE, THE NEW SPAN STRETCHES 35,830 FEET—6.7 miles—but when viewed from its northern end, it looks as if it runs all the way to Cuba. The bridge's opening in 1982 meant the retirement of its then 70-year-old predecessor, which still runs alongside it and is sometimes described as the world's largest fishing pier. Though the old bridge is missing sections here and there, and in places appears to be little more than a guano-spattered pelican roost, it's plain to see why, upon its completion in 1912, newspapers proclaimed it the Eighth Wonder of the World.

Seven Mile Bridge

184 A1

The bridge was in fact one of the most ambitious endeavors of its time, for despite seductively pretty aquamarine seas and the Keys' ever moderate clime, swift-running tides and an unstable sea bottom challenged the skills of Flagler's engineers. The tycoon personally exhorted his managers to attack the project as if on a military campaign and spared no expense. Historical photographs in Pigeon Key's museum (see p. 189) document the intensity of the effort: Large warehouses, four dormitories, a kitchen and dining hall, and an encampment of military-style tents for the construction crews, with building materials piled up almost everywhere else.

Still impressive, it runs southwest atop 546 concrete piers and 210 arches, some of them reaching nearly 30 feet underwater to anchor on limestone bedrock. It was one of the few man-made things to withstand the winds and tidal surges of the 1935 hurricane.

Time was when you had to stop at a drawbridge over Moser Channel at MM 43.5 while boats and small ships passed below. Those unscheduled stops were a part of Keys life, an opportunity for people to leave their cars on the roadway and chat with neighbors and travelers. The new bridge simply vaults the channel, clearing the high tide mark by 65 feet. ■

The Lower Keys take a sudden westerly bend just below Seven Mile Bridge, and just as abruptly the islands take on a different look and feel. They have a wilder appearance, and are less developed and more densely wooded.

Lower Keys

**Preparing for a dive,
Bahia Honda State Park**

Lower Keys

A GOOD PORTION OF THE LOWER KEYS FALLS WITHIN THREE DESIGNATED refuges that comprise the Florida Keys Wilderness and enclose 6,170 acres of pristine subtropical pineland, mangrove, and hammock habitats, virtually all of which lie marooned on islands accessible only by boat. The southernmost haven is the Key West National Wildlife Refuge, lying just west of Key West and embracing 2,019 uninhabited acres of red, white, and black mangrove in the Marquesas Keys.

Gulf of Mexico

Johnston Key

3▷

Snipe Keys

GREAT WHITE HERON NATIONAL WILDLIFE REFUGE

Perk Ba Tov P

Saddlebunch

OVERSEAS

Keys

2▷ Cottrell Key

Fleming Key

Dredgers Key

Big Coppitt Key

East Rockland Key

El Chico

KEY WEST NATIONAL WILDLIFE REFUGE

Stock Island

U.S. Naval Air Station

941

Saddlehill Key

5

Key West

Key West International Airport

Boca Chica Key

FLORIDA KEY

Key West

Barracouta Keys

1▷

Marquesas Keys

Straits

△A △B △C △D

Most of the larger islands in the Lower Keys, such as the Torches, Sugarloaf, and Saddlebunch, have convoluted shorelines that can create the illusion that they're small. Big Pine Key, for example, runs to nearly 8 miles in length, and at one point is 2 miles wide. Where the Overseas Highway negotiates an isthmus, however, it's easy to underestimate the possibilities lying alongside the road and down humble lanes that wander off into woods. Follow a dirt road here or there, and if you do not find yourself in a cul-de-sac of gates to private hideaway retreats, you'll probably wind through brush and scrub and slash pine, past explosions of scarred cactus to a rocky beach of broken shells and coral, or perhaps a mudflat, or a mangrove wilderness stretching west to the horizon.

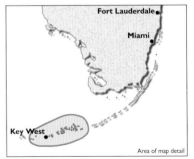

Fort Lauderdale
Miami
Key West
Area of map detail

You'll find one of the Keys' few truly sandy beaches at Bahia Honda State Park, which also encloses a mangrove forest and a hardwood hammock stippled with West Indian exotics like the sanguine red bougainvillea, the buttery alamada, the Jamaican morning glory, and the Geiger tree, whose startling flowers resemble small orange artillery bursts.

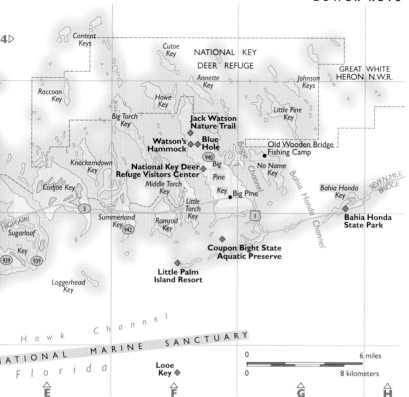

As travelers near Key West, the Keys' top-billed star, they exhibit a tendency to drive faster, particularly after crossing Seven Mile Bridge, as if that were the last point of worthwhile interest before heading for Jimmy Buffet's Margaritaville and ordering a margarita (what else?) to celebrate their arrival at Mile Zero.

But while it is understandable, it would be a mistake, at least if you value natural places and opportunities to wander in them—which in the Lower Keys are numerous and memorable. Look again at your map: The Great White Heron National Wildlife Refuge sprawls from the latitude of Marathon as far southwest as Key West; from there, out past the uninhabited Marquesas Keys, the great watery rectangle of the Key West National Wildlife Refuge takes over the custody and care of the myriad creatures within.

A further glance at your map reveals another wildlife preserve: the National Key Deer Refuge on Big Pine Key, where several hundred miniature versions of the Virginia white-tailed deer dart through slash pine. The tips of these tiny, skittish deer's ears barely reach the level of your belt. You can wander here, too, under a 50-foot canopy of hardwood trees in Watson's Hammock, another remnant of the primordial Keys, filled with gumbo limbo and Jamaican dogwood, spiky century plants (despite their name they usually bloom every decade or so), orchids, and ferns.

Look due south of Big Pine Key, about 7 miles south in shallow, remarkably clear Gulf Stream waters, and you have the Looe Key National Marine Sanctuary, whose 5 square miles protect a complex coral reef that is prized as the most vibrantly healthy and biologically diverse reef in the entire island chain. The other Lower Keys—No Name, Summerland, Ramrod, Cudjoe, Sugarloaf, Saddlebunch, Big Coppitt, and Boca Chica—are distinguished more by their histories and man-made eccentricities than by nature. All it takes to experience them is a bit of time and a willingness to spend it here. ■

Bahia Honda Key

Bahia Honda Key
◪ 193 G3

Bahia Honda State Park
www.bahiahondapark.com
✉ Park entrance,
36850 Overseas
Hwy., Big Pine Key,
MM 36.9
☎ 305/872-2353
$ $–$$

ENVIRONMENTALISTS TREASURE BAHIA HONDA (DEEP BAY) because most of the island is claimed by Bahia Honda State Park and thereby protected from commercial development. Most day-trippers, from Key West and Greater Miami, come here for the park's graceful Atlantic-facing beach, the Keys' longest naturally sandy strand, which has been rightly described as one of America's most appealing, and has excellent snorkeling just offshore.

BAHIA HONDA STATE PARK

Although most of the 524-acre park is intentionally allowed to remain in a wild state, Bahia Honda is nevertheless one of the most accommodating in the Keys, with such unusual amenities as a half-dozen two-bedroom waterfront housekeeping cabins (each sleeping eight) rising on stilts to take in a paradisiacal ocean view. Tucked away elsewhere are 80 campsites, a marina (where you can rent Windsurfers), a boat-launching ramp, and a dive shop where you can rent scuba and snorkeling gear.

Treat yourself to a half-hour respite at a shaded picnic table on **Sandspur Beach,** or a stroll along Bahia Honda's northeastern shore. A self-guided nature trail flirts with a lagoon and winds through a hardwood hammock dense with exotic Caribbean trees and bushes: gumbo limbo, the Jamaica morning glory, the West Indies yellow satinwood (found nowhere else in the Keys), Geiger trees, sea lavender, bay cedar, and thatch and silver palm. Resident birds include pelicans, white-crowned pigeons, laughing gulls, ospreys, herons, and smooth-billed anis, joined seasonally by migratory birds such as ibis, willets, sandpipers, and terns. Ask a ranger to point out the remnant of Henry Flagler's railroad rusting in the undergrowth.

The channel between the old and new Bahia Honda bridges is one of the deepest in the Florida Keys, attracting divers to the bridge pilings, which create a habitat for coral, sponges, spiny lobsters, and myriad species of varicolored fish. Be sure to check at the dive shop for current conditions and advice, which will certainly include a warning to watch out for stinging fire coral, sea urchins, and the Bahia Honda Channel's powerful currents, the swiftest in the Keys.

The tarpon fishing in this area is especially good. Charter fishing boats operate from here—the fee provides everything except the tarpon—so if you're planning on visiting, consider trying your hand at the recreation that Ernest Hemingway credited with renewing his energy and creative powers between intensive days of writing.

Ask at the park headquarters about daily snorkeling programs on the reef at nearby **Looe Key National Marine Sanctuary** (see p. 203). The Bahia Honda Dive Shop *(tel 305/872-3210)* in the concession building is the place to inquire about snorkeling and scuba diving trips to offshore reefs. You can also rent a small boat or kayak here. Sunset cruises depart from here as well, except in the depths of the hurricane season *(Oct.–Nov.).* One-half of the park's campsites are offered on a first-come first-served basis. Stop by in the morning to put your name on a waiting list, and be present when names are called in the afternoon. Oceanfront cottages are also available. ∎

**Opposite:
Despite extensive development, some Keys retain substantial tracts of native jungle. On Bahia Honda, a state-protected wilderness flanks the Overseas Highway.**

Big Pine Key

UPON LANDING ON BIG PINE KEY—THE KEYS' SECOND
largest island after Key Largo—you will encounter the on-going tug-
of-war between those who love concrete and those who prefer their
Keys au naturel. Pinelands once shared much of the island with
tropical hardwood and shoreline mangrove forests. More than 5,000
people live on the island today, and development has gone danger-
ously far, encouraged in part because Big Pine is one of the few keys
with a natural year-round supply of fresh water. Although houses,
condos, shopping centers, marinas, and parking lots claim more of Big
Pine than is desirable, you can still sense the natural order of things.

Big Pine Key
🏕 193 F5

**National Key
Deer Refuge
Visitors Center**
www.fws.gov/national
keydeer
🏕 193 F3
✉ MM 28.5–31.5
☎ 305/872-0774

NATIONAL KEY
DEER REFUGE

What acreage that does not lie
beneath some improvement
belongs mainly to the pine, palm,
and hardwood hammocks of the
8,700-acre National Key Deer
Refuge on Big Pine, established in

1957 to protect the dwindling population of Key deer. The largest
among these odd creatures might
stand 32 inches at the shoulder and
weigh 85 pounds. Biologists have
listed them as a pint-size sub-
species of the Virginia white-tailed
deer, rendered small by eons of

environmental stresses, including limited water and forage, and a small habitat. They're found nowhere else but in the Keys, and are further distinguished by their ability to drink brackish water. It is supposed that their ancestors ranged south before the melting of the ancient Wisconsin ice age glacier, which elevated sea levels and turned what had been a tenuous peninsula into an archipelago. Whatever produced these carefully stepping miniatures, whose newborns weigh two to four pounds and leave a postage-stamp-size hoofprint, their numbers were reduced by hunting and poaching to a mere 50, from which the herd has slowly grown to something near 800. That's a peak population for the size of the habitat. As you drive across Big Pine, observe the slow speed limit (45 by day, 35 at night). Until early 2003, when a fence was built along US 1 as it crosses the island, approximately 20 Key deer were killed by automobiles annually. In the year after the fence was built, one was killed.

Right: Once considered a unique species, Key deer are now believed to be related to better nourished, hence larger, northern cousins.

To get to the refuge, turn west off the highway just south of MM 31 onto Key Deer Boulevard (Fla. 940), where you'll soon see a sign pointing the way. Turn right into a shopping center for the refuge's **Visitors Center**; stop to pick up information and a map. Return to Key Deer Boulevard and turn right, and after 1.5 miles turn right onto Watson Boulevard to reach **No Name Key** (see p. 199).

While at the Visitors Center, look for the general brochure and information on the mile-long loop of the **Jack Watson Nature Trail,** which lies ahead. (The trail is named for the refuge manager who campaigned successfully to ban the hunting of Key deer.) Return to the intersection and continue on Key Deer Boulevard for another

1.5 miles to a former quarry known as the **Blue Hole,** now naturally filled with fresh groundwater and alligators of various sizes. You can leave your car here, take a look at the torpid reptiles, and then stroll a short way to the head of the Jack Watson Nature Trail (made more

interesting by consulting the brochure you picked up, which refers to signs along the trail). Along the path you'll find water-filled sinkholes and stands of thatch and silver palm rising above a riot of subtropical plants. Come evening, you might see a Key deer lurking in the shadows. Without a doubt it will see you first. Be aware that feeding Key deer is against the law.

Walk along the Watson Nature Trail, which cuts through a hardwood forest of mostly gumbo limbo and Jamaican dogwood that rise 50 feet to create an oasis of shade. Then walk or drive to the nearby Mannillo Nature Trail. In addition to the flora, some unique to the Lower Keys, the wildlife includes a marsh rabbit, the silver rice rat, alligators, Eastern diamondback rattlesnakes, hognose snakes, and raccoons.

A great white
heron on watch

Bud Boats

✉ Big Pine Key, via
Key Deer Blvd.
from MM 31, BS

☎ 305/872-9165

**Big Pine Kayak
Adventures**

www.keyskayaktours.com

✉ Big Pine Key

☎ 305/872-7474

Reflections

www.floridakeyskayaktours
.com

✉ Parmer's Place
Resort at MM 28.5,
group kayak trips

☎ 305/872-2157

GREAT WHITE HERON NATIONAL WILDLIFE REFUGE

You probably won't see a sign announcing this federal sanctuary, home to the Keys' flying, feathered ballet troupe and the only nesting place in the United States for great white herons and the endangered white-crowned pigeon. Glance at your map, however, and you'll notice ruler-straight boundary lines embracing much of the bay side of the Lower Keys nearly to Key West.

These nearly 192,600 back-country acres of shallow water, fringe and scrub mangrove wetlands, low hardwood hammocks, and salt marsh also provide a haven for ospreys, reddish egrets, mangrove cuckoos, black-whiskered vireos, green- and blue-winged teal,

red-breasted mergansers, and coots. Bird-watchers consider themselves especially fortunate to record sightings of the gawky-beautiful roseate spoonbill, the ibis, and the double-crested cormorant, among many other uncommon species. In other words, it's wild out there.

You can't drive to the 1,900 acres of land included in the refuge, but you can explore them by boat, and if you have the time (at least a half day) you ought to consider it. There is profoundly affecting primordial beauty here, and local fishing guides offer day-trips aboard shallow-draft boats for those who simply want to observe. Within the refuge you'll find a fertile world where native seabirds and migratory waterfowl breed, many roosting on floating nests. Once you wander into its maze of mangrove islands, you get the pleasant sense of entering a magical kingdom. And it is—a place where the Earth abides simply by being left alone.

If you're reasonably good at handling a canoe or kayak, it's a fairly easy paddle from Big Pine Key (see p. 196) or the Torch Keys (see p. 202) out into the **Content Keys,** inside refuge boundaries. If you motor out, keep your noise and speed at a minimum to avoid frightening birds from their nests or creating wakes that swamp low-lying and floating nests. Be sure to take binoculars, for within the shaded mangroves you'll see dark beady eyes fixed on you, watching your approach. You're also likely to encounter sea turtles and bottle-nose dolphins. Stay about 200 feet away from the islands—causing a roosting bird to flee its nest leaves eggs or nestlings unshaded in the sun's killing glare.

There aren't any facilities within the refuge, so be sure to take water and food. ■

No Name Key

THIS ISLAND ONCE HOSTED A CLANDESTINE TRAINING base for anti-Castro Cuban guerrillas. The base failed, as did No Name's only settlement. This small village was served in the 1920s by a ferry from Marathon, then a torturous route of dusty crushed rock roads and wooden bridges hopscotching between Big Pine, Ramrod, and Summerland Keys.

To get to No Name today, take US 1, then turn west off the highway just south of MM 31 onto Key Deer Boulevard (Fla. 940) and follow it about 1.5 miles to its intersection with Watson Boulevard. A right turn onto Watson leads to a concrete bridge across Bogie Channel to No Name's old ferry slip. (You might find Key deer, so drive slowly.)

The only vestige of the community era is the **Old Wooden Bridge Guest Cottages & Marina,** a cluster of one- and two-bedroom housekeeping cottages *(1791 Bogie Dr., tel 305/872-2241, www.oldwooden-bridge.com).* The local hangout is the humble beer- and pizza-serving No Name Pub *(N. Watson Blvd., tel 305/872-9115, www.nonamepub .com)* on Big Pine, just across the bridge that links it with No Name.

Though some back roads here— some paved, others not—lead to the remnants of failed enterprise and broken dreams, you can explore scenic areas in and around the National Key Deer Refuge (see pp. 196–98). The Big Pine Bicycle Center at MM 30 on the ocean side of the highway *(tel 305/872-0130)* rents single-gear, fat-tire bikes for adults and children with safety helmets included.

A pleasant route departs from MM 30.3 on US 1's bay side and follows Wilder Road across the bridge to No Name. Or pedal along Key Deer Boulevard into the refuge on Big Pine. Avoid walking trails leading through wetlands, as bike tires cut into their loam, causing damage and encouraging erosion. ∎

Key deer are protected in Big Pine's National Key Deer Refuge, but they can swim between the surrounding keys. Feeding them is illegal.

No Name Key
△ 193 G3

Tropical hardwood hammocks

The image is appealing: drowsing in a hammock in the shade of a tropical glade to the rustle of palms and the lapping of gentle waves. In the Keys, however, there are hammocks (a word adopted by 16th-century Spanish explorers from the language of native Caribbeans, who invented them for more comfortable sleeping in their humid clime) and there are hammocks, a term that first appeared in English among 18th-century mariners who used it to designate a low rise or hillock on a sea coast.

Along the coasts of southern Florida throughout the Everglades, and in the Florida Keys, hammocks refer to the dense, vine-entangled forests that geologists believe arose here between 120 and 110 thousand years ago, after the Keys' coral reef foundation was left high and dry when ancient seas receded. A curious mix of plant and animal communities evolved along with them and competed with populations of hardy South Florida slash pines that thrive atop fossilized coral limestone and are known as pine rocklands.

The hammocks support over 20 species of broad-leafed trees, shrubs, and vines, most of them native to the West Indies. Biologists assume their seeds were washed ashore, arrived on driftwood, or were left in the droppings of migratory birds. Those exotics able to cope with scant rainfall and thin soil eventually landscaped the once-barren coral knobs, forming a low canopy of live oak (their deeply furrowed bark fringed with lacy resurrection fern), red mulberry, and palm over a dense, often impenetrable tangle of vines and shrubbery whose names are whimsically charming: catbrier, Virginia creeper, pepper vine, possum grape, beautyberry, shiny sumac, redbay, Simpsons stopper, marlberry, wild coffee, wild lime, coralbean, torchwood. And below these, Spanish moss, ball moss, quill wild pine, the cardinal air plant, the green wild pine, and, if you're lucky, butterfly orchids.

Tropical hammocks sprang up as far north as Cape Canaveral on the Atlantic shoreline, and as far west as the mouth of the Manatee River on the Gulf Coast. Most of these have been destroyed, leaving just a few beleaguered remnants, most of them in the Florida Keys.

The lack of a primordial physical connection between the landmasses of Florida and the West Indies barred most earthbound West Indian wildlife from colonizing the Keys. The hammocks drew their roster of animals from mainland North America, the creatures arriving in improbable ways—clinging to trees washed out to sea by flooding, arriving as captives of the Calusa, or as tiny stowaways on their dugout canoes. The West Indies white-crowned pigeon made the crossing as well, and so did the Jamaican fruit bat and its Caribbean cohort, the Wagner's mastiff bat, the latter two thriving on the mosquitoes that swarmed here then.

Poke around long enough in a hammock and you're likely to come nose to nose with raccoons, rough green snakes, green tree frogs, red-bellied woodpeckers, cotton mice, and white-tailed deer. If you chance across a Florida tree snail—you'll know it from the dazzling variety of colored bands covering its whorled shell—let it be. Until recently the ranks of this little spectral riot were decimated by collectors. Should you spot a flutter of blue, brown, and orange overhead, that's the Schaus' swallowtail butterfly, another living rarity. (An officially designated endangered species, its populations were unintentionally depleted by pesticides sprayed for mosquito control.)

Other primeval forests in the Keys are John Pennekamp Coral Reef State Park (see pp. 163–66), Lignumvitae Key Botanical State Park (see pp. 178–79), and the National Key Deer Refuge on Big Pine Key (see pp. 196–97). ∎

Right: In hammock communities, where ground area is often in short supply, some plants actually grow atop others in symbiotic relationships.

Left: Paurotis palms rise
like green aerial explosions.
Above: Gleaming red bark
identifies a gumbo limbo tree.

Torch Keys

Peace and quiet, plus the appeal of a luxury resort and fine dining, are the main attractions of the Torch Keys.

THE TORCH KEYS—LITTLE, BIG, AND MIDDLE—WERE NAMED for the sappy torchwood tree found here. You'll also notice a sprinkling of key lime trees, the offspring of failed efforts to raise a cash crop. The Torches' heyday was in the 1920s. Ironically, the arrival of the Overseas Highway in the late 1930s concentrated traffic along the new road, and starved the little communities that sprang up at the ends of the Torches' humble marl lanes. But that's mostly gone now, and if you drive the so-called scenic road that slaloms for some 8 miles across Big Torch's swampy interior, you will discover this yourself before coming to its end among a mixed mangrove jungle.

Torch Keys
193 F3

Little Palm Island Resort
www.littlepalmisland.com
193 F2
305/343-8567

It is this out-of-the-way atmosphere that boosts the appeal of the **Little Palm Island Resort** (see p. 255), a 5-acre retreat with a reputation for luxury and privacy. Coconut palms sway above open-air thatched-roof huts set up on stilts. Beds are draped in mosquito netting; overhead ceiling fans stir the balmy air. There are no televisions, and there is only one telephone. The point is to leave the world behind, thus the islet is accessible only by a private launch shuttling back and forth hourly from the Dolphin Marina on Little Torch Key at MM 28.5.

Many people make the effort to visit because the resort's Dining Room at Little Palm (see p. 254), whose bamboo and rattan tables overlook the water, is consistently rated the Keys' premier dining spot outside of Key West. It serves modern tropical cuisine, has a very respectable wine list, and is renowned for its first-class level of service. Despite their exotic isolation, both the resort and restaurant are wheelchair accessible. The fishing and diving here are superb, as Little Palm's isle lies within **Coupon Bight Aquatic Preserve.** ∎

Looe Key

JUST SOUTH OF THE 720-FOOT-LONG TORCH-RAMROD Bridge, MM 27 confirms that you've reached Ramrod Key. This smallish limestone knob is best known as a staging area for eager divers headed out to the reefs of Looe Key, part of the Florida Keys National Marine Sanctuary, just over 5 miles out in the Atlantic. The 5.3-square-mile preserve encloses the most diverse coral community in the Lower Keys, a wonderland teeming with fish and other sea creatures, with shallow depths suitable for snorkelers and scuba divers of all skill levels. Many underwater enthusiasts rate it North America's premier dive spot.

Looe Key
www.floridakeys.noaa.gov
🗺 193 F2
✉ Off Big Pine Key, MM 28.5–31.5 (Key West headquarters, 216 Ann St.)
☎ 305/292-0311
💲 Free admission

Looe Key—not really a key but a reef—commemorates the unfort-unate H.M.S. *Looe*, a British warship that foundered here in the 1700s. (Look carefully at the bottom and you might notice some of the frigate's ballast stones, their shapes at odds with the natural detritus.) From the air the key sprawls darkly atop pale coral sand in the shape of a bent Y, roughly 800 yards long and 200 yards wide. Its massive accretions or spurs of pillar coral rise up from depths as great as 35 feet nearly to the surface. Lying in sandy grooves between these great spurs are bulky, dome-shaped brain corals, patrolled by skulking lobsters and bottom-skimming sea rays. Varicolored fish by the thousands congregate here, moving in precision-swimming schools and darting among the antlerlike branches of elkhorn coral. Purple sea fans sway languidly in the Gulf Stream, which surges above clusters of sponges and sea urchins. The blue-tinted scene is otherworldly.

Virtually every dive shop in the region offers half-day excursions to Looe Key twice daily (*8 a.m. & 1:30 p.m.*), providing all equipment. Although the water is comfortably warm, you will slowly lose body heat as you explore the reef. For many, a wet suit vest rented at nominal cost prevents the weakness, shortness of breath, and occasional nausea that some experience after an otherwise perfectly delightful hour of leisurely paddling. If you're prone to motion sickness, consider starting your medication the night before your trip. ∎

A marine patrol puts out a warning to snorkelers and divers at the reefs of Looe Key.

Sugarloaf Key & Big Coppitt Key

ANGLO-AMERICAN SETTLERS FIRST STAKED OUT HOME-steads on these two small isles in the late 19th century. Then in 1912, an English-born entrepreneur named Charles Chase established a sponge farm on Sugarloaf Key's shore, attaching live pieces of sponge to fragments of concrete submerged in saltwater pens. Chase soon owned most of the key, which also bought the privilege of naming its first town in honor of himself. Two years later, beset with banking troubles in Britain, Chase's Florida Sponge & Fruit Company failed. He sold out to R. C. Perky, a real estate salesman who had a vision of developing Sugarloaf. Perky renamed his newly acquired hamlet Perky, but his fortunes foundered like Chase's.

Sugarloaf Key
🅜 193 E2

Big Coppitt Key
🅜 192 D2

It's easy to imagine why Chase and Perky had big dreams. Sugarloaf's pleasant somnolence tends to clear the mind and allow you to think.

To experience the homey serenity along the island's shaggy, overgrown back roads, leave US 1 at MM 20 (OS)—the turnoff is hard by Mangrove Mama's *(tel 305/745-3030; see p. 254)*, a charming, funky restaurant and bar—and take either Fla. 939 or 939A, which loop back to the highway at MM 17. A turn onto Old State Road (Fla. 4A) wanders through mangrove thickets broken

by bright blue-jade flashes of the tropical Atlantic, crosses a narrow channel, and delivers you to Upper Sugarloaf Key and a dead-end at Sugarloaf Boulevard. This is how the Keys looked to motorists in the early 1930s.

South of **Perky's Bat Tower,** at MM 17, are the popular Sugarloaf Lodge resort and restaurant *(tel 305/745-3211)*, and marina and airstrip. A mere 11 bridges separate you from Key West. The longest runs a half-mile; the shortest and last—the bridge from Stock Island to Key West—a mere 159 feet. Six of the spans are necessary to complete a crossing of the low-lying **Saddlebunch Keys,** which are little more than coral mounts topped by mangroves.

South of Sugarloaf, separated by the Saddlebunch Keys, is **Big Coppitt Key,** most of which is a bedroom community for the naval air station on adjoining **Boca Chica Key** farther south, whose beaches, enticing when viewed from offshore, are mostly off-limits. Like Boca Chica, **Rockland Key** has been claimed by industry, namely a cement plant. Ahead lies Key West and the terminus of the Overseas Highway. ∎

PERKY'S BAT TOWER

Real estate salesman R.C. Perky dreamed of turning Sugarloaf into South Florida's finest resort, but there was a problem —mosquitoes. He read a book by a Texas health official named Dr. Charles Campbell, who claimed to have developed a system by which bats could be enlisted to rid the Earth of mosquitoes. Following instructions, Perky built a 35-foot-tall bat tower, using Campbell's secret-formula bat bait to entice the creatures into adopting the tower as their home. They didn't, and Perky went bankrupt, leaving his empty obelisk bat tower as an exotic monument to his entrepreneurial dreams. ∎

Left: A mosquito abatement apparatus proved effective only at exterminating its builder's fortune.

There is probably no community in America remotely like Key West, an odd, beguiling, eccentric, raffishly charming end-of-the-road outpost set apart from all others.

Key West & Dry Tortugas

A pineapple motif in a Key West fence

Key West & Dry Tortugas

KEY WEST IS THE SOUTHERNMOST CITY IN THE CONTINENTAL UNITED States—45 miles above the Tropic of Cancer, a mere 90 from Cuba—and is South Florida's oldest, established in 1829. Many find its isolated island setting irresistibly exotic. The town's slow-paced, shorts-and-sandals lifestyle has compelled more than a few travelers to read the house rental ads in the *Key West Citizen*. Most Americans vaguely associate Key West with literary personages (Ernest Hemingway in particular) and unusual news items—boatloads of Cuban and Haitian refugees, hunters of sunken Spanish treasure galleons, Coast Guard interceptions of drug runners, a new sportfishing record.

But Key West's day-to-day reality is so ineffably different from mainstream American life that it defies any glib summing up. Even locals will, in moments of affectionate exasperation, shake their heads and mutter, "Key Weird." The island is a surprise to first timers. Many newcomers are put off by its apparent disregard for notions of conventional behavior. The prim consider it dissolute, despairing of its never-quite-correct ways: Its

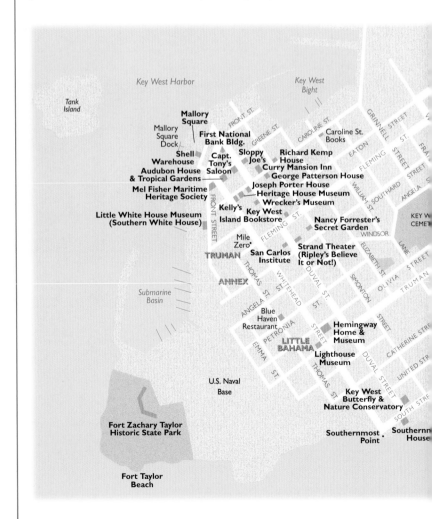

sidewalks are broken by banyan tree roots; its houses overgrown with vines and bowers of orange-petaled royal poinciana trees, suggesting a local law against painting. Whether you will like it depends largely upon the expectations you bring with you. It's probably best to bring none at all, save a willingness to sample the unfamiliar and indulge the eccentric.

Nineteenth-century Cubans called the island Stella Maris, Star of the Sea. It was for them a prosperous place, where fishing and cigarmaking offered a good living and an escape from Cuban sugarcane fields and heavy handed Spanish colonial rule. Early Spanish explorers found it littered with bleached human skeletons, and charted it as Cayo

Hueso, Island of Bones. Why these remains were there, no one knows. Some speculate Key West was a Calusa burial ground, or perhaps a battlefield. Whatever it was once called, Key West is still a place of mystery and contradiction, of extremes and contrasts.

A hedonistic, self-absorbed island, it has no natural fresh water. Bedeviled by its own

Caribbean colors decorate a house in Old Key West.

popularity as a tourist destination, it lies within a vast watery wilderness. It is by turns refined and tawdry: For every fine art gallery, bookstore, and antique showroom, there are a dozen T-shirt shops. For every linen-covered restaurant table, on which candle-burning hurricane lamps illumine dishes that would compete nicely in Manhattan, there is a much-beloved greasy spoon shoveling conch fritters and french fries onto paper trays for patrons crowding picnic tables under tin roofs. Parts of the downtown Mallory Square area, full of glitzy tourist attractions and gimcrack vendors, resemble a theme park. But look beyond that—past the jewelry stands and the cotton candy and saltwater taffy carts and the crowds applauding street performers —to the untrammeled and gorgeous subtropical sea shimmering below a pollution-free sky, and you reconnect with the natural

U.S. Naval Air Station

0   500 yards
0   500 meters

Garrison Bight

PALM AVENUE

ROOSEVELT BLVD.

PETRONIA ST.
FLORIDA ST.

Riggs Wildlife Refuge, Little Hamaca Park

OLIVIA ST.

LEON STREET
STREET
DUNCAN STREET
UNITED STREET
SOUTH ST

AVENUE
STREET
ST

VIRGINIA
CATHERINE ST.

Tennessee Williams' Home

FLAGLER AVE.

area of map detail

Miami

LAIRD ST.

Dry Tortugas
Key West

ATLANTIC BLVD.

Smathers Beach,
Fort East Martello,
Fort East Martello Museum
& Gardens

Higgs Beach
West Martello Tower
Key West International Airport

Key West African Cemetery
White St. Pier

setting that underlies all that is here. Wander away from Old Key West's gentrified 19th-century houses and mansions, and its new condominium developments, and you'll find overgrown lanes and bungalow neighborhoods that are downright shabby, survivors of the wild dream-busting swings of the island's historically mercurial economy. (During the Depression, Key West went bankrupt, and state officials proposed abandoning the isle and relocating residents to the mainland.) In old Cuban and Bahamian neighborhoods only a few blocks from the bustle of Duval Street's retail bazaar, chickens scratch and cluck amid modest cottages where Caribbean families sit on porches to talk and watch life go by.

Pronounced "konk," the term Conch today refers to a person born on Key West, and implies a free-thinking, prickly, independent-minded political sentiment. The nickname traces to 1646, when a group of British subjects established a Bahamian colony, declaring themselves exempt from royal taxation and free to worship as they pleased. When the Crown attempted to tax them, they defiantly declared themselves more willing to eat conch meat (which they did anyway) than pay it. Thereafter they were known as Conchs. The creature for which they are named, however, is no longer plentiful. It's officially an endangered species; the conch meat served in the Keys is shipped fresh-frozen from the Bahamas, Belize, or the Caribbean.

Today, native Conchs are outnumbered by so-called freshwater Conchs, people who, for a number of reasons, have adopted the town with a vengeance. Key West particularly attracts those who find comfort in knowing that they live in a place as unconventional as they are. As a consequence it has a significant cadre of artists, writers, musicians, lifestyle devotees, and others who are probably best described as eccentric. The island is also home to a sizable gay community, credited for leadership roles in civic improvements, historic preservation, and the revival of the town's hospitality industry. A good many Key Westers are embarked on new lives—urban professionals-turned-innkeepers, entrepreneurs, or artists—encouraged by the island's air of isolation that produces a bracing sense of personal freedom

and possibility. For these people, despite the impact of tourism and the island's vulnerability to hurricanes, Key West remains an immensely desirable place to live and work, a truism confirmed by the steady inflation of real estate prices.

Above all, Key West engages the senses. Come evening, the subtropical light off the water boosts colors to a fabulous intensity, the reason why crowds gather at Mallory Square for the Sunset Celebration, to applaud as the sun eases into the sea. The air is redolent of brine, perfumed by flowering vines and wild orchids, laced with the scent of old wood and damp gardens, and humid. The island's temperature averages a balmy 79°F, and the ocean is warm and clear blue, like old glass. Smoke from the braziers of open-air backyard restaurants fills the streets with the burnt spice of Bahamian and Cuban fare, often served to the strum of guitars. There are menus for every taste, bistros for every mood, people for every adventure.

A somnolent afternoon on Smathers Beach, a popular windsurfing spot

Old Key West is best (and most easily) explored on foot, its streets lined by a picturesque collection of indigenous architecture and historical monuments, tropical gardens, arcane museums, and a waterfront that is always interesting. A raffish maritime heritage accounts for an abundance of saloons. The variety of catches brought in by the town's fishing fleet enables local chefs to create fresh seafood dishes almost impossible to find elsewhere. Out-of-the-way places like the beach and tree-shaded picnic area inside Fort Zachary Taylor Historic State Park, the old Key West Lighthouse, the town cemetery, and the Audubon House gardens offer quiet respites from the bustling downtown. There are upscale resort hotels and elegant bed-and-breakfasts in refurbished Victorian houses, and there are modestly priced inns whose friendly panache makes up for facilities that,

although comfortable, elsewhere might be considered a bit scruffy. As with most towns where the living is not always easy, there are districts where you probably ought not wander at night. By day and in the evening, the Little Bahama neighborhood south of downtown is charming. Locals, however, advise against strolling its unlighted back streets later at night.

Surrounding all is the sea. A fleet of charter boats offers day-long snorkeling trips to the reefs that garland Key West. There are quiet beaches to drowse on, and busy ones where you can rent sailboats. And though a marker at the corner of Whitehead and Fleming Streets proclaims this Mile Zero, the Keys do not really end here, but rather 70 miles west in the Dry Tortugas (see pp. 234–38). This lonely scattering of small atoll-like islands among sandy shoals and coral reefs is watched over by a colossal Civil War fortress and a 19th-century lighthouse whose beacon sweeps the sea at night. ■

THE LURE OF TREASURE

"There is not a diver, not an adventurer, not a hunter after fame and fortune, who has not, at some time, dreamed of striking it rich." So wrote French adventurer Jacques-Yves Cousteau, whose invention of the "self-contained underwater breathing apparatus"—the SCUBA—opened up Florida's shallow, treasure-strewn reefs to a postwar generation of dreamers. ∎

Entering Key West

WHETHER YOU ARRIVE BY CAR OR PLANE, THERE ARE TWO routes leading to Old Key West, one more scenic and interesting than the other. If you're driving and haven't visited the island before, Stock Island's commercial clutter can be alarming. It's practical—there are good marine supply and sporting goods stores, but they give no hint of the older, far more charming city ahead.

Just after you cross the bridge from Stock Island to Key West, you'll reach a T-shaped intersection with Roosevelt Boulevard. Look for highway signs indicating Fla. A1A and pointing left (south) to "Beaches/Airport." Turn left and follow S. Roosevelt Boulevard's palmy corridor south past the Key West International Airport and then west along the Atlantic Ocean side of the island. This part of Key West lying east of White Street is considered its New Town, much of it created by filling wetlands. Officially speaking, the neighborhoods west of White Street constitute Old Town.

Inland, as you drive along S. Roosevelt, are the marshy **Salt Ponds,** used commercially in the mid-1800s to evaporate water and create sea salt. The ponds nowadays teem with crustaceans and small fish, attracting seabirds, especially in the early morning hours when

Above: Formerly a morgue, Captain Tony's bar later became a regular haunt of Ernest Hemingway.

Key West
Map pp. 206–207

Above right: The Overseas Highway nears Mile Zero toward Key West's northern stretch.

avid bird-watchers gather here. Part of the grassy wetland is enclosed by the **Riggs Wildlife Refuge—** look for a green gate—which has a nicely designed observation platform. Across the briny bog is another wildlife sanctuary known as **Little Hamaca Park,** located just off Flagler at Government Road. This unusual preserve encloses a pristine enclave of living biological history. A boardwalk lets you examine and explore the sanctuary without disturbing the delicate wetlands below.

The 2-mile-long strand opposite is **Smathers Beach,** popular among windsurfers and Hobie Cat sailors. You can rent two-person catamarans here. They're inexpensive, easy to sail, and quite stable unless the wind is whipping up whitecaps, but you're not allowed to take them out of sight of the vendors, meaning you can't use them to explore other parts of the island.

This approach to Old Key West takes you past the **Fort East Martello,** one of the oldest brick structures on the island, a cylindrical Civil War-era fort that houses

the eclectic collection of the **Fort East Martello Museum and Gardens** *(3501 S. Roosevelt Blvd., tel 305/296-3913, www.kwahs.com/ martello.htm, $–$$).* Besides being a singularly pleasant place to stretch your legs after your long drive, it also gives human faces to the historical eras that make up the branches of Key West's complex family tree of pirates, soldiers, railroaders, spongers, rumrunners, shipbuilders, cigarmakers, shrimpers, and Caribbean political refugees who survived the crossing. There are exhibits of local artists' work, and a room devoted to Key West's lengthy roster of accomplished writers, including seven honored with the Pulitzer Prize. Be sure to climb the 48 steps to the tower's observation platform, an exertion that rewards with a splendid ocean view.

Just down the road from the museum, S. Roosevelt Boulevard becomes Atlantic Boulevard and enters a neighborhood of condominium apartments. Atlantic ends at White Street, which is considered the northern boundary of Key West's Old Town district. ■

Key West's
Historic Old Town

Key West
Map p. 206

KEY WEST'S HISTORIC CENTER ISN'T ITS GEOGRAPHIC center, but rather it lies hard alongside Key West Harbor and the old city's commercial moorage, Key West Bight. The official center of downtown is Mallory Square, where the Mallory Steamship Company once boarded Cuban-bound travelers.

History states that in 1822, a U.S. Navy party led by a lieutenant named Matthew Perry (who later as a commodore opened Japan to American commerce) raised the Stars and Stripes over the island for the first time. The swampy, malarial place had been purchased that year by an Alabama speculator named John Simonton from Spanish land grantee, Juan Pablo Salas, for $2,000. Simonton got real estate, and the U.S. its southernmost deep-water anchorage, something rare on Florida's shallow coastline. Key West became the forward base of the Navy's pirate-hunting West India Squadron, which mounted a brutal eight-year campaign to root the murderous buccaneers from their hideaways deep in mangrove creeks up and down the Keys. Meanwhile, a few hundred settlers, mostly New Englanders and English Bahamian whalers, merchant mariners, and marine salvagers, began to build houses and a multicultural community.

As America's merchant fleet grew and its reach extended, the reefs around Key West claimed an ever-increasing number of ships. In calm weather and bright sunlight these jagged coral rasps are virtually invisible until the moment before impact. In the hurricane season, howling gales make evasive maneuvering impossible. Then, as now, this was one of the busiest sea lanes in the Western Hemisphere. As a result, hundreds of sailing ships came to grief on the reefs. Their cargoes, often strewn along Key West's shores, produced a phenomenal economic boom. American maritime salvage law, fundamentally based on the notion that finders are keepers, was largely written by Key West judges. The island's "wreckers" literally furnished their ornate mansions with the spoils of disaster.

This run of luck ended in the 1850s with the installation of lighthouses. As wrecking declined, the harvesting of sponges picked up, followed in the late 19th century by the arrival of Cuban immigrants skilled in the art of cigarmaking. Commercial fishing began to pay, and by 1890 Key West was Florida's wealthiest city, with a population of 25,000.

That all ended during the Great Depression. The sponges were gone, the cigar companies had moved north to Tampa, and ships bypassed the harbor for points north. Even the Navy had closed its base here. By 1934, four out of every five Key Westers were on the dole. The town fathers declared Key West a ward of the State, which promptly handed the starving waif over to the federal government. It was decided that Key West would be made over with public funds and volunteer work into a tourist destination.

Some 4,000 islanders labored for half a year to smarten up the town. Trees were planted, houses repaired, mountains of trash removed, and beaches raked clear of seaweed.

KEY WEST IN LITERATURE

Ernest Hemingway's novel *To Have and Have Not*, published in 1938, tells the tragic story of a Conch fisherman and smuggler named Henry Morgan, evoking the desperation of Key West's Depression years and the self-reliance Hemingway admired in his fellow townsfolk. Another Pulitzer Prize-winning Key Wester was poet and writer Elizabeth Bishop, who lived at 624 White Street from 1938 to 1942. Much of her work is set here and elsewhere in the Keys. ∎

Federal grants reopened hotels staffed by graduates of the government-funded Key West Maids' Training School. Unemployed musicians were hired to form the Key West Hospitality Band, which serenaded travelers as they stepped from trains and ships' gangways. Other locals were trained in handicrafts, including weaving sun hats from coconut palm fronds. (Stroll Duval Street and you'll see sidewalk vendors still weaving them.)

A tourist guide was written, and nearly everything of remotely possible interest to a visitor was pointed out. A "Typical Old House" was Sight No. 12, the "Abandoned Cigar Factory" No. 35. Number 18 was Ernest Hemingway's house at 907 Whitehead Street. In "A Key West Letter" written for the April 1935 *Esquire,* he declared himself besieged by sightseers, situated as he was "between Johnson's Tropical Grove (No. 17) and Lighthouse and Aviaries (No. 19)." It was "all very flattering to the easily bloated ego of your correspondent," he allowed, "but very hard on production."

So began Key West's career in tourism, with this recommendation to travelers, which was written by the federal agent in charge of the island's makeover: "To appreciate Key West with its indigenous architecture, its lanes and byways, its friendly people and general picturesqueness, the visitor must spend at least a few days in the city; a cursory tour of an hour or two serves no good purpose. Unless a visitor is prepared to spend at least three full days here, the Key West Administration would rather he did not come." ∎

Jugglers perform for the nightly gathering who come to Mallory Square to applaud the often fiery sunsets.

Mallory Square

HUNDREDS OF CRUISE SHIPS EASE UP TO MALLORY SQUARE Dock every year. Legions of voyagers are met here by purveyors of ice cream, sea shells, T-shirts, balloons, and baubles of every kind. In open-air bars, bartenders working rows of blenders pour bright-colored slurries of ice, fruit juice, and alcohol—Key West versions of the daiquiri and the piña colada—into goblets. There are magicians, jugglers, tap dancers, mimes, portrait artists, flame-eaters, musicians, fortune-tellers—even an occasional tightrope walker.

Mallory Square
www.mallorysquare.com
Map p. 206

SUNSET WATCHING

The ritual of gathering to cheer the sun's descent into the Gulf of Mexico entered Key West lore in the 1960s at Mallory Square. The sunsets are indeed spectacular—Audubon rhapsodized over them in his journal, nearly running out of adjectives—but the carnival atmosphere of Mallory Square's Sunset Celebration is not for everyone. ■

There are freelance tour guides on pedal-powered jitneys eager to take you away, but don't leave too quickly, as there is much of interest here. The square commemorates Stephen Mallory, a Key Wester who, in 1861, served as secretary of the Confederacy's short-lived navy. Set back off Front and Greene Streets is the red and terra-cotta brick Customs House, Florida's premier example of Romanesque Revival architecture, a vogue of America's Gilded Age. Now home to the **Key West Museum of Art & History** *(tel 305/295-6616, www.kwahs.com/customhouse.htm, $$)*, it was built in the 1880s and served as a post office and federal

courthouse, where Key West's cadre of judges set salvage law precedents. The smaller brick edifice adjoining it is the island's oldest naval structure, completed in 1856 to cache coal for ships' boilers. The florid **First National Bank Building** nearby owes its gaudy brickwork and intricate facade to the tastes of the 19th-century Cuban cigar-makers who commissioned it.

Fronting the square is Key West's oldest commercial edifice, built of coral rock quarried from the site it occupies. Originally used for storing ice, it's now the Shell Warehouse, a bazaar-in-a-building filled with the delicate cacophony of wind chimes for sale within. ■

Mel Fisher Maritime Heritage Society

 Map p. 206
✉ 200 Greene St.
☎ 305/294-2633
www.melfisher.org
$ $$

CAPTAIN GEIGER WASN'T THE ONLY KEY WEST ENTREPRE-
neur to make himself wealthy through salvage (see p. 219). In recent
times the most successful salvor, albeit at bitter personal cost, was
the late Mel Fisher, whose quest for a pair of Spanish treasure galleons
sunk in a 1622 hurricane is part of local folklore.

The *Nuestra Señora de Atocha* and
the *Santa Margarita* eluded Fisher
for 16 years, but on July 20, 1985,
his divers found treasure valued at
400 million dollars.

It's a short walk from Mallory
Square to "Treasure Exhibit" at
Front and Greene Streets, where
newly recovered loot is exhibited.
Here you'll find a modest sampling
of the gold, silver, jewelry, and rare
nautical artifacts recovered from
the two shipwrecks, which lay scattered at depths nearing 60 feet.
There are gold and silver ingots,
intricate gold chains stretching

nearly 9 feet, uncut emeralds of
colossal size, and ornate jeweled
crucifixes. One exhibit permits you
to grasp a seven-pound gold bar;
another displays a 77-carat raw
emerald worth a quarter-million
dollars. Historical exhibits tantalize
with promises of greater finds,
while others present the sobering
reality of treasure hunting: breath-
taking expense, years of back-
breaking labor, and the innate
perils of working underwater.
(Early in the quest, Fisher lost a
son and daughter-in-law when
their ship capsized.) ∎

**Mel Fisher was
Key West's best
known treasure-
hunter.**

**Recovered
Spanish treasure**

Exploring Old Key West

The best way to see Old Key West is on foot—so that all of your senses get to take in all of the sights, sounds, and smells. But there are also other ways to experience Key West first-hand.

The most popular self-guided tour is the 25-block Pelican Path, mapped out by the Old Island Restoration Foundation, which acquaints you with a dozen streets and 50 architecturally significant and historic buildings in the city. Pick up "A Guide to Historic Key West on the 'Pelican Path'" at the Chamber of Commerce (*402 Wall St., tel 305/294-2587, www.keywestchamber.org*) where the walk begins and ends. The free brochure is also available at the Wreckers Museum (*322 Duval St.*), or contact the Old Island Restoration Foundation for more information (*tel 305/294-9501, www.oirf.org*). The walk takes several hours, including a stop for lunch along the way. Most buildings are privately owned and not open to visitors; however, in February and March, during the Old Island Days celebration, the foundation offers several guided themed house and garden tours.

The Cuban Heritage Trail is another intriguing walk featuring nearly 40 houses, buildings, and locales, all of them historical footnotes to the history of the island's Cuban connections. For this you'll need the guide and map, available free from the Historic Florida Keys Foundation (*510 Greene St., tel 305/292-6718, www.historicfloridakeys.org*). While you are here, have a look at the excellent annotated map of Key West's historic district, a well-researched guide to the relics of island history, which includes a driving tour of the Overseas Highway up to Key Largo. Included are evocative descriptions of Pigeon Key and the Bat Tower on Sugarloaf Key. You'll also find a brochure you can use to visit the historic cemetery (*Tours Tues. & Thurs. at 9:30 a.m. by volunteers, from the sexton's office at the Margaret St. entrance, tel 305/292-6718*). The cemetery is also covered in Sharon Wells's free, widely available "Walking & Biking Guide to Historic Key West." Her website, www.seekeywest.com, includes several of the tours, as well as information on guided tours (*tel 305/294-8380*).

As an alternative to walking, board the Conch Train for a 90-minute, 14-mile narrated island tour. This gasoline-powered, open-air trolley, pulled by a tractor fancifully disguised as a miniature locomotive, leaves from Mallory Square at 303 Front Street every half hour (*9:30 a.m.–4:30 p.m., tel 305/294-5161, www.conchtourtrain.com, $$–$$$$$*). You can also board at Flagler Station at 901 Caroline Street.

Similar to the Conch is the Old Town Trolley, small, trolleylike buses that depart from the square at Roosevelt Boulevard on the half hour (*9 a.m.–4:30 p.m., tel 305/296-6688, www.trolleytours.com/Key-West*). The 90-minute tours take a somewhat different route, and allow you to disembark at any stop, and continue when you wish by catching a later trolley. ∎

The Conch Republic

On April 20, 1982, the U.S. Border Patrol, seeking to catch undocumented aliens and drug runners, blocked the Overseas Highway below Florida City. Motorists were asked to prove U.S. citizenship, and their vehicles were searched. The resulting traffic jam was a public relations disaster, and Keys residents were outraged at being treated like criminal suspects. After three days, Key West officials announced the island's secession from the Union. A raucous Mallory Square rally proclaimed Key West an independent nation to be known as the Conch Republic. A Conch flag was raised, visas and border passes were issued, and Conch currency was printed. The rebel nation then promptly "surrendered," requested U.S. foreign aid, and partied for a week. The Conch Spring is commemorated every April during the week-long Conch Republic Independence Celebration. ∎

Above: Tin roofs, plantation shutters, and clapboard siding typify Old Key West buildings.
Below: The popular Conch Train departs for an island-wide sight-seeing trip.

Audubon House & Tropical Gardens

JUST OFF MALLORY SQUARE IS A HANDSOME, WHITE-painted, three-story house at the corner of Whitehead and Greene Streets, situated amid a lush, neatly tended garden of trees, plants, and flowering bushes, a tropical garden some insist is Florida's finest.

It is arguably the most elegant historic house on the island, filled with a marvelously attractive mix of period domestic furnishings and decorative pieces—paintings, porcelains, clothing, children's dolls, and toys. Its name, however, is misleading; the house's connection with the famed ornithologist and painter of wild birds is sentimental, not historical.

John James Audubon, who briefly visited Key West and the Dry Tortugas in 1832, never stayed here; the house was home to John Geiger, a sea captain who, like many Key West residents, made a fortune salvaging cargo from ships wrecked on the Florida Reef. He built this immaculately maintained residence for his family some time in the 1830s. His heirs lived here for more than 120 years, until 1958. Its prox-

imity to Mallory Square brought the threat of demolition, thwarted by local preservationists who refurbished the building and its garden as a museum to commemorate Audubon's stay in Key West. The restoration of the house inaugurated a movement to save other historically significant Key West buildings.

Visitors are free to wander throughout the spacious manse. The children's room on the top floor is filled with toys from the 1830s, including two pairs of antique roller skates. Throughout the house are original Audubon engravings and paintings, and, on the second floor, porcelains with motifs of birds and wildlife. The brick-laid garden, stippled with orchids and with a nursery maintained in the style of the 1840s, is a lovely spot in which to linger. ∎

Above: Table settings like these were often the spoils of salvage. Opposite: The prosperous Geiger family home

Audubon House & Tropical Gardens
www.audubonhouse.com

🅰 Map p. 206
✉ 205 Whitehead St. at Greene St.
☎ 305/294-2116
💲 $$. Audio tours available.

Caroline Street

THERE ARE MANY FINE REASONS FOR STROLLING THIS picturesque core sample of Old Key West, which runs from the President's Gate to Truman Annex on upper Whitehead Street, and to the waterfront clutter of Key West Bight. Across the street from the ceremonial entrance to the old Navy base (opened only for the Commander in Chief and ranking dignitaries) is a white-painted, much renovated clapboard house that once headquartered Aeromarine Airways.

In the early 1920s the pioneering airline flew passengers and bags of mail aboard ex-Navy Curtiss F5-L coastal patrol flying boats to Cuba. Each carried a homing pigeon in the event of a ditching at sea. Aeromarine's inaugural hop to Havana, on November 1, 1920, established one of America's first officially recognized international air mail routes. The seaplane company located here as it was near the waterfront—Navy landfill eventually extended the island several hundred yards to the old Navy submarine pens, now a posh marina and promenade. Aeromarine charged $50 for the 105-mile flight to Havana, which, depending upon winds and weather, took from 90 minutes to two hours. (Passage aboard a Mallory

Key West Lighthouse

At night, the treetops in Ernest Hemingway's yard would catch the light from the old Key West Lighthouse, just down Whitehead Street. The stocky tower, originally 57 feet tall, went on duty in 1848, tended by a lighthouse keeper who lived with his family in a pretty clapboard cottage near its base. (Local salvors, however, were not amused; the navigational aid meant fewer wrecks and the decline of their trade.) As the island's trees and buildings grew taller, masons returned to increase the tower's height. It was eventually raised to 92 feet, allowing mariners to see it from every compass point.

The light went out in 1969, replaced by automated beacons installed elsewhere, but you can climb the 88-step steel spiral staircase inside the tower to its encircling catwalk. The 360-degree panorama is splendidly photogenic, even though it's not the highest in town. That honor belongs to the Top, a lounge on top of the seven-story Crowne Plaza Key West La Concha *(430 Duval St., tel 305/296-2991)*. The keeper's 1887 house is so thoroughly refurbished it looks brand new. It is filled with ship models, nautical charts, old photographs, and antique equipment from retired lighthouses throughout the Keys. There are a few artifacts from the U.S.S. *Maine,* which took on coal in the Dry Tortugas before steaming south to its explosive fate in Havana Harbor in 1898 (see p. 231). The beacon's original Fresnel lens is here as well, demonstrating the ability of its ingenious geometry to amplify a lantern's flicker into a lifesaving beacon visible far out at sea. ■

**Key West
Lighthouse &
Keeper's Quarters
Museum**
www.kwahs.com/lighthouse
.htm

Map. p. 206

938 Whitehead St.

305/295-6616

$$

San Carlos Institute

Until 1961, when Cuba and the Unites States severed diplomatic relations, Havana supported the San Carlos Institute, a political and social center. In its youth it was also an opera house, with what some insist is the South's most acoustically perfect hall. The Cuban patriot José Martí (see p. 231) spoke words from its balcony that still arouse Miami's expatriate Cuban community. The San Carlos is back in business as a museum and archive whose focus is the role of Cubans in Key West history and culture.

The institute's first permanent building went up in 1884 on Fleming Street, named for Carlos Manuel de Cespedes, a Cuban plantation owner credited with the revolutionary slogan "Cuba libre!"—now more associated with a tall iced glass of rum and coke. On weekends the stirring hour-long documentary *Nostalgia Cubano,* about Cuba from the thirties to the fifties, is screened. The social unrest that led to Castro's overthrow of the Batista regime is obscured by the film's gorgeous images of Cuba's still-vibrant culture. Be sure to look into the theater, whose backdrop paintings have been painstakingly restored to their original splendor. The lobby is decorated with beautifully detailed, hand-painted Spanish majolica tiles. There are also exquisite hand-colored prints of Cuban wildfowl and fascinating historical exhibits. ■

**San Carlos
Institute**
www.institutosancarlos.org

Map p. 206

516 Duval St.

305/294-3887

Open Fri.–Sun.,
noon–6 p.m.
Closed a.m. and
Mon.–Thurs.

$

**Above: The
old Key West
Lighthouse**

Hemingway Home & Museum

WHEN ERNEST HEMINGWAY AND PAULINE PFEIFFER SET UP
housekeeping in December 1931, this was the only house in Key West
with a basement, created when the coral bedrock for its walls was
quarried there. Set back a hundred feet on a deep one-acre corner lot
among banyan trees, date palms, sago, and palmetto, it is one of the
island's most distinctive houses, a two-story villa with thick limestone
walls, mansard roof, French windows, tall green shutters, and encircling iron-railed balconies.

**Hemingway Home
& Museum**
www.hemingwayhome.com
🅜 Map p. 206
✉ 907 Whitehead St.
☎ 305/294-1136
💲 $$

When the Hemingways bought
it (for $8,000), it was a decrepit
ruin known as the Asa Tift House,
named for the shipbuilder who built
it in 1851. Hemingway—or more
accurately his wealthy spouse—set
to restoring the house into a ser-
vant-staffed domestic enclave and
a creative sanctuary for a mercurial
genius, whose application to his
craft was so intense that the writing
of 500 words could leave him physi-
cally drained. Hemingway needed
undisturbed quiet, and found it in a
study installed above the backyard
carriage house. Pauline (a former
Paris correspondent for *Vogue*)
spent $20,000 to create a 65-foot-
long saltwater swimming pool out
of the site's limestone bedrock, a
breathtaking extravagance in
Depression-era Key West.

Right: Hemingway's stylish second wife added formal furnishings and decorations to their Key West mansion.

He lived in the house until his divorce from Pauline in 1940. During his 12 years in Key West (eight of them at this address) his life of writing, famously mixed with interludes of fishing, hunting, drinking, travel, war reporting, and romance, produced much of his best work, including *Death in the Afternoon*, *The Green Hills of Africa*, *To Have and Have Not*, and an enduring collection of extraordinary short stories, most notably "The Short Happy Life of Francis Macomber" and "The Snows of Kilimanjaro."

For those fascinated by Hemingway's prose and near-mythic life, there's magic in the air as they pass through the brick wall surrounding the house. Guided half-hour tours roam the house, which holds some of Hemingway's furniture and fixtures, including ornate Venetian glass chandeliers that Pauline installed in the dining room to replace ceiling fans she considered unattractive. There is a small bookstore featuring Hemingway's work and a souvenir shop. These

additions give the downstairs a slightly institutional look that disappoints some aficionados. Better, perhaps, to wander the grounds on your own and ponder the master's red-tiled, book-lined, backyard aerie, little changed from his days of solitary labor seated on a cigar-maker's chair at a small circular drop-leaf table. The period Smith-Corona, however, is misleading; Hemingway wrote almost exclusively in longhand and had others type his manuscripts. ■

Key West bight

Desperate characters prowled Old Town's waterfront in Hemingway's gritty hard-times novel *To Have and Have Not*. The boardwalks are the last vestige of those days—but perhaps not for long, as renovations progress. They call it the Harborwalk now, and you should take it, wandering docks where treasure hunting ships moor alongside charter boats and pleasure yachts. ■

Duval Street

NAMED FOR THE FIRST GOVERNOR OF THE FLORIDA Territory, Duval Street has everything, from Spanish silver pieces of eight and jewels salvaged from sunken galleons to designer sunglasses and cookies. There are probably more T-shirts and bikinis for sale along its Old Town stretch than on any other six blocks in the United States. There is fast food and there are attempts at haute cuisine, but most eateries fall somewhere in between, made pleasant if not memorable simply because they are in Key West.

Until the 1920s, Duval Street was dirt. Bricks were laid during the islanders' Depression-era campaign to dress up the town for tourism. When the street was finally paved in the 1930s, many of the bricks ended up in the wall around Hemingway's home. Older Conchs remember when Duval was a street of raucous bars. They speak fondly of vanished flophouse hotels and Cuban cafés and cigarmakers' homes, and of seeing movies at the old **Strand Theater** (527 Duval St.). Built by Cuban artisans in 1918, it later held **Ripley's Believe It or Not!** until the museum of the absurd moved to 108 Duval Street. The Strand Theater's facade remains as the front of a Walgreen's. Conchs remember the days when Duval was a street that intimidated more visitors than it amused, and they miss them.

Today Duval is a street of friendlier but no less noisy bars, filled mainly with tourists and vacationing students instead of out-of-work railroaders, sunburned fishermen, and merchant mariners looking for a ship. You can drive Duval in minutes, but you really ought to walk it, from Mallory Square to Truman Avenue, where the retail frenzy peters out. Depending on your mood and attitude toward the free market system, Duval will strike you as either horribly fascinating or fascinatingly horrible. During spring break, college students swarm into town, swilling beer, margaritas, and

piña coladas and buzzing around on mopeds whose tiny, snarling two-cycle engines are the bane of the island. If you want to be treated with respect by anyone over the age of 19, rent a bicycle not a moped.

Between Greene and Caroline Streets, Duval is a street of bars, saloons, pubs, and more bars. **Sloppy Joe's,** at 201 Duval Street (www.sloppyjoes.com), is beat-up, popular, and usually crowded with tourists examining the many photographs of Hemingway, long ago a regular of the original Sloppy Joe's around the corner at 428 Greene Street—a location now occupied by **Captain Tony's Saloon,** another vintage spirit house (www.capttonyssaloon.com). Sloppy Joe was Joe Russell, a sometime rumrunner described by Hemingway biographer Carlos Baker as a "tough little slab-faced man," locally nicknamed Josie Grunts. Russell and Hemingway hit it off, and the author took to chartering Russell's 32-foot cabin cruiser for fishing trips. On one of these Hemingway had his first taste of marlin fishing, a sport that would enthrall him ever after. More importantly for literature, the author's observations of Russell eventually distilled into the tragic hero of one of Hemingway's short stories that evolved into the novel *To Have and Have Not.*

On the southwest corner of Duval and Caroline Streets stands

Duval Street
🗺 Map. p. 206

Wrecker's Museum
www.oirf.org
✉ 322 Duval St.
☎ 305/294-9502
💲 $$

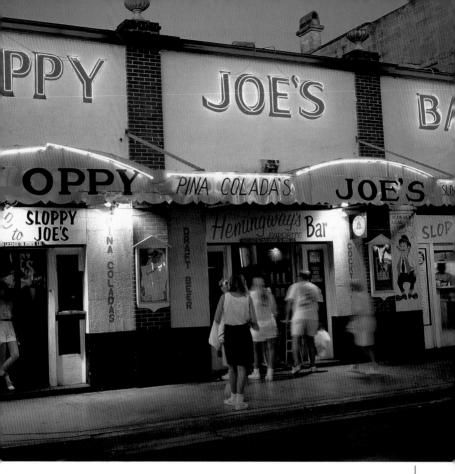

the **Joseph Porter House** (*No. 10 on the Pelican Path home tour),* one of the island's best examples of conch architecture's peculiar blend of New England, Bahamian, and creole styles. Though part private, the lower level is occupied by a pair of boutiques, permitting you to linger outside on the veranda. The graceful home is named for a physician, born here in 1847, who did pioneering work in the prevention and treatment of yellow fever, and was Florida's first public health officer. He died here at the age of 80, in the same room in which he was born.

Just down the street is the **Wrecker's Museum,** which occupies another conch classic known as Key West's Oldest House.

This white clapboard building is a classic example of an early resident's home. (Its original occupant was a sea captain, Francis Watlington.) Built in 1829 on Whitehead Street, it was moved here three years later (something done fairly often in those days), and set atop 3-foot-high pier posts to keep it dry when storm surges flooded the downtown area. The little museum occupies six rooms, displaying 18th- and 19th-century antiques, model ships, and exhibits explaining how "wrecking" became not only a respectable trade here but, for a time, a fabulously lucrative one. Be sure to visit the backyard, where you'll find Key West's last outdoor kitchen, once common here. ∎

Under the roof of the original Sloppy Joe's, Hemingway met third wife Martha Gellhorn. Walls within are a picture gallery of the author's friendship with the bar's founder.

Amid the green kaleidoscope of Nancy's Old Town hideaway

Nancy Forrester's
Secret Garden

ONE BLOCK FROM DUVAL STREET IS A GORGEOUS ONE-acre botanical garden of extraordinary quality. This quarter-century labor of love overflows with orchids, ferns, bromeliads, cycads, flowering plants, vines, and more than 150 species of palm.

**Nancy Forrester's
Secret Garden**
www.nfsgarden.org
🅰 Map. p. 206
✉ 1 Free School Lane,
off Simonton St.
between Fleming &
Southard Sts.
☎ 305/294-0015
💲 $$

Nancy Forrester's garden is not really secret, of course, but you'll feel a sense of discovery as you venture down Free School Lane to her private jungle. You might want to stay, and you can, for in the garden's heart is an exquisitely renovated little antique cottage, suitable for two. The garden is open daily from mid-morning to evening, after which it becomes a secluded retreat for the cottage's tenants. You can rent the air-conditioned house, which has a screened-in porch, for an overnight stay, or for a week or a month. Walking from Duval to Nancy's along Fleming Street you pass **Key West Island Bookstore** *(513 Fleming St., tel 305/294-2904),* perhaps Key West's premier vendor of new and fine used books. Admirably loyal to the island's literary cadre, past and present, it displays their portraits and stocks their books, some of which you'll find in the rare book room. ∎

Key West Cemetery

LIKE MANY THINGS ORIGINALLY LOCATED ELSEWHERE IN Key West, the city's burial ground was moved (a consequence of an 1846 hurricane that flooded the grounds and opened graves) to the edge of Old Town, in a quiet neighborhood of cottages, some elegantly refurbished, others untouched by a paintbrush in decades.

Generations of Key West's founding families rest here.

Because the "new" cemetery lies atop coral rock and a shallow water table, its graves are above-ground vaults reminiscent of New Orleans' crypts. Key West's mordant humor is evident in its epitaphs: "I told you I was sick," one scolds. Mourning stone angels, downcast swans, and melancholy lambs grieve over untimely ends: "The Day is Gone and Tomorrow Shall Never Be Mine." Within a small fenced enclosure, surrounding a flagpole styled like a ship's mast and a stalwart stone sailor with oar held at the ready, are the graves of 22 Navy tars who died when the U.S.S. *Maine* exploded in Havana Harbor in 1898, igniting the Spanish-American War.

There is a separate monument commemorating Cubans who died fighting for their island's independence from Spain, and a section of Jewish graves, the diversity of monuments revealing chapters of Key West's cultural history not evident elsewhere. If your schedule permits, take a guided tour with one of the knowledgeable volunteer members of the Historic Florida Keys Foundation, starting from the sexton's office at the Margaret Street entrance. The walk takes 90 minutes and is wisely conducted before the sun begins to broil the unshaded gravel lanes. Gates are open sunrise to sunset. ∎

Key West Cemetery

- 🗺 Map p. 206
- ✉ Angela, Frances, Olivia, & Windsor Sts.
- ☎ 305/292-6718 or 305/292-6829
- 🕐 Open daily. Tours Tues. & Thurs. at 9:30 a.m.

Key West's Cuban heritage

By 1890 Key West was Florida's wealthiest city. Among its leading citizens were Cuban bankers, shippers, and cigar manufacturers. They were joined by hundreds of self-exiled Cubans opposed to Spain's colonial rule and led by the charismatic José Martí, who adopted Key West as the base of his Partido Revolucionario Cubano. In early April 1895, Martí and Gen. Máximo Gómez set off from Santo Domingo for their homeland's coast, sparking Cuba's War of Independence. All but forgotten after decades of antipathy between Washington and Havana is the fact that Key West was once known as the Cradle of Cuban Independence. ∎

West Martello Tower

WEST MARTELLO TOWER HAS A RATHER TUMBLE-DOWN appearance that stems from a time when Army artillerymen at Fort Zachary Taylor across the island used the construction for target practice. Built as a coastal lookout and battery in 1861, it survived this not-so-friendly fire to serve again as a lookout during the Spanish-American War, and is now in the kinder hands of the Key West Garden Club, which has filled it with plants, books on horticulture, and artworks, and every spring hosts an orchid show here. The old sentinel's greenery is a living encyclopedia of tropical plants and orchids that adjoins a pleasant beach. Its opening times vary; if it's closed when you come by, call for information.

West Martello Tower
www.keywestgardenclub.com
 Map p. 207
 Atlantic Blvd. & White St.
☎ 305/294-3210

PLAYWRIGHT'S RETREAT

From the tower, White Street leads inland to Old Town, a pleasant route through vintage neighborhoods that ends a few short blocks from the Mallory Square area. En route, take a four-minute side trip off White Street by turning right onto Duncan Street for a drive-by look at the unassuming but inviting compound at No. 1431, once the home of Tennessee Williams. The writer of *A Streetcar Named Desire* owned it from 1949 until his death in 1983. It is not open to the public;

however, the author's stature as one of America's most gifted playwrights makes the two-story Bahamian-style house an intriguing sight. Williams added a writing studio and a swimming pool to the backyard, and lived and wrote enjoyably and productively here. The house, near Leon Street, was used as a set during the filming of Williams' play *The Rose Tattoo* (1955), which starred Burt Lancaster and Anna Magnani. Even in black and white, Williams' vision of Key West looks sultry and overheated. ■

Southernmost Point & the Southernmost House

Cuba lies some 90 miles beyond the posing couple.

IF YOU PEER SOUTH DOWN DUVAL STREET, YOU WILL SEE AT its end the bright blue of sea and sky, where at high tide the Atlantic splashes against a concrete barrier erected to keep people from driving onto South Beach. Duval dead-ends beside a large, buoy-shaped, concrete marker proclaiming this the southernmost point of the United States. Across the intersection stands a magnificent turreted Queen Anne-style manse, a museum and inn flanked by palms and known as the Southernmost House. The house and the marker make for memorable and dramatic photographs, but Southernmost Point isn't really what it claims to be.

Key West's farthest reach toward Cuba is a knob of land about a half-mile west, inside the U.S. Naval Base and thus off-limits to the public. That this distinction is claimed by a part of the island denied to most citizens of the Conch Republic offends local sensibilities. And as the difference between fact and fiction is a matter of only a few hundred feet, it strikes most as a technicality only the hopelessly unromantic would raise. Never mind that a far humbler house at the intersection of Whitehead and South Street one block west is itself more southerly than the handsome Victorian at Duval's end. The actual southernmost point on American soil is far, far from here in the Hawaiian Islands, on a latitude shared with Mexico City. However, we are speaking of the continental United States. Yet, on days when the surf runs high, seawater surges onto the street, wetting the tires of passing vehicles and adding an aura of credibility to the notion that this is where America ends and the Caribbean begins. ∎

Southernmost Point
 Map p. 206

Southernmost House
www.southernmosthouse.com
✉ 1400 Duval St.
☎ 305/296-3141

Dry Tortugas National Park

A FEW WEEKS AFTER ARRIVING IN KEY WEST IN 1928, Ernest Hemingway hired a guide and boat and led two friends on a fishing trip to the Dry Tortugas, a 7-mile-long archipelago of seven low-lying sandy coral spits and crescents about 68 miles west of Key West. He would return many times, captivated by the Tortugas' desert-island wildness, star-filled nights, swirling seabird populations, and vivid, clear waters teeming with fish. There was also the astonishing ruin of Fort Jefferson, a 16-million-brick colossus started in 1846 and never completed, still the largest brick fortress in the Western Hemisphere.

Here, in 1930, Hemingway, his legendary editor Maxwell Perkins, and three others spent 17 happily storm-bound days casting lines in the blue lagoon lying beneath the fort's mammoth guns. There is a photograph of the writer and the editor standing near the old fort's entrance, the gun ports behind them as empty as the eyes of a skull. If you stand there today, nothing in the background will have changed much, nor for that matter anything within the vast blue line of the encircling horizon.

In 1992 the islands were made the centerpiece of one of America's newest and most unusual national parks, a bird and marine life sanctuary whose 100 square miles enclose some of the healthiest coral reefs remaining off North American

shores. Unless you take the 40-minute hop by seaplane, a visit to the Tortugas requires a full day, about half of it spent aboard one of the excursion boats that make the three-hour voyage from Key West. Either way, it will be a day you will not forget.

It should be noted that only 85 acres of this 65,000-acre park are above water, and that your visit will land you on 16-acre **Garden Key,** 11 acres of which are claimed by Fort Jefferson's massive hexagon. Three easterly islands are little more than sand spits, and the two isles adjoining Garden Key, **Bush Key** and **Long Key,** are both wildlife refuges, Long being permanently off-limits. (In recent years, a sand bar has connected Bush and Garden Keys). The Tortugas end 3 miles west with 30-acre **Loggerhead Key,** where, since 1858, a 151-foot-high lighthouse has warned mariners away from reefs and shoals known

Construction of Fort Jefferson increased Garden Key's area nearly by half. A moat and seawall constructed as a killing ground now nurtures abundant sea life.

Dry Tortugas National Park
www.nps.gov/drto
✉ P.O. Box 6208, Key West, FL 33041
☎ 305/242-7700
$ $$

to have claimed more than 200 ships since the 1600s.

GARDEN KEY

Garden Key is the place to be. Its tree-shaded picnic area adjoins a lovely swimming beach of soft white sand that slants gently down into crystalline shallows, deep enough near the shore to invite those who haven't snorkeled before. Behind the fort's seawall, depths increase to about six feet, supporting sea-grass "meadows" where brightly colored tropical fish dart about.

Allow at least an hour to explore ghostly **Fort Jefferson,** built to anchor American control of the Straits of Florida. Proclaimed the Gibraltar of the Gulf, it still looks the part: eight-foot-thick walls rising 50 feet, forming a

hexagon whose 2,000 massive brick arches support three tiers of gun emplacements running a half-mile around and designed for 450 guns, including huge Rodmans able to heave a 300-pound shell 3 miles. But the fort was a fiasco in almost every sense, literally cracking apart under its own weight as the island's crumbly coral rock gave way underneath. Fortunately, the citadel's intimidating bulk spared it from being tested in battle.

Undermanned, and with only one gun operational when the Civil War broke out, the garrison answered a Confederate navy demand to surrender with a threat to blow it out of the water. A 450-gun barrage would have certainly been lethal, had the dark gun ports concealed anything

A hypnotizing view down a second-floor gun deck corridor

Fort Jefferson's 19th-century iron-plate lighthouse, now retired, rises above the visitor center. A beacon on nearby Loggerhead Key alerts mariners to the Tortugas' reefs and shoals.

but a few soldiers peering out apprehensively at the rebel fleet. The Confederates prudently retreated, then sailed away forever, leaving the lonely outpost to serve mainly as a prison for Union deserters. After the war, the inmates included four men convicted of complicity in Abraham Lincoln's murder. One was the hapless physician Samuel Mudd who—unknowingly, he insisted—set the broken leg of the assassin John Wilkes Booth.

After 30 years of intermittent construction, the citadel fell in 1874 to yellow fever, the ravages of a hurricane, and the new rifled cannon, which rendered even those eight-foot-thick walls obsolete. Revived in 1898 as a Navy coaling station, the fort was permanently abandoned in 1907.

When you arrive, take a look at dockside announcement boards for ranger-led activities. If you intend to camp, check campground availability immediately, as the sites are allotted on a first-come, first-served basis. The **visitor center** is just inside the fort entrance, and a Florida National Parks and Monuments Association bookstore opens upon request. Take a few minutes to view an orientation videotape on a self-operated VCR, then follow interpretive signs on a self-guided tour of Fort Jefferson's impressive architecture and park-like parade ground.

Granite spiral staircases lead to open-air battlements and a 360-degree panorama that's ideal for binocular-aided bird-watching. (The Tortugas' populations of terns, cormorants, gulls, boobies, plovers, pelicans, peregrine falcons, and twin-tailed frigate birds induced ornithologist and painter John James Audubon to sail out from Key West in 1832 to study them.) If you stroll the grassy parapet you will find several burly Civil War-era coastal guns on display near the fort's long-retired 19th-century lighthouse. To sit up here and watch dark frigate birds swoop by, riding the wind currents on graceful, slender wings, is a sublime experience.

SNORKELING

It would be a shame to travel this far and deny yourself the experience of snorkeling here. The ferry services try to keep a few goggles, snorkels, and flippers on hand for loan, but it is better to bring your own if you have them. If you prefer not to go in the water, pick up a copy of the brochure entitled "Walking the Seawall," and then do exactly that: stroll the 0.6-mile-long brick wall enclosing Fort Jefferson's defensive moat, a sheltered habitat adopted by the queen conch, yellow stingray, gray snapper, and other creatures.

The island's best close-to-shore snorkeling is on the sea side of the wall, in chest-deep water covering a sandy shoal thick with sea fans, brain coral, and turtle grass, and patrolled by many of the 442 species of fish identified here. If you have a companion or can enlist one for mutual safety, consider paddling from the campground's swimming beach along the wall, where fish tend to congregate. Watch for barracuda, which, though seldom aggressive, are territorial and should be given a wide berth.

Thanks to a sand bar that has developed in recent years, you can walk to Bush Key's primordial garden of bay cedar, seagrape, mangrove, sea oats, and prickly pear cactus—a landscape exactly like the one Spanish explorer Juan Ponce de León encountered when he first dropped anchor here in 1513. Ponce de León found the waters

teeming with turtles—greens, hawksbills, leatherbacks, and loggerheads—and so named these *cayos* las Tortugas. The turtles are now scarce, decimated by four centuries of over-hunting, but every year between March and September an estimated 100,000 sooty and noddy terns return to Bush Key to roost in sandy nests. (During these months, Bush is closed to visitors.)

HOW TO GET THERE

Access to the Dry Tortugas is by boat or floatplane, and is subject to weather conditions. If you are contemplating a visit, call the Dry Tortugas National Park headquarters *(tel 305/242-7700)* for current information and a list of authorized air taxi and charter boat companies serving the islands, then contact carriers directly. Be aware, however, that the Dry Tortugas administrative center is actually located at Everglades National Park *(40001 Fla. 9336, Homestead, tel 305/242-7700)*. There is currently no park office in Key West, but inquiries may be addressed to P.O. Box 6208, Key West, FL 33041-6208.

Boat passage from Key West takes about three hours. Private boaters should refer to NOAA (National Oceanic and Atmospheric Administration) Chart No. 11434 ("Sombrero Key Dry Tortugas") and Chart No. 11438 ("Dry Tortugas"). There are no public boat moorings or slips; private boats must anchor offshore in designated areas. The crossing should be attempted only by seasoned, fully equipped mariners in appropriate and sea-

Snorkelers explore pellucid shallows off Loggerhead Key and its Civil War-era lighthouse. The island is being stripped of nonnative trees and vegetation and returned to an approximation of its natural state.

By far the greater part of the Dry Tortugas National Park is underwater, so the best way to explore is by diving or snorkeling.

worthy craft, as these waters are often shallow and subject year-round to strong winds that can bring rough seas. If you go by air, expect round-trip fares of about $229 per person for a half-day idyll (which is rushing it), and around $405 for a day-long stay *(Sea Planes of Key West, tel 305/294-0709)*. Excursion boat round-trips typically cost in the neighborhood of $120 *(Fast Cat II, tel 800/236-7937)*. Some include a buffet lunch; others don't, or charge extra for food, so check when booking.

The park is open year-round. Visitation peaks in spring, when advance boat or airplane reservations are advised. Only Garden Key is open for overnight stays; Loggerhead and Bush Keys open for day use only. Bush Key is closed from February to September (the migratory terns' nesting season). There is no admission fee for a day visit. Pets permitted only in the campground and must be leashed at all times.

CAMPING

Garden Key has ten primitive tree-shaded sites with picnic tables and grills, available on a first-come, first-served basis. There are compost toilets on the public dock. The park charges a small camping fee per person per night, with a 14-day limit. Groups of ten or more must obtain a special use permit in advance from the Dry Tortugas administrative center in Everglades National Park(see p. 237).

SPECIAL ADVICE

The dock, the visitor center, and the ground level of Fort Jefferson are wheelchair accessible, as is the campground. However,brick pathways in the fort and sandy soil in the campground may impede your mobility. It's a good idea to confirm charter boat and departure dock accessibility when you make reservations.

The Dry Tortugas are indeed dry: Except for one public drinking fountain, there is no fresh water available for campers and there are no showers. If you plan to camp, you must bring water, fuel, food, and supplies. Day-trippers should bring plenty of water, a swimsuit and towel, a sweater or jacket for the evening (the boat trip back can be breezy, damp, and cool), snorkeling equipment, and binoculars for bird-watching and scouting nearby islands. Experienced campers enthusiastically recommend the solar-heated shower—a durable plastic water bag with sprinkler attachment for rinsing off after swimming. Make sure you fill it in Key West.

A final note: For however long you choose to linger in this excellent little fragment of sub-tropical paradise, you will be beyond the reach of worldly cares, as there is no public telephone service to the Tortugas. ∎

Travelwise

Umbrellas, Miami Beach

TRAVELWISE INFORMATION

PLANNING YOUR TRIP

Miami has a strong image as a sunny, water-oriented resort with 354 square miles of coastal waters, 60 marinas, some 90,000 registered boats, nearly 12,000 acres of parks, and a mean annual temperature of 75°F.

The climate is unique, extremely tropical with hot muggy summers balanced by warm winters—70°F January days are quite common. But in winter cold snaps can plunge temperatures to a low of 50°F.

The period from November to mid-May is considered high season, when South Beach is at its most active with film and fashion shoots scheduled, and many of the major events take place. The weather is at its best, with hot days, cool evenings, and low humidity; but many hotel and car rental prices shoot up during this time, lowering by the end of May. May to October brings hotter, more humid weather, with frequent, heavy showers, but these are usually brief. Most tropical storms and hurricanes occur between August and November.

The average daytime temperature in the Keys is 78°F, with night temperatures about 66°F. Cool winds across the Atlantic and Gulf keep the heat down. Key West is also the driest city in Florida and sunny nearly year-round, although December and January are the coldest months of the year and temperatures can drop to the 50s.

GETTING TO MIAMI

BY AIR

Miami International Airport (MIA), tel 305/876-700

Centrally located about 7 miles northwest of Downtown Miami.

Tourist information counters are located outside the customs exits at the main information counter on the upper level on Concourse E, and on Concourse D and G on the lower level of the terminal.

BY TRAIN

Although Henry Flagler opened up Florida with the railroad, visitors are only now rediscovering the ease of rail travel, primarily on the east coast, with Amtrak's Silver Service from New York to Miami.

GETTING TO THE KEYS

BY AIR

There is frequent air service to both Key West and Marathon municipal airports from Miami International Airport, Orlando, Tampa, and Fort Lauderdale. Flights between Miami and Key West take 45 minutes.

BY CAR

From Miami International Airport, take LeJeune Road south to Fla. 836 west. This connects with the Fla. 821 west tollway, which will take you south to Florida City, where it leads into US 1. (See opposite for car rental details at Miami International Airport.)

It can feel as if you're on a ship as you cruise down US 1 over the 42 bridges linking the Keys with the mainland. On the driver's side are the turquoise waters of the Atlantic; on the passenger's side the bold blue of Florida Bay. From Key Largo to Key West this Overseas Highway is the only road to the Keys, and includes the famous Seven Mile Bridge.

Mile markers (MM) are small green signs beside the road, which start in South Miami at MM 126 and end at Key West at MM 0. Addresses along the way are followed by their mile marker location.

BY SHUTTLE

Visitors arriving at Miami International Airport can take a shuttle service to Key West, which stops at various points throughout the chain of islands. The trip to Key West takes about four-and-a-half hours. Departures from Miami International Airport are scheduled daily at 6:30 a.m., 12:45 p.m., 4:00 p.m., and 7:00 p.m. The round-trip costs around $36 to and from Marathon and around $70 to and from Key West. Or shuttle down and fly back.

Greyhound Keys Shuttle, tel 800/410-5397

GETTING AROUND

BY CAR

CAR RENTALS
Most rental companies operate off-site branches that are reached by shuttle from the airport terminals. If you are arriving at night, take a taxi to your hotel and arrange for the car rental firm to deliver a car to the hotel the next day.

Pick up a "Follow The Sun" guide at the airport information kiosks, car rental counters in baggage claim, or off-airport car rental facilities. The guide features special amplified maps and multilingual instructions that are designed to help get you to your destination.

When traveling around Greater Miami, watch for the Follow The Sun bright "sun" road signs. These will lead you to primary tourist destinations such as

Miami Beach, Coconut Grove, and Downtown Miami.

Alamo Rent A Car
3355 N.W. 22nd St., Miami, FL 33142, tel 305/633-4132 or 800/327-9633, www.alamo.com

Avis Rent-A-Car
2318 Collins Ave., Miami Beach, FL 33139, tel 305/538-4441 or 800/331-1212, www.avis.com

Budget Car and Truck Rental
3901 N.W. 28th St., Miami, FL 33142, tel 800/527-0700, www.budget.com

Dollar Rent-A-Car
Miami International Airport 3670 N.W. South River Dr., Miami, FL 33142, tel 866/434-2226, www.dollar.com

Enterprise Rent-A-Car
3975 N.W. South River Dr., Miami, FL 33142, tel 305/633-0377 or 800/325-8007, www.enterprise.com

Excellence Luxury Car Rental
3851 Bird Rd., Miami, FL 33146, tel 305/526-0000, www.excellenceluxury.com

Hertz Rent-A-Car
3795 N.W. 21st St., Miami, FL 33142, tel 305/871-0300 or 800/654-3131, www.hertz.com

National Car Rental
2301 N.W. 33 Ave., Miami, FL 33142, tel 305/423-2104, www.nationalcar.com

Royal Rent A Car
3650 NW South River Dr., Miami, FL 33166, tel 305/871-3000 or 800/314-8616 www.royalrentacar.com

Wheelchair-accessible van rentals
Wheelchair Getaways, 8 Bay Harbour Rd., Tequesta, FL 33469, tel 561/748-8414 or fax 561/748-8677

PARKING
The fine for an expired meter is $18; $45 if not paid within 30 calendar days.

Garages
Contact the Miami Parking Authority, 190 N.E. 3rd St. (Downtown Miami), for locations, rates, and hours of parking garages. (Open Mon.–Fri. 7:30 a.m.–5:30 p.m., tel 305/373-6789.)

Tow-away zones
If your car has been towed, contact the municipality where it was parked for further details. In Miami Beach call Beach Towing, tel 305/534-2128.

AAA EMERGENCY ROAD SERVICE
Members receive free towing and roadside service. Non-members can join over the phone, but existing members have priority. tel 800/222-4357, or 800/618-8734 in Miami.

TRANSPORTATION TO & FROM AIRPORT
Public transportation is not recommended for getting from the airport to your hotel. Buses heading downtown from the arrivals level are hourly, with poor connections.

SUPER SHUTTLE
2595 N.W. 38th St., Miami, FL 33142. tel 305/871-2000. A shared-ride van service to and from Miami International Airport. Reservations are required only for services to the airport. Per-person rates from MIA to hotels/attractions in the greater Miami area range from $15–$20.

TAXIS
From the airport to Downtown Miami, the trip is approximately 8 miles and costs about $18; Miami Beach is 14 miles and costs about $24; northern Miami Beach costs about $38. tel 305/375-2460 with any concerns, complaints, or comments about the taxi service.

Flamingo Taxi
198 N.W. 79th St., Miami, FL 33150, tel 305/759-8100

Florida Keys Taxi Dispatch
6631 Maloney Ave., Key West, FL 33040, tel 305/296-6666

Friendly Cab Co.
800 14th St., Key West, FL 33040, tel 305/295-5555

Metro Taxi
1995 N.E. 142nd St., North Miami, FL 33181, tel 305/888-8888

TRANSPORTATION IN & AROUND MIAMI
Metro-Dade Transit runs Miami's public transportation system. For information on Metrobus, MetroMover, and Metrorail routes and schedules, tel 305/770-3131. Information is also available on the website: www.co.miamidade.fl.us/transit. Tickets and tokens can be bought at any Metrorail station.

METROBUS
More than 19 routes serve Greater Miami and the Beaches. Fares are $1.50 each way, exact change only. Seniors, persons with disabilities, and students pay 75 cents with a bus permit or Medicare card.

METROMOVER
Miami's high-tech electric monorail with individual motorized cars runs atop a 4.4-mile elevated track looping around Downtown Miami and on

to the Brickell and Omni business districts. It offers great views of Biscayne Bay, and a cool, clean, comfortable ride. MetroMover operates every 90 seconds daily, from 6 a.m. to midnight. The MetroMover fare is free. It connects with Metrorail at Government Center and Brickell Avenue stations.

METRORAIL
Miami's very expensive and very underused rapid transit system, a 21-mile elevated rail system. Stations include Coconut Grove, Vizcaya, Brickell Avenue, and Government Center. Trains operate approximately every 20 minutes (5 minutes during peak hours), 6 a.m. to midnight. The fare is $1.50 (75 cents reduced fare); exact change only . Passengers can transfer directly onto MetroMover free of charge at Government Center and Brickell Avenue stations.

SOUTH BEACH LOCAL
The South Beach Local, operated by Miami-Dade Transit, is a bi-directional circular service to the entire South Beach area.
Mon.–Sat. 7:45 a.m.–1 a.m.
Sun. 10 a.m.–1 a.m.
For a map, visit www.miamibeachfl.gov/NEW CITY/sobe_local.asp

KEY WEST TRANSPORTATION

Driving can be more trouble than it is worth, especially around the narrow streets of the Old Town. It is far better to explore Key West on foot, or rent a bike or moped. Trolleys and trains are another way of getting around and seeing the sights.

Old Town Trolley Tours 1910 N. Roosevelt Blvd., Key West, FL 33040, tel 305/296-6688 or 800/868-7482, www.trolleytours.com/Key-West The Old Town Trolley fleet provides narrated tours of the city's historic landmarks.

Conch Tour Trains 1805 Staples Ave., Key West, FL 33040, tel 305/294-5161 or 800/868-7482, www.conchtourtrain.com The Conch Tour Trains consist of small canvas canopied cars that are pulled by tractors disguised as miniature locomotives, and tour all the historic sites.

PORT OF MIAMI CRUISES

Miami is known as the Cruise Capital of the World. The Port of Miami (tel 305/371-7678; www.co.miami-dade.fl.us /portofmiami) is the embarkation point for 15 cruise ships operated by 10 cruise lines—the world's largest year-round fleet. The port's 12 air-conditioned terminals offer duty-free shopping, wheelchair access, and ground-level customs clearance.

Cruise Travel Specialists Cruises Only, 150 N.W. 168th St., North Miami Beach, FL 33169, tel 305/653-6111.

PRACTICAL ADVICE

COMMUNICATIONS

NEWSPAPERS
The *Miami Herald* is South Florida's main newspaper. The Friday edition includes a good section on weekend events, restaurants, movies, music, and night life. Miami's alternative newspaper is the free weekly *New Times* with a comprehensive listing of restaurants, arts, and entertainment.

POST OFFICE
General Mail Facility 2200 N.W. 72nd Ave., Miami, FL 33126, tel 305/470-0222 or 800/275-8777. Call for postal information and branch locations.

BOOKS
South Florida has been the source of inspiration for many writers. The following are just a few of the authors who have set all or some of their work in South Florida.
John D. MacDonald, *The Deep Blue Goodbye* (Florida-based thriller); Elmore Leonard, *La Brava* (South Beach mystery); Carl Hiaasen, *Striptease* (by the famous *Miami Herald* columnist—great book, dumb movie); Jimmy Buffett, *Where is Joe Merchant?* (rock guitarist missing in the Keys); John Hersey, *Key West Tales* (short stories set in Key West); Tom McGuane, *92 in the Shade* (set in Key West); Ernest Hemingway, *To Have and Have Not* (famous Keys resident); and Marjorie Kinnan Rawlings, *The Yearling* (classic novel set in central Florida).

FISHING & HUNTING LICENSES

Tax Collector's Office 140 W. Flagler St., Room 101, Miami, tel 305/375-5452. Hunting, fishing, and saltwater fishing licenses are required and available at the above address, or some tackle shops, discount retail stores, and sporting goods stores. Nonresident licenses are valid for three to ten days; freshwater and saltwater licenses are valid three to seven days or for one year.

TRAVELERS WITH DISABILITIES

Miami-Dade Transit Agency, Special Transportation Service 2775 S.W. 74th Ave., Miami, FL 33155, tel 786/469-5000 Mon.–Fri. 8 a.m.–5 p.m.

Miami Lighthouse for the Blind 601 S.W. 8th Ave., Miami, FL 33130, tel 305/856-2288. Mon.–Fri. 8 a.m.–5 p.m.

Tri-Rail
A commuter rail line to West Palm Beach at the Tri-Rail/Metrorail Transfer station, near the Hialeah end of the Metrorail. All trains and stations are accessible via a ramp to travelers with disabilities; www.tri-rail.com.

VISITOR INFORMATION & RESERVATION SERVICES

Greater Miami Convention & Visitors Bureau
701 Brickell Ave., Suite 2700, Miami, FL 33131,
tel 305/539-3063,
www.TropicoolMiami.com

Miami Beach Chamber of Commerce
1920 Meridian Ave., #3A, Miami Beach, FL 33139,
tel 305/674-1300,
www.miamibeachchamber.com

Miami Visitor Center at Aventura Mall
19501 Biscayne Blvd., Aventura, FL 33180, tel 305/935-3836

Miami Visitor Center at Bayside Marketplace
401 N. Biscayne Blvd., Miami, FL 33132, tel 305/539-8070

Sunny Isles Beach Resort Association Visitor Information Center
16701 Collins Ave., Suite 219, Sunny Isles, FL 33160,
tel 305/947-5826

Tropical Everglades Visitor Association
160 US 1, Florida City, FL 33030, tel 305/245-9180,
www.tropicaleverglades.com

Greater Fort Lauderdale Convention & Visitors Bureau,
100 East Broward Blvd., Ste. 200, Fort Lauderdale, FL 33301, tel 954/765-4466 or 800/22-SUNNY, www.sunny.org

Key Largo Chamber of Commerce/Florida Keys Visitor Center
106000 Overseas Hwy., Key Largo, FL 33037, tel 305/451-1414 or 800/822-1088,
www.Floridakeys.org

Islamorada Chamber of Commerce
82185 Overseas Hwy., Islamorada, FL 33036, tel 305/664-4503 or 800/322-5397, www.fla-keys.com

Marathon Chamber of Commerce
12222 Overseas Hwy., Marathon, FL 33050, tel 305/743-5417 or 800/262-7284, www.floridakeysmarathon.com

Lower Keys Chamber of Commerce
MM31/Overseas Hwy., Big Pine Key, FL 33043, tel 305/872-2411 or 800/872-3722, www.lowerkeyschamber.com

Key West Welcome Center
3840 N. Roosevelt Blvd., Key West, FL 33040, tel 305/296-4444 or 800/284-4482, www.Keywestinfo.com

Historic Tours of America
tel 305/292-TOUR, fax 305/745-4220.

Art Deco Welcome Center
Miami Design Preservation League, 1001 Ocean Dr., Miami Beach, FL 33139, tel 305/672-2014, fax 305/672-4319, www.mdpl.org
Call to reserve art deco tours

Dragonfly Expeditions
1825 Ponce de Leon Blvd., Suite 369, Coral Gables, FL 33134-4418, tel 305/774-9019, www.dragonflyexpeditions.com

Greater Miami and The Beaches Hotel Association
407 Lincoln Rd., Suite 10G, Miami Beach, tel 305/531-3553 or 800/SEE-MIAMI, fax 305/531-8954, www.gmbha.com

Miami-Dade Gay & Lesbian Chamber of Commerce,
3510 Biscayne Blvd., # 02, Miami, FL 33137, tel 305/573-4000, www.gogaymiami.com

Surfside Tourist Board
9301 Collins Ave., Surfside, tel 305/864-0722 or 800/327-4557, fax 305/993-5128

EMERGENCIES

Call **911** in case of police, ambulance, or fire emergency. Nonemergency police inquiry: 305/595-6263.

LOST CREDIT CARDS

To report lost or stolen credit cards or travelers' checks, contact the following:

Credit cards
American Express, tel 800/528-4800
Diners Club, tel 800/234-6377
Discover, tel 800/347-2683
MasterCard, tel 800/826-2181
Visa, tel 800/336-8472

Travelers' checks
American Express, tel 800/221-7282
MasterCard, tel 800/223-9920
Thomas Cook, tel 800/223-7373
Visa, tel 800/227-6811

HOTELS & RESTAURANTS

Accommodations listed below range from bed-and-breakfast, small establishments with the emphasis on personal attention rather than, say, room TVs or phones, to one- or two-story motels that offer limited service, to full service hotels that are usually multistory buildings and include a coffee shop and restaurant.

All hotels and restaurants are listed by price category. Unless otherwise stated, all the following hotels have private bathrooms with shower and/or bathtub. Prices quoted do not include taxes. Most municipalities levy special taxes on hotel rooms and food and beverages served in hotels and restaurants, on top of the 6 percent sales tax and 0.5 percent local sales tax. In South Beach and Miami-Dade County combined taxes are 12.5 percent, in Surfside 10.5 percent, in Bal Harbour 9.5 percent. Most hotels charge extra for breakfast.

Reservations are recommended for restaurants, but a special note has been made of those places where it is essential. Few restaurants offer fixed-price menus, but some do so for Sunday brunch, or offer "early bird" specials (between 4 and 6 p.m.). Many restaurants open early for dinner (5 p.m.) and close late.

Water defines the Keys, and whether you're staying in a glitzy resort or a simple bed-and-breakfast, all Keys' accommodations offer access to some of the best water sports facilities in South Florida. Those down for the fishing may like to get to bed early, but for the rest, late night bars and restaurants are part of the Keys way of life. It may be the fact that this is the southernmost tip of the continental U.S., but the Keys always give a feeling that it is perched precariously on the edge of the world, and it seems to boost appetites—for food and drink.

Not all of the hotels and restaurants listed are readily accessible to people with disabilities. Many buildings, especially in South Beach and Key West, may have one or more steps to negotiate before entering. Visitors are advised to check when booking to make sure the hotel or restaurant meets their specific needs.

PRICES

HOTELS

An indication of the cost of a double room without breakfast is given by $ signs.

$$$$$	Over $280
$$$$	$200–$280
$$$	$120–$200
$$	$80–$120
$	Under $80

RESTAURANTS

An indication of the cost of a three-course dinner without drinks is given by $ signs.

$$$$$	Over $80
$$$$	$50–$80
$$$	$35–$50
$$	$20–$35
$	Under $20

MIAMI'S CENTRAL DISTRICTS

From the fountains of the cultural center to the excitement of the commercial district, the downtown area of Miami has benefited from the multicultural population. Some bay side restaurants here offer the freshest fish in the city.

Little Havana's Calle Ocho (8th St.) is noted for restaurants specializing in *mojito*-laced *lechón* (rum and lime marinated pork) and *carne asada* (roast meats). Although high-style Cuban SoBe (South Beach) experiences such as Yuca, or Larios on the Beach, are making waves with their innovative cuisine, the more traditional eateries still offer good value for the dollar with traditional dishes of pork, chicken, or seafood, and yellow or white rice, with yucca, black beans, plantains, or fried bananas on the side. The residential area of North Miami offers some of the city's better restaurants and shops.

DOWNTOWN MIAMI

🏨 INTERCONTINENTAL 🍽 MIAMI
$$$$$
100 CHOPIN PLAZA
FL 33131
TEL 866/327-3005 or 866/396-7606
FAX 305/577-0384
www.icmiamihotel.com
Deluxe, newly renovated high-rise on Biscayne Bay, adjacent to Bayside Marketplace and Bayfront Park. Elegantly appointed rooms, full range of first-class services. This is the place to stay downtown.
🛏 675 rooms & suites
🅿 Valet 🔁 🅢 🅢 🌊 🌊 🔽 🄰 All major cards

🏨 HOLIDAY INN 🍽 PORT OF MIAMI - DOWNTOWN
$$
340 BISCAYNE BLVD.
FL 33132
TEL 305/371-4400
www.ichotelsgroup.com
An economically priced hotel minutes from all the activity.
🛏 200 rooms 🅿 🔁 🅢 🌊 🔽 🄰 All major cards

🏨 RIVER PARK HOTEL 🍽 & SUITES
$$
100 SE 4TH ST., FL 33131
TEL 305/374-5100
www.river-park-suites-hotel-miami.com
In the heart of downtown, next to the MetroMover, the River Park reflects Miami's international sophistication. Spacious rooms and suites feature cable, data port, voice mail, and coffee maker.
🛏 149 🅿 🔁 🅢 🌊 🔽 🄰 All major cards

🍴 BRISA BISTRO
$$-$$$
HILTON MIAMI DOWNTOWN
1601 BISCAYNE BLVD.
TEL 305/374-0000
High standards in an elegant
mirrored, marbled dining
room tucked away in a corner
of the hotel lobby. Seafood
seldom comes better than
this with dishes such as
seared swordfish with
Oriental vinaigrette.
🪑 100 🅿 Valet 🔒 Closed
Sun. & L Sat. 🚭 ❄ 🅰 All
major cards

LITTLE HAVANA 33130

**🏨 MIAMI RIVER INN
BED & BREAKFAST**
$$
118 S.W. SOUTH RIVER DR.
TEL 305/325-0045 or
800/468-3589
FAX 305/325-9227
www.miamiriverinn.com
Historic inn made up of five
restored clapboard buildings
dating from 1906. Charming
rooms, styled individually but
retaining a traditional look.
Lush garden.
ⓘ 40 rooms & suites 🅿
🚭 ❄ ☎ 🅰 All major
cards

🍴 LA ESQUINA DE TEJAS
$$
101 S.W. 12TH AVE.
TEL 305/545-5341
Fast-food, inexpensive Cuban
restaurant made famous by
President Ronald Reagan—
his lunch choice is on the
menu. Great sandwiches.
🪑 210 🚭 🅰 All major
cards

🍴 LA CARRETA
$
3632 S.W. 8TH ST.
TEL 305/444-7501
Old-style Cuban restaurant,
part of a chain. Large portions
of classic dishes, and a
backroom cafeteria for strong
coffee, sweet pastries, and
sugarcane juice.
🪑 300 🚭 🅰 All major
cards

🍴 VERSAILLES
$
3555 S.W. 8TH ST.
TEL 305/444-0240
Famous Cuban landmark with
kitsch decor and wall-to-wall
mirrors—a must for tourists.
Menu offers every Cuban dish
imaginable in hearty portions.
🪑 400 🚭 🅰 All major
cards

NORTH MIAMI 33180

**🏨 THE FAIRMONT
TURNBERRY ISLE
RESORT & CLUB**
$$$$$
19999 W. COUNTRY CLUB DR.
AVENTURA, FL
TEL 305/932-6200 or
800/327-7028
FAX 305/933-6554
www.fairmont.com/turnberryisle
This is the grandest of the
grand Miami resorts, a
stunning Mediterranean-style
hotel set in a secluded oasis
of 300 tropical acres by the
bay. Oversize rooms, large
terraces, two golf courses,
and moorings for 117 boats.
ⓘ 392 rooms & suites 🅿
🔗 🚭 ☎ 🏋 🅰 All
major cards

**SOMETHING
SPECIAL**

🍴 CHEF ALLEN'S
South Florida dining at its
best. Allen Susser's artfully
conceived New World cuisine is
a must. The open kitchen lets
diners see all, from pompano in
parchment with black truffles
and yellow tomato to great
desserts. Fixed-price menu.
$$$
19088 N.E. 29TH AVE.
NORTH MIAMI BEACH
TEL 305/935-2900
🪑 140 🅿 Valet 🔒 Closed
L, except Fri. 🚭 ❄
🅰 All major cards

🍴 PASHA'S
$
14871 BISCAYNE BLVD.
NORTH MIAMI BEACH

TEL 786/923-2323
www.pashas.com
This Miami chain serves fast,
casual, healthy Mediterranean
meals including hoummus
wraps, kebabs, and tatziki soup.
🪑 90 🚭 🅰 All major
cards

MIAMI BEACH

SoBe (South Beach) offers an
entirely new world of sleek,
chic cuisine, backed by cool art
deco hotels and hyper-designed
fantasies—the undoubted king
of which is Ian Schrager. His
showpiece Delano Hotel opened
in mid-1995, just as a major
renovation project began on the
Lincoln Road pedestrian mall
between Washington Avenue
and Lenox Street.

MIAMI BEACH 33139

🏨 CASA GRANDE
$$$$$
834 OCEAN DR.
TEL 305/672-7003
FAX 305/673-3669
www.casagrandesuitehotel.com
At this deluxe, all-suite hotel,
ocean views are standard, and
stunning contemporary
amenities such as carved teak
and mahogany furnishings and
Indonesian batiks capture the
SoBe look exactly.
ⓘ 34 🅿 Valet 🔗 🚭
🅰 All major cards

🏨 DELANO
🍴 $$$$$
1685 COLLINS AVE.
TEL 305/672-2000 or
800/697-1791
FAX 305/532-0099
www.delano-hotel.com
Understated luxury is reflected
in designer Philippe Starck's
blinding white decor, offset by
billowing curtains, antique
pieces, and the Granny Smith
apple, replaced daily, in every
one of the rooms. See Blue
Door restaurant, p. 247.
ⓘ 194 rooms, suites & lofts
🪑 200 🅿 Valet 🔗 🚭
🚭 ❄ 🏋 🅰 All major
cards

🚭 Non-smoking ❄ Air-conditioning 🏊 Indoor/🏊 Outdoor swimming pool 🏋 Health club 🅰 Credit cards **KEY**

HOTELS & RESTAURANTS

🏨 **THE NATIONAL HOTEL**
🍴 **$$$$$**
1677 COLLINS AVE.
TEL 305/532-2311 or
800/327-8370
www.nationalhotel.com
A beachfront landmark, The
National has been restored
to its chic art deco glamour.
Complimentary poolside yoga
and luxurious amenities,
including flat-screen TVs.
🛏 151 rooms & suites
🅿 Valet 🔼 ⦾ ⦾ ⊠
⦿ All major cards

🏨 **SEA VIEW**
$$$$$
9909 COLLINS AVE.
BAL HARBOUR, FL 33154
TEL 305/866-4441 or
800/447-1010
FAX 305/866-1898
www.seaview-hotel.com
European-style beachfront
hotel and resort with
Mediterranean cabanas
directly across from the
famous Bal Harbour shops.
Attracts a conservative
clientele who want the
beach but not South Beach.
🛏 220 rooms & suites
🅿 🔼 ⦾ ⦾ ⊠ ⦿
⦿ All major cards

🏨 **THE TIDES**
$$$$$
1220 OCEAN DR.
TEL 305/604-5070
FAX 305/604-5180
www.tidessouthbeach.com
One of the most beautiful
hotels that South Beach has
to offer, The Tides features
suites overlooking the ocean;
those on the ninth and tenth
floors are among the highest
points on Ocean Drive.
🛏 45 rooms & suites
🅿 Valet 🔼 ⦾ ⦾ ⊠
⦿ All major cards

🏨 **HOTEL OCEAN**
$$$$
1230 OCEAN DR.
TEL 305/672-2579
FAX 305/672-7665
www.hotelocean.com
A full renovation has resulted
in a French Riviera feel to this

hotel. The owners and managers
are French, as is the food.
🛏 27 🔼 ⦾ ⦿ All
major cards

🏨 **HOTEL IMPALA**
🍴 **$$$$**
1228 COLLINS AVE.
TEL 305/673-2021
FAX 305/673-5984
www.hotelimpalamiamibeach.com
Diminutive, discreet
celebrity hideaway, offering
Mediterranean flair, custom
furnishings, original art-
work, and European-style
service. Rooms are small
but elegant. Spiga is a note-
worthy restaurant, see p. 249.
🛏 17 rooms & suites
🍴 100 🅿 Valet 🔼 ⦾
⦾ ⦿ All major cards

🏨 **ALBION**
$$$
1650 JAMES AVE.
TEL 305/913-1000
FAX 305/531-4580
www.rubelhotels.com
White-sand beach, a poolside
outdoor living room, and
contemporary deck and
rooftop solarium suites define
this trendy hotel, attracting a
cosmopolitan crowd.
🛏 96 🅿 Valet 🔼 ⦾ ⦾ ⦿
⊠ ⦿ ⦿ AE, MC, V

🏨 **BAY HARBOR INN
& SUITES**
$$$
9660 E. BAY HARBOR DR.
BAY HARBOUR ISLANDS,
FL 33154
TEL 305/868-4141
FAX 305/867-9094
www.bayharborinn.com
Waterfront inn on scenic
Indian Creek in a quiet
neighborhood. Walking
distance to fishing and scuba
charters. Close to Bal
Harbour shops.
🛏 38 🅿 🔼 ⦾ ⊠
⦿ AE, MC, V

🏨 **CARDOZO**
$$$
1300 OCEAN DR.
TEL 305/535-6500 or
800/782-6500

FAX 305/532-3563
www.cardozohotel.com
Classic art deco hotel, the
informal headquarters of
owners Gloria and Emilio
Estefan. Stylish and modern
rooms featuring handcrafted
furniture. Great location.
🛏 43 🅿 Valet 🔼 ⦾
⦿ All major cards

🏨 **CAVALIER**
🍴 **$$$**
1320 OCEAN DR.
TEL 305/531-3555
www.cavaliermiami.com
This renovated and
redecorated prime deco
building is popular both for
its hotel and the Lotus
Lounge restaurant and bar.
🛏 45 rooms & suites
🅿 Valet 🔼 ⦾ ⦾
⦿ All major cards

🏨 **ESSEX HOUSE**
$$$
1001 COLLINS AVE.
TEL 305/534-2700
FAX 305/531-3953
www.essexhotel.com
European charm, modern
conveniences, and affordable
luxury at this Hohauser-
designed deco hotel. The
pastel-colored rooms are
stylish and soundproof.
Complimentary continental
breakfast and wi-fi.
🛏 74 rooms & suites 🔼
⦾ ⊠ ⦿ All major cards

🏨 **GREENVIEW HOTEL**
$$$
1671 WASHINGTON AVE.
TEL 305/531-6588
FAX 305/531-4580
www.greenviewhotel.com
Extraordinary Henry
Hohauser deco building
brought up to date by the
Rubell family. Cool, urbane
interior of exceptional
tranquility from Parisian
designer Chaban Minassian.
🛏 45 🔼 ⦾ ⦿ AE,
MC, V

🏨 **HOTEL ASTOR**
🍴 **$$$**
956 WASHINGTON AVE.

TEL 305/531-8081
FAX 305/531-3193
www.hotelastor.com
Another great deco building,
built in 1936 and magnificently
renovated with attention to
detail. Blond wood furniture,
original, polished terazzo
floors, and restful colors
define the look. See Joley
Restaurant & Lounge, p. 248.
(1) 41 rooms & suites
144 P Valet 🔄 🚭
🚗 All major cards

🏨 KENT
$$$
1131 COLLINS AVE.
TEL 305/604-5068
FAX 305/604-5180
www.thekenthotel.com
A striking deco hotel, the
lobby is popular with fashion
shoots, and the style is
contemporary chic. An
affordable retreat in
South Beach.
(1) 54 rooms & suites
P Valet 🔄 🚭
🚗 All major cards

🏨 PARK CENTRAL
$$$
640 OCEAN DR.
TEL 305/538-1611 or
800/727-5236
FAX 305/534-7520
www.theparkcentral.com
Authentically restored to
reflect the 1940s, this
Hohauser beachfront hotel
boasts wraparound corner
windows and sleek, modern
touches. The lobby bar
attracts a cool fashion crowd.
(1) 125 rooms & suites
P 🔄 🚭 🏊 🏋
🚗 All major cards

🏨 PELICAN HOTEL
$$$
826 OCEAN DR.
TEL 305/673-3373 or
800/7-PELICAN
FAX 305/673-3255
www.pelicanhotel.com
Four-story deco-inspired
frivolity with wonderful,
eclectic styling in custom-
designed themed rooms
such as Leafforest and Best

Whorehouse. The bath-
rooms are amazing.
(1) 30 rooms & suites
P Valet 🔄 🚭 🚭
🚗 All major cards

🏨 AVALON
🍴 $$
700 OCEAN DR.
TEL 305/538-0133 or
800/933-3306
FAX 305/534-0258
www.avalonhotel.com
Classic deco-style hotel. Tidy,
small rooms offer simple
modern amenities, but the
main attraction is that this is a
friendly place to stay in a great
beachside location. Complimentary continental breakfast
and wi-fi.
(1) 108 P Valet 🔄 🚭
🚗 All major cards

🏨 BEACHCOMBER
$
1340 COLLINS AVE.
TEL 305/531-3755 or
888/305-HOTEL
FAX 305/673-8609
www.beachcombermiami.com
Quaint art deco hotel in the
heart of SoBe with functional,
small rooms and a tropical,
carefree atmosphere. The
breakfast buffet is a bargain,
the beach a block away.
(1) 28 P 🔄 🚭 🚭
🚗 All major cards

🏨 CARLTON
$
1433 COLLINS AVE.
TEL 305/672-5858
FAX 305/534-6855
www.carltonsouthbeach.com
Central location in the
heart of the Art Deco
District. Quaint, family-run
hotel with emphasis on
personalized attention.
(1) 67 rooms & suites
P 🔄 🚭 🏊
🚗 All major cards

🏨 CLAY HOTEL &
INTERNATIONAL
HOSTEL
$
1438 WASHINGTON AVE.
TEL 305/534-2988 or

800/379-CLAY
FAX 305/673-0346
www.clayhotel.com
Listed on the National
Register of Historic Places,
the place throbs with youth
and vitality. However, guests
of all ages are welcome and
stay here. All the rooms are
clean and quiet in this classic
part dormitory-style hostel
and part hotel.
(1) 106 🔄 🚭 🚭
🚗 MC, V

🍴 ESCOPAZZO
$$$$
1311 WASHINGTON AVE.
TEL 305/674-9450
Intimate, passionately run, and
offering some of the best
Italian food on South Beach.
Soufflés are recommended—
seafood in herb-infused
fumé—or there's arugula and
goat cheese risotto.
Reservations required.
65 🕐 Closed L, Mon.
🚭 🚗 All major cards

SOMETHING
SPECIAL

🍴 THE BLUE DOOR
High-style experience set in
the sensational white-on-
white Delano Hotel (see p. 245).
Creative fusion menu from
Claude Troisgros—basically
French techniques, South
American/ local ingredients, and
a few Asian twists. Magic desserts;
try the passion fruit crêpe soufflé.
Reservations required.
$$$$
DELANO HOTEL
1685 COLLINS AVE.
MIAMI BEACH
TEL 305/ 674-6400
FAX 305/674-5649
www.delano-hotel.com
195 P Valet 🚭 🚭
🚗 All major cards

🍴 THE FORGE
$$$$
432 41st ST.
TEL 305/538-8533
Classic, expensive, rococo
restaurant serving excellent

Continental American cuisine that includes scrambled eggs with caviar served in the eggshells, 16-ounce steaks, and organic arugula salad, escargot, and soufflé. Club with disco and cigar room every Wed. Reservations required.
🔾 275 🅿 Valet
🕔 Closed L 🔾 🔾
🔾 All major cards

🍴 B.E.D.
$$$
929 WASHINGTON AVE.
TEL 305/532-9070
www.bedmiami.com
This is the ultimate "South Beach" dining experience. B.E.D., a restaurant/bar, serves global fusion cuisine fare that includes ceviche and goat cheese fig fritters. Yes, you are served in a king-size bed.
🔾 156 🕔 Closed L, & Tue., Wed. , & Sun. 🅿 Valet 🔾
🔾 All major cards

🍴 CHINA GRILL
$$$
404 WASHINGTON AVE.
TEL 305/534-2211
Lively, upscale, new wave Asian/Chinese restaurant cloned from New York City's East-Meets-West. Try seared rare tuna with spicy Japanese pepper and avocado sashimi, and mushroom fettucine in sake-Madeira-cream sauce. Great for celeb-spotting. Reservations required.
🔾 500 🅿 Valet 🔾 🔾
🔾 All major cards

🍴 GRILLFISH
$$$
1444 COLLINS AVE.
MIAMI BEACH
TEL 305/538-9908
www.grillfish.com
Serving healthy and tasty seafood, this eatery is popular with locals.
🔾 130 🔾 🔾 🔾 All major cards

🍴 JERRY'S FAMOUS DELI
$$$
1450 COLLINS AVE.
TEL 305/532-8030

www.jerrysfamousdeli.com
This historic restaurant, which is open 24 hours a day, is a great place to slow down after an evening out.
🔾 70 🔾 🔾 All major cards

🍴 NEMO
$$$
100 COLLINS AVE.
TEL 305/532-4550
Nemo is loved for organic New American cuisine at this this see-and-be-seen art deco building. Ideas range from pan-roasted chicken with olive mashed potato and garlic sauce to spicy Vietnamese salad. Reservations required.
🔾 300 🅿 Valet 🔾 🔾
🔾 AE, MC, V

🍴 OSTERIA DEL TEATRO
$$$
1443 WASHINGTON AVE.
TEL 305/538-7850
It's elbow room only at Dino Pirola's intimate gray-on-gray North Italian restaurant. The homemade bread is great, the pasta exceptional, the fish imaginative (try halibut with sliced garlic and olives), and the desserts a must. Reservations essential.
🔾 60 🕔 Closed L & Sun. 🔾 🔾 All major cards

🍴 SUSHISAMBA DROMO
$$$
600 LINCOLN RD.
TEL 305/673-5337
A colorful hotspot that mixes Japanese, Brazilian, and Peruvian dishes, SushiSamba dromo is a New York transplant like so many Miamians. The caiprinhas and various sakes are great for wahing down sushi and livening up the evening.
🔾 300 🔾 🔾 🔾 All major cards

🍴 NOBU MIAMI BEACH
$$$
1901 COLLINS AVE.
TEL 305/695-3232
A celebrity/fashion model

hangout that serves what's considered the ultimate sushi and sashimi, as well as the newest cocktails.
🔾 125 🅿 Valet
🕔 Closed L 🔾 🔾
🔾 All major cards

🍴 NEXXT CAFÉ
$$
700 LINCOLN RD.
TEL 305/532-6643
One of the busiest spots on Lincoln Road for dining and people-watching, the portions are always large and delicious. Serves a variety of American sandwiches and entrees.
🔾 400 🔾 🔾 🔾 All major cards

🍴 JOLEY RESTAURANT & LONGUE
Joley is a stunning restaurant in an innovative setting under a glass atrium. Chef John Suley's newest hotspot features American cuisine with a European influence.
$$$
HOTEL ASTOR
956 WASHINGTON AVE.
SOUTH BEACH
TEL 305/672-7217
🔾 200 (plus 80 outdoors)
🕔 Closed L 🔾 🔾 All major cards

🍴 TALULA
$$
210 33RD ST.
TEL 305/672-0778
Creative American cuisine served inside or on the patio. Inviting and eclectic decor, and weekly wine specials.
🔾 130 🕔 Closed Mon., L Sat. & Sun. 🔾 🔾
🔾 All major cards

🍴 JOE'S STONE CRAB
$$
11 WASHINGTON AVE.
TEL 305/673-0365
www.joesstonecrab.com
This South Beach landmark hasn't looked back since

opening in 1913 (although it did change locations a few years ago). Stand in line for stone crabs and mustard sauce (available Oct.–May), fried green tomatoes, and perfect key lime pie. No reservations taken.
🛏 475 🕐 Closed Aug. 1 to Oct. 15 🅿 Valet 🚭 💧
🏧 All major cards

🍴 LARIOS ON THE BEACH
$$
820 OCEAN DR.
TEL 305/532-9577
Quintin Larios is backed by Gloria and Emilio Estefan at this Cuban restaurant with South Beach attitude that's crowded with Cuban Americans hungry for their grandmother's cooking. Sidewalk tables are best for people-watching.
🛏 114 🚭 🏧 All major cards

🍴 A FISH CALLED AVALON
$$
700 OCEAN DR.
TEL 305/532-1727
A casual restaurant/bar with indoor and outside seating, A Fish Called Avalon offers fresh local seafood and live music in an art deco hotel setting.
🛏 200 🕐 Closed L 🅿 Valet 🚭 💧 🏧 All major cards

🍴 MANGO'S TROPICAL CAFÉ
$$
9004 OCEAN DR.
TEL 305/673-4422
www.mangostropicalcafe.com
Pulsing with Cuban bartenders and waitresses who double as table-top dancers, Mango's has some of the best desserts on the beach. Entrees include Caribbean mahi mahi and margarita chicken.
🛏 570 🚭 🏧 All major cards

🍴 SPIGA
$$
HOTEL IMPALA
1228 COLLINS AVE.
TEL 305/534-0079
Pastas, breads, and desserts are all homemade at this great Italian spot set in the tiny Hotel Impala (see p. 246). Seafood is a specialty. Reservations required.
🛏 75 🅿 🕐 Closed L 💧 🏧 All major cards

🍴 SUSHI DORAKU
$$
1104 LINCOLN RD.
TEL 305/695-8383
Benihana owns this new concept sushi spot, part of the regal South Beach movie complex. Watch plates of sushi roll by on a conveyor belt and pick what you want. Best bets: South Beach roll and Spider roll.
🛏 130 🕐 Closed L Sat. & Sun. 🚭 💧 🏧 All major cards

SOMETHING SPECIAL

🍴 YUCA
Upscale restaurant for fun Nuevo Latino food with attitude from Ramon Medrano. That means Caribbean and South American influences in dishes such as sweet plantains wrapped around a savory cured beef filling and steamed yuca filled with a truffle scented wild mushroom picadillos. Reservations required.
$$$
501 LINCOLN RD.
MIAMI BEACH
TEL 305/532-9822
www.yuca.com
🛏 190 🅿 Valet 🚭 🏧 AE, MC, V

🍴 BALANS
$
1022 LINCOLN RD.
TEL 305/534-9191
British-owned eatery that hits the spot. Try a tasty sampler of goat cheese and

portobello, don't miss the herb-crusted Chilean sea bass, and leave room for desserts such as baked chocolate cheesecake.
🛏 140 🚭 🏧 All major cards

🍴 CAFÉ PRIMA PASTA
$
414 71ST ST.
NORTH MIAMI BEACH
TEL 305/867-0106
Tiny budget Italian restaurant with a great combination of beach location, top-notch service, and a reputation for the best Italian food in the area. Pasta is homemade, veal dishes recommended.
🛏 150 🚭 💧 🏧 No credit cards

🍴 LEMON TWIST
$
908 71ST ST.
NORTH MIAMI BEACH
TEL 305/868-2075
Ultra cool hangout for Mediterranean food built around olives, anchovies, tomatoes, and lemons. Gazpacho is fabulous.
🛏 60 🕐 Closed L 💧 🏧 AE, MC, V

🍴 NEWS CAFÉ
$
1300 OCEAN DR.
TEL 305/538-6397
More Euro than American, this is the people-watching place. Wait for an outside table, choose a burger, omelette, or salad, and browse the national and international press while you wait.
🛏 150 🅿 Valet 🚭 🏧 All major cards

🍴 VAN DYKE CAFÉ
$
846 LINCOLN RD.
TEL 305/534-3600
From the owners of the News Café (see above), a jazzier version on two floors. The same Euro-American style, identical menu, and a great people-watching venue.
🛏 200 🚭 🏧 All major cards

🚭 Non-smoking 💧 Air-conditioning 🏊 Indoor/🏊 Outdoor swimming pool 💪 Health club 🏧 Credit cards **KEY**

HOTELS & RESTAURANTS

This former coconut plantation has been given over to rows of luxury high-rises with wonderful beaches and multimillion-dollar waterfront estates. Ocean views are paramount with restaurants and hotels offering some of the most superb settings imaginable.

KEY BISCAYNE 33149

🏨 SONESTA BEACH RESORT KEY BISCAYNE
$$$$$
350 OCEAN DR.
TEL 305/361-2021 or
800/SONESTA
FAX 305/361-3096
www.sonesta.com
Secluded deluxe resort, dramatically set on a wide, white-sand beach. Caribbean-style rooms with balconies, and impressive sports facilities are keynotes.
ⓘ 300 rooms & suites P
🔁 🛇 🛇 🍴 ⏻ 🛇 All major cards

🍴 RUSTY PELICAN
$$
3201 RICKENBACKER CAUSEWAY
TEL 305/361-3818
Landmark waterfront restaurant serving continental seafood against the stunning backdrop of the Downtown Miami skyline. Sunday brunch is best, or just go for a drink and soak up the view.
🍴 450 P Valet 🛇 🛇 All major cards

🍴 SUNDAYS ON THE BAY
$$
5420 CRANDON BLVD.
TEL 305/361-6777
Lives up to its name. Lively waterfront seafood restaurant, popular with a young crowd. Great sunset views but at its best for Sunday brunch.
🍴 100 🛇 🛇 All major cards

Once a colony of artists and writers, Coconut Grove is now a base for wealthy winter and year-round residents. A few craft shops remain next to the expensive boutiques and smart restaurants. Luxurious yachts lie in Biscayne Bay, and a young weekend crowd hangs out in the CocoWalk shopping and entertainment complex.

COCONUT GROVE 33133

🏨 GRAND BAY HOTEL
$$$$$
2669 S. BAYSHORE DR.
TEL 305/858-9600
FAX 305/859-2026
www.wyndham.com
Upscale luxury hotel in the heart of Coconut Grove. Distinctive style, restful atmosphere; many celebrities prefer this hotel to any other in Miami.
ⓘ 178 rooms & suites
P Valet 🔁 🛇 🛇 🎐
⏻ 🛇 All major cards

🏨 MAYFAIR HOUSE
$$$$$
3000 FLORIDA AVE.
TEL 305/441-0000 or
800/433-4555
FAX 305/447-9173
www.mayfairhotelandspa.com
Intimate all-suite hotel, despite hectic Streets of Mayfair Mall setting. Most suites have private terraces facing the street, screened by plants; some have a Japanese hot tub on the balcony.
ⓘ 179 P 🔁 🛇 🛇
🎐 ⏻ 🛇 All major cards

🏨 GROVE ISLE CLUB & RESORT
$$$$
4 GROVE ISLE DR.
TEL 305/858-8300 or
800/88-GROVE
FAX 305/858-5908
www.groveisle.com
This comfortable hotel is on Biscayne Bay, over the bridge onto the island. Popular with families and

HOTELS
An indication of the cost of a double room without breakfast is given by **$** signs.
$$$$$	Over $280
$$$$	$200–$280
$$$	$120–$200
$$	$80–$120
$	Under $80

RESTAURANTS
An indication of the cost of a three-course dinner without drinks is given by $ signs.
$$$$$	Over $80
$$$$	$50–$80
$$$	$35–$50
$$	$20–$35
$	Under $20

for small conferences, and with a wide range of sports facilities.
ⓘ 50 🔁 🛇 🎐 🛇 All major cards

🏨 SONESTA BAYFRONT HOTEL
$$$
2889 MCFARLANE RD.
TEL 305/529-2828 or
800/SONESTA
www.sonesta.com/CoconutGrove
Your stay will be enhanced by beautifully appointed rooms (many with balconies) and bay views. Art by Lynne Golub Gelfman, Frank Stella, and Robert Rauschenberg graces public areas. Rooms have flat-screen tvs and free wi-fi. Enjoy dining or lounging at Panorama or Nikki Coconut Grove. This hotel stands across from the CocoWalk shopping mecca.
ⓘ 210 rooms & suites
P Valet 🔁 🛇 🛇 🎐
⏻ 🛇 All major cards

🍴 CAFÉ TU TU TANGO
$$
3015 GRAND AVE.
(COCOWALK)
TEL 305/529-2222
People-watching becomes a way of life at this arty, cosmopolitan tapas bar on the second story of CocoWalk.

While watching, graze on the eclectic offerings of crab cakes, frittatas, empanadas, and paella. Best sangria in town.

🛏 200 🚭 🌀 AE, MC, V

🍴 GROVE ISLE
$$
4 GROVE ISLE DR.
TEL 305/858-8300
Wonderful waterside setting. Modern American cuisine is served in either the indoor dining area or the tented terrace, a favorite.

🛏 100 🌀 All major cards

CORAL GABLES

Coral Gables offers a more conservative dining experience compared to the glitzy chic of South Beach. Some of Miami's most acclaimed establishments are here, and the food offered is among the best in the city.

CORAL GABLES 33134

🏨 BILTMORE
$$$$$
1200 ANASTASIA AVE.
TEL 305/445-1926 or
800/727-1926
FAX 305/913-3152
www.biltmorehotel.com
National historic landmark that oozes Old-World Mediterranean elegance. Roman columns, hand-painted ceilings, Spanish tiles, and marble floors add to the style. The pool has to be seen to be believed.

ⓘ 280 rooms & suites 🅿
🚭 🌀 🌀 🏊 🎾 🌀 All
major cards

🏨 HOTEL PLACE
🍴 ST. MICHEL
$$$
162 ALCAZAR AVE.
TEL 305/444-1666 or
800/848-HOTEL
FAX 305/529-0074
www.hotelstmichel.com
Sophisticated European-style hotel in the heart of the Gables. The building dates from 1926, and it's filled

with antiques, dark paneling, and fresh flowers. See Restaurant St. Michel, below.

ⓘ 27 🅿 🚭 🌀 🌀 All
major cards

🏨 WESTIN
COLONNADE HOTEL
$$$
180 ARAGON AVE.
TEL 305/441-2600
www.westin.com/coralgables
Former home of Coral Gables founder George Merrick, now an elegant hotel with upscale decor and service. Central location between business and retail districts ensures a mainly business clientele.

ⓘ 157 rooms & suites
🅿 Valet 🚭 🌀 🌀 🏊
🎾 🌀 All major cards

🍴 RESTAURANT
ST. MICHEL
$$$
HOTEL PLACE ST. MICHEL
162 ALCAZAR AVE.
TEL 305/444-1666
Historic Gables hotel restaurant with European feel—excellent on every count. Crêpes are the best in town; fish dishes are outstanding. Romantic setting, charming service. Reservations required. Early bird specials.

🛏 92 🅿 🌀 🌀 🌀 All
major cards

🍴 CACAO 1737
$$$
141 GIRALDA AVE.
TEL 305/445-1001
Named for the year of chocolate's discovery, this is a chocoholic's dream. It's popular for Nuevo Latino dishes, including the Peruvian crayfish and yellow potato Napoleon.

🛏 85 🕐 Closed Sun.
🅿 Valet 🌀 🌀 🌀 All
major cards

🍴 ORTANIQUE
ON THE MILE
$$
278 MIRACLE MILE
TEL 305/446-7710

www.cindyhutsoncuisine.com
Named after a hybrid fruit (orange and tangerine), this restaurant resonates with Floribbean cuisine such as candied pecans, jerk pork loin and yellowtail snapper.

🛏 120 🕐 Closed Sat. & Sun. L 🌀 🌀 All major cards

SOMETHING SPECIAL

🍴 LA PALMA
RISTORANTE & BAR

Serves Northern Italian delicacies like lobster La Palma and clams with fettuccine. Also try the Maine lobster sautéed with white wine and the 14-ounce veal chop.

$$$
116 ALHAMBRA CIRCLE
CORAL GABLES
TEL 305/445-8777
www.lapalmarestaurant.net

🛏 150 🅿 Valet 🌀 🌀
🌀 All major cards

SOUTH MIAMI

See hotel and restaurant listings under Excursions from Miami, below.

EXCURSIONS

Homestead and Florida City are both starting points for those visiting the shallow "river of grass," the Everglades. In both places there are numerous shops and small restaurants, although accommodations tend to be of the standard chain motel variety.

🏨 EVERGLADES MOTEL
$$
605 S. KROME AVE.
HOMESTEAD, FL 33030
TEL 305/247-4117
Small, well-run motel with bright contemporary look to well-maintained rooms.

ⓘ 14 🅿 🌀 🌀 🏊
🌀 All major cards

🚭 Non-smoking 🌀 Air-conditioning ⓘ Indoor/🏊 Outdoor swimming pool 🎾 Health club 🌀 Credit cards   **KEY**

HOTELS & RESTAURANTS

🏨 RIVERSIDE HOTEL
🍴 $$

620 E. LAS OLAS BLVD.
FORT LAUDERDALE, FL 33301
TEL 954/467-0671 or
800/325-3280
FAX 954/462-2148
www.riversidehotel.com
The location in the
fashionable historic district
with lush gardens along the
New River is the draw. Old
World charm, some rooms
with canopy beds, plus free
transportation to beach.
🛏 217 rooms & suites
🅿 Valet 🅂 🅂 ☎
🅂 All major cards

🍴 MICCOSUKEE RESORT
& GAMING
$–$$$$

500 S.W. KROME AVE.
HOMESTEAD
TEL 877/242-6464
www.miccosukee.com
This huge modern complex
has plenty to do other than
eat, but if you want to play at
a casino while seeing a
modern take on one of
America's smallest Indian
tribes, try the resort's
restaurant, buffet, deli, or
snack bar.
🍽 372 (in buffet) 🅿 Valet
🅂 🅂 All major cards

🍴 MARK'S LAS OLAS
$$–$$$

1032 E. LAS OLAS BLVD.
FORT LAUDERDALE
TEL 954/463-1000
Mark Militello is one of South
Florida's hottest chefs. His
showpiece restaurant attracts
a smart crowd for New
World cuisine built around
unique flavor combinations.
Reservations required.
🍽 150 🅿 Valet 🅂 🅂
🅂 All major cards

🍴 EL TORO TACO
$

I S. KROME AVE.
HOMESTEAD
TEL 305/245-8182
Authentic home-style
Mexican cooking from
the Hernandez family.

Expect chile rellenos, chicken
fajitas, grilled T-bone with
fiery salsa verde, and
great guacamole.
🅿 🅂 🅂 🅂 DC, MC, V

UPPER KEYS

The 1948 film, *Key Largo*, in
which Humphrey Bogart and
Lauren Bacall fought crime and
hurricanes, put the place on the
tourist map, although only a few
scenes were shot here. Visitors
can experience a bit more old
movie magic by checking out
that other famous movie prop,
the *African Queen*, memorably
dragged by Bogey in the film,
now moored in the marina of
the Holiday Inn at MM 99.7.

KEY LARGO 33037

🏨 JULES' UNDERSEA
LODGE
$$$$$

51 SHORELAND DR., MM 103.2
TEL 305/451-2353
FAX 305/451-4789
www.jul.com
The only underwater hotel in
the world. Guests swim down
to the unit, comprising two
bedrooms and galley. Popular
with diving honeymooners.
Staff deliver anything to your
room—including dinner—in
waterproof containers.
🛏 2 🅂 🅂 All major cards

🏨 MARRIOTT KEY
🍴 LARGO BAY RESORT
$$$$

OVERSEAS HWY., MM 103.8
TEL 305/453-0000 or
800/228-9290
FAX 305/453-0093
www.marriottkeylargo.com
For island glitz, one of the
Keys' latest resorts, only 55
minutes south of Miami
International Airport. Rooms
are oversized, some deluxe
two-bedroom suites, all with
wi-fi. Great range of facilities.
See Gus' Grille, this page.
🛏 147 rooms and suites 🅿
🔁 🅂 🅂 ♨ 🔻 🅂 All
major cards

🏨 SUNSET COVE BEACH
RESORT
$$

OVERSEAS HWY., MM 99.6
TEL 305/451-0705 or
877/451-0705
FAX 305/451-5609
www.sunsetcovebeachresort.com
Mom-and-pop place with a
feel of Old Florida. Cottages,
palm-thatched chickee huts,
a wooden fishing pier, canoes,
and pelicans that gather twice
daily for feeding. Reasonably
priced rooms.
🛏 11 🅿 🅂 🅂 All major
cards

🍴 GUS' GRILLE
$$$

MARRIOTT KEY LARGO BAY
RESORT
OVERSEAS HWY., MM 103.8
TEL 305/453-0000
Creative, seafood-inspired
Floribbean cooking, which
translates as yellowtail
snapper with almond crust,
topped with avocado, orange,
and chive sweet-butter sauce.
Pizzas are recommended.
Terrific view of the Gulf.
🅿 🅂 ☎ 🅂 All major
cards

SNAPPER'S WATERFRONT SALOON
$$$
139 SEASIDE AVE., MM 94.5
TEL 305/852-5956
Dine on the water in an Old Florida atmosphere with Caribbean-style seafood.
🅿 💺 🔲 All major cards

THE FISH HOUSE ENCORE!
$$–$$$
OVERSEAS HWY, MM 102
TEL 305/451-0650
Spawned from the historic Fish House, ENCORE! has a piano bar, indoor and outdoor seating, and an ultra-casual outlook. But the food is first-rate with fresh stone crab (from Oct.–May), Cayman chicken and rack of lamb.
🍴 125 🕐 Closed L 💺
🅿 💺 🔲 All major cards

PILOT HOUSE
$$
BAYSIDE CAY CLUB RESORT & MARINA
13 SEAGATE BLVD., MM 100
TEL 305/451-3142
www.baysideresort.us/pilothouse
A 1950s old stager, famous for Harvey's fish sandwich. Seafood takes in snapper stuffed with lobster, topped with shrimp, and served on homemade Florentine pasta; steak Diane and New York strip are just as popular.
🅿 💺 🔲 All major cards

SUNDOWNERS ON THE BAY
$
OVERSEAS HWY., MM 104
TEL 305/451-4502
www.sundownerskeylargo.com
A great eatery for watching the sun set while eating solid pub grub. Vegetarian options.
🅿 💺 🔲 All major cards

PLANTATION KEY

MARKER 88
$$$
MM 88
TEL 305/852-9315

Legendary, innovative Upper Keys landmark. Banana, papaya, pineapple, mango, currant jelly, and cinnamon butter accompany fish Rangoon, or there are great Florida lobster, stone crab, and shrimp. Key lime-baked Alaska is a must-have dessert. Rustic decor, romantic sunsets.
🅿 🕐 Closed L 💺 🔲 All major cards

UPPER MATECUMBE KEY 33036

CHEECA LODGE & SPA
$$$$$
OVERSEAS HWY., MM 82
ISLAMORADA
TEL 305/664-4651 or
800 327-2888
FAX 305/664-2893
www.cheeca.com
Top-rated Upper Keys resort noted for first-rate fishing and diving programs. Blue-and-white plantation-style buildings on 27 lush beachfront acres. Low-key luxury in simply furnished but spacious rooms. See Atlantic's Edge restaurant below.
🛏 199 rooms & suites
🅿 🔄 💺 💺 🌊 🏊
🔲 All major cards

PELICAN COVE RESORT
$$$
84457 OLD OVERSEAS HWY.
MM 84.5
ISLAMORADA
TEL 305/664-4435 or
800/445-4690
FAX 305/664-5134
www.pcove.com
Contemporary decor, balconies, and ocean views define the look at this pleasant, well-run resort hotel. Wide range of activities in and out of the water.
🛏 50 🅿 💺 🌊 🔲 All major cards

ATLANTIC'S EDGE
$$$
CHEECA LODGE & SPA, MM 82
ISLAMORADA
TEL 305/664-4651

www.cheeca.com/atlanticsedge
Classy resort hotel backdrop for executive chef Barry Walling's cuisine features wild, exotic and naturally farmed meats and fish and organically grown Florida produce fused with a unique Florida Keys twist.
🅿 🕐 Closed L; Mon.–Tue. 💺 🔲 All major cards

ZIGGIE'S CONCH RESTAURANT
$$$
OVERSEAS HWY., MM 83.5
ISLAMORADA
TEL 305/664-3391
Memorable seafood amid laid-back '50s decor. Stone crab; conch fritters; cracked conch; yellowtail meunière, almondine, or veronique; oysters stuffed a half-dozen ways; Florida lobster in a mustard sauce. A must.
🅿 🕐 Closed L, Wed. Labor Day–Oct. 💺 🔲 All major cards

SMUGGLER'S COVE
$$–$$$
MM 85.5
ISLAMORADA
TEL 800/864-4363
The name lets you know you're in for colorful characters at this waterside eatery. Clams, oysters, conch, and fish—you can even bring in the fish you just caught and the chef will cook it up.
🛏 150 💺 💺 🔲 All major cards

LOR-E-LEI RESTAURANT & CABANA BAR
$$
MM 82
ISLAMORADA
TEL 305/664-4656
Serving some of the Keys' best seafood, and live rock music, Lor-e-Lei has been an Islamorada landmark for decades..
🛏 330 outside, 250 inside
🅿 💺 💺 🔲 All major cards

HOTELS & RESTAURANTS

🍴 LAZY DAYS OCEANFRONT BAR & SEAFOOD GRILL
$$
79867 US 1, MM 79.9
ISLAMORADA
TEL 305/664-5256
Directly on Atlantic shore, elevated, plantation-style property offering great water views as well as some creative Floribbean seafood dishes. Dolphin (the fish) with tropical fruit salsa and mango rum sauce sums it all up.
🅿 🌀 All major cards

🍴 PAPA JOE'S LANDMARK RESTAURANT
$$
MM 79.7
ISLAMORADA
TEL 305/664-5599
Built in 1937, this down-to-earth fish house of long standing specializes in lobster and catches of the day, especially your own. Steaks, prime ribs, and veal also.
🅿 🌀 All major cards

🍴 MANNY & ISA'S KITCHEN
$
MM 81.6
ISLAMORADA
TEL 305/664-4767
Unassuming mom-and-pop restaurant, with less than ten tables but some of the best Cuban home cooking in the Keys. Black bean soup, paella, and lobster enchiladas pack them in. The fame of Manny's Key lime pie is legendary.
🅿 ⊕ Closed Mon.–Tue.
🌀 All major cards

LONG KEY 33001

🍴 LITTLE ITALY
$
MM 68.5
TEL 305/664-4472
Good, hearty, home-style Italian cooking at this reasonably priced family favorite. Extensive menu takes in linguine with red clam sauce, seafood, veal Parmesan, and chicken dishes. Huge portions.
🅿 🌀 All major cards

MIDDLE KEYS

The Middle Keys stretch from MM 85 to MM 45 and are considered the fishing and diving capital of America, as well as a year-round refuge for South Floridians who take full advantage of the Keys' proximity to the mainland. But don't expect to find any beaches here. There are no natural ones, and sand is shipped in from the Caribbean to create tiny stretches near the sea.

DUCK KEY 33050

🏨 🍴 HAWK'S CAY RESORT & MARINA
$$$$$
MM 61
TEL 305/743-7000
FAX 305/743-0641
www.hawkscay.com
Spacious rooms await the guests at this West Indies-style resort on a private island. The amenities include a marina and watersports center, plus sandy beach, saltwater lagoon, and kids' club, Dolphin Connection, offering interactive program.
🛏 193 🅿 🔁 🌀 ⊞
🔽 🌀 All major cards

KEY VACA 33050

🍴 KEYS FISHERY MARKET AND MARINA
$$$
OFF MM 49.2 ON 35TH STREET
MARATHON
TEL 866/743-4353
Although relatively unknown, Keys Fishery is an outdoor, casual eatery famous for lobster reuben sandwich and coconut shrimp.
🍴 250 🅿 🌀 All major cards

🏨 SOMBRERO REEF INN & FISHING LODGE
$$
500 SOMBRERO BEACH RD.
MM 50
MARATHON
TEL 305/743-4118
www.sombreroreefinn.com
Relaxed bed-and-breakfast on the water's edge overlooking the Atlantic Ocean. The style is Florida casual; all rooms have private entrances and water views. Ramp and dockage for boats.
🛏 4 suites 🌀 🌀 MC, V

LOWER KEYS

The Lower Keys start at the end of the Seven Mile Bridge. Big Pine, Sugarloaf, Summerland, and the other Lower Keys are less developed and therefore more peaceful than the Upper Keys. Pride of the place goes to the Bahia Honda State Park on the ocean side of Big Pine Key; it has one of the loveliest beaches in South Florida and one of the most beautiful coastlines.

BIG PINE KEY 33050

🏨 BARNACLE BED AND BREAKFAST
$$
1557 LONG BEACH DR.
MM 33
TEL 305/872-3298
FAX 305/872-3863
www.thebarnacle.net
Caribbean-style home set off by a beautiful garden—with hot tub, hammock, and private beach—cherished eclectic furnishings and just two rooms in the main house, two in the cottage.
🛏 4 🅿 🌀 🌀 MC, V

SUGARLOAF KEY

🍴 MANGROVE MAMA'S RESTAURANT
$$
19991 OVERSEAS HWY.
TEL 305/745-3030
Landmark old timer—a plain

shack that survived the 1935 hurricane. You will find simple tables inside and out, shaded by a banana grove. Fresh seafood, chowders, and great Key lime pie, as well as teriyaki chicken and spicy barbecued baby back ribs.

P 🚭 🕲 All major cards

LITTLE TORCH KEY

🏨 LITTLE PALM
🍴 ISLAND RESORT & SPA

Holiday heaven. Private island accessible only by seaplane, boat or 15-minute water taxi ride. Individual, luxury palm-thatched suites are dotted about five lush acres; all with sun decks with hammocks. There are no phones, no TV. In the dining room, executive chef Luis Pous uses local ingredients to create mouthwatering European, Caribbean, and Asian dishes. Reservations only. Thursday is gourmet night.

$$$$$
MM 28.5, LITTLE TORCH KEY, FL 33042
TEL 800/343-8567 (reservations), 305-515-4004 (front desk), or 305/872-2551 (dining room)
FAX 305/872-4843
www.littlepalmisland.com
🛏 30 suites 🕲 🏊
🚭 All major cards

KEY WEST & DRY TORTUGAS

There are more guest houses, inns, and B&Bs per capita in Key West than in any other city in the country. Quaint and eccentric inns are what Key West is known for.

KEY WEST 33040

🏨 WYNDHAM CASA
🍴 MARINA
$$$$
1500 REYNOLDS ST.
TEL 305/296-3535 or 800/626-0777

FAX 305/296-4633
www.casamarinaresort.com
Romantic seaside classic, the oldest hotel in all of the Keys, built in 1921 by railway magnate Henry Flagler. There are a private beach, a choice of two pools, and a restaurant noted for its Sunday brunch.
🛏 314 **P** 🚭 🕲 🏊
🚭 All major cards

🏨 OCEAN KEY HOUSE SUITE RESORT & MARINA
$$$$$
ZERO DUVAL ST.
TEL 305/296-7701 or 800/328-9815
FAX 305/295-7016
www.oceankey.com
For those who prefer lots of room and modern convenience, this five-story hotel at the foot of Duval Street is the place. The hotel's Dockside Bar has the best seats in town for sunsets.
🛏 100 suites **P** 🚭 🕲
🏊 🚭 All major cards

🏨 PIER HOUSE
🍴 $$$$$
1 DUVAL ST.
TEL 305/296-4600 or 800/327-8340
FAX 305/296-7569
www.pierhouse.com
Stylish, deluxe, Old Town property with Caribbean flavor, discreetly screened by lush tropical gardens. Enjoy a health spa, man-made sand beach, and a choice of bars and restaurants. Highly rated restaurant, see p. 256.
🛏 142 rooms & suites **P** 🚭 🕲 🏊 ⛹ 🚭 All major cards

🏨 CHELSEA HOUSE
$$$
709 TRUMAN AVE.
TEL 305/296-2211 or 800/845-8859
FAX 305/296-4822
www.historickeywestinns.com
Laid-back, relaxed gray-and-white jewel of a house, surrounded by lush tropical

plants. Rooms in the main house have antique touches, and those by the pool are Mediterranean in style. The sundeck is clothing optional.
🛏 37 🚭 🕲 🏊 🚭 All major cards

🏨 THE MARQUESA
🍴 HOTEL

Luxury hotel converted from two 1880s private homes (listed on the National Register of Historic Places) and two recently constructed buildings. Tasteful blend of contemporary and antique furnishings, marble baths, two pools, and a rated restaurant, Café Marquesa (see p. 257).
$$$$
600 FLEMING ST.
KEY WEST, FL 33040
TEL 305/292-1919 or 800/869-4631
FAX 305/294-2121
www.marquesa.com
🛏 27 🛏 50 🕲 🚭 🏊 🚭 AE, MC, V

🏨 CURRY MANSION INN
$$$
511 CAROLINE ST.
TEL 305/294-5349 or 800/253-3466
FAX 305/294-4093
www.currymansion.com
Rambling, historic, classy Victorian mansion, a masterpiece of belle epoque grandeur. Open to the public for guided tours. Bedrooms are in a modern wing, accented with antiques and wicker.
🛏 28 🚭 🕲 🏊 🚭 All major cards

🏨 HERON HOUSE
$$$
512 SIMONTON ST.
TEL 305/294-9227 OR 800/294-1644
FAX 305/294-5692
www.heronhouse.com
Comfortable inn, simply but tastefully styled. Generous

HOTELS & RESTAURANTS

private decks and balconies to large rooms that merge with private gardens. Detailed interiors feature walls of teak, oak, and cedar.

🚹 25 🛗 🅢 🖨 🆑 All major cards

🏨 ISLAND CITY HOUSE HOTEL
$$$
411 WILLIAM ST.
TEL 305/294-5702
FAX 305/294-1289
www.islandcityhouse.com
Of the three converted 1880s houses that make up this unique hotel, the Arch House is the sole surviving carriage house in the Keys. There's a choice of suites and studios.
🚹 24 rooms & suites 🅢 🖨 🆑 All major cards

🏨 SIMONTON COURT HISTORIC INN
$$$
320 SIMONTON ST.
TEL 305/294-6386
FAX 305/293-8446
www.simontoncourt.com
Nine buildings full of character on this former cigar factory site are set into the gardens. There are four swimming pools to choose from—one is lit at night. For adults.
🚹 26 🅢 🖨 🆑 AE, MC, V

🏨 CONCH HOUSE HERITAGE INN
$$
625 TRUMAN AVE.
TEL 305/293-0020
FAX 305/293-8447
www.conchhouse.com
One of the island's earliest historic family estates, listed on the National Register of Historic Places. Spacious, elegant bedrooms in the main house or Caribbean-style wicker rooms in the tropical poolside cottage.
🚹 8 🅿 🅢 🖨 🆑 All major cards

🏨 DUVAL HOUSE
$$
815 DUVAL ST.

TEL 305/294-1666
FAX 305/292-1701
www.duvalhousekeywest.com
No phones or radios, though there is cable TV. Simple wicker furniture, some antiques, and a pool crowded by luxurious hibiscus are the keynotes to this laid-back Victorian gingerbread house.
🚹 31 🛗 🅢 🖨 🆑 All major cards

🏨 EDEN HOUSE
$$
1015 FLEMING ST.
TEL 305/296-6868
FAX 305/294-1221
www.edenhouse.com
Lovingly restored, well-run 1920s hotel. Reasonably priced rooms in wicker-filled main house; pricier private suites in three adjoining tin-roofed conch houses.
🚹 40 🅢 🖨 🆑 AE, MC, V

🏨 THE MERMAID AND THE ALLIGATOR
$$
729 TRUMAN AVE.
TEL 305/294-1894
FAX 305/295-9925
www.kwmermaid.com
A 1904 former city attorney's home, now an unusual inn with Oriental and art deco accents, book-lined hallway, and lots of open space. The Conch House annex has more economical rooms. Breakfast served poolside.
🚹 9 🅢 🖨 🆑 AE, MC, V

🍴 CAFÉ DES ARTISTES
$$$$
1007 SIMONTON ST.
TEL 305/294-7100
Longstanding French restaurant with a reputation for first-rate cooking. Formal, pricey, but strong on creativity. Try the snapper sautéed in tarragon butter with shrimps and scallops. Also has an excellent wine list.
🆑 Closed L 🅢 🆑 AE, MC, V

🍴 PIER HOUSE RESTAURANT
$$$$
1 DUVAL ST.
TEL 305/296-4600 or 800/327-8340
FAX 305/296-7569
Stunning, glass-enclosed waterfront dining room, great backdrop for upbeat, ambitious American cooking with strong Caribbean accents. Menu built around local seafood. Good wines.
🅿 🅢 🆑 All major cards

🍴 MICHAEL'S RESTAURANT
$$$
532 MARGARET ST.
TEL 305/295-1300
Nestled along the back streets of Key West's Old Town District, Michael's Restaurant serves island elegance both inside and next to a fountain outside. Meals are on the heavy side with prime beef, pasta and the local seafood, as well as cheese fondues.
🍴 100 🆑 Closed L 🅢 🆑 All major cards

SOMETHING SPECIAL

🍴 LOUIE'S BACKYARD
Prime piece of Atlantic oceanfront property. Stunning outdoor dining room, exquisite interior, new Caribbean cuisine centered on local seafood. Try Bahamian conch chowder with bird-pepper hot sauce. Reservations essential.
$$$$
700 WADDELL AVE.
KEY WEST
TEL 305/294-1061
🆑 Closed L Sept. 🅢 🆑 All major cards

🍴 SQUARE ONE
$$$
1075 DUVAL ST.
TEL 305/296-4300
Stylish, sophisticated bistro offering innovative New World cooking. Signature dishes of sautéed sea scallops

on poached spinach with mustard cream sauce set the pace. Reservations required.
P Access Simonton St. 🚭
🔥 All major cards

🍴 BLUE HEAVEN
$$$
729 THOMAS STREET
TEL 305/296-8666
Located behind a rickety old house, the restaurant features fresh fish, vegetarian dishes, and various salads. It's best to walk or bike to this famous restaurant, whose motto is "Blue Heaven: You don't have to die to get there."
🚭 🔥 All major cards

SOMETHING SPECIAL

🍴 CAFÉ MARQUESA
⊞

One of Key West's most imaginative restaurants with the air of a European brasserie. Innovative cuisine and stunning presentation; try the seared yellowfin tuna in salsa verde, or the spicy Jamaican barbecued prawns. Reservations essential.
$$$
600 FLEMING ST.
KEY WEST
TEL 305/292-1244
🔒 Closed L 🚭 🔥 All major cards

🍴 DUFFY'S STEAK AND LOBSTER HOUSE
$$
1007 SIMONTON ST.
TEL 305/296-4900
Steaks, ribs, and lobster are always good, and reasonably priced at this art deco-style off-shoot of Café des Artistes next door (see p. 256). All dishes are simply prepared with salad, freshly baked bread, and choice of potato.
🚭 🔥 All major cards

🍴 KELLY'S CARIBBEAN BAR & GRILL
$$
301 WHITEHEAD ST.

TEL 305/293-7897
www.kellyskeywest.com
Set in historic old Pan Am office, and themed with flying memorabilia. Also the home of Southernmost Brewery—try Havana Red Ale with your jerk chicken. No reservations.
🚭 🔥 All major cards

🍴 MANGOES
$$
700 DUVAL ST.
TEL 305/292-4606
Caribbean-style seafood served indoors or out. Specialties take in pan-seared yellow snapper with passion fruit. Super thin crust pizzas. Great for people-watching.
P Valet 🚭 🔥 All major cards

🍴 SIAM HOUSE
$$
829 SIMONTON ST.
TEL 305/292-0302
Suriya Siripant is from Bangkok, and his Thai cuisine has the ring of authenticity. Herbs are home-grown, the lunch buffet is good value, and reservations are recommended.
🚭 🔥 All major cards

🍴 ORIGAMI
$$
1075 DUVAL ST.
TEL 305/294-0092
One of Key West's best Japanese restaurants, Origami is renowned for its sushi deluxe dinner and Origami super special.
⊞ 60 **P** Valet 🔒 Closed L 🚭 🔥 All major cards

🍴 CAMILLE'S RESTAURANT
$
1202 SIMONTON ST.
TEL 305/296-4811
A local favorite open from breakfast through dinner. A hefty full rack of lamb is served with garlic-oregano marinade or raspberry

coulis, or try stone crab clawmeat cakes with spiced rum-mango sauce.
⊞ 150 **P** Valet 🚭 🔥 All major cards

🍴 EL SIBONEY
$
900 CATHERINE ST.
TEL 305/296-4184
www.elsiboneyrestaurant.com
Simple decor defines this great neighborhood hangout serving authentic Cuban food. Enormous portions at low prices. Ropa vieja, paella, boliche, plus an array of sandwiches and much more.
🚭 🔥 All major cards

🍴 HALF SHELL RAW BAR
$
231 MARGARET ST. 1
TEL 305/294-7496
Old Key West-style waterside hangout, noted for casual, laid-back atmosphere, simply prepared local seafood, and reasonable prices. Stone crabs in season and Maine lobsters.
P 🚭 🔥 All major cards

🍴 HOG'S BREATH SALOON
$
400 FRONT ST.
TEL 305/296-4222
Built to resemble an authentic surfer's bar, packed with tourists and locals drawn by laid-back Keys' atmosphere. Grilled fish sandwiches are sold by the ton; also good burgers and seafood, plus the T-shirt. Happy hour 5–7 p.m.
P Valet L 🚭 🔥 All major cards

🍴 PEPE'S CAFÉ
$
806 CAROLINE ST.
TEL 305/294-7192
Oldest restaurant in Key West for traditional American-style home-cooking of steaks, pork chops, and burgers, as well as Apalachicola oysters in season. Breakfast is a Keys' tradition.
🚭 🔥 DC, MC, V

SHOPPING

As a result of relatively low rents and a sales tax of 6.5 percent on top of the retail price, goods are generally cheaper than in New York or Los Angeles. South Beach, Coconut Grove, Coral Gables, and Downtown Miami are the few spots in Miami where walking is really encouraged. Here the shopping is diverse and individual.

Elsewhere, the majority of shopping is in air-conditioned mega-malls, offering department store fare from the likes of Macy's and JC Penney, and chains such as the Gap, Banana Republic, and Victoria's Secret, as well as food courts, and possibly a movie mall of six or more screens.

But the current trend is also toward upscale, open-air shopping malls with a directory of designer names in deluxe settings. These places are popular with wealthy South Americans, lured by names such as Gucci, Bulgari, Prada, and Vuitton, which they buy in bulk.

Shopping in Key West is expensive, especially for clothes. The shops worth checking out offer something more unusual than the regular close encounters with Key West's over-prolific T-shirt shops. Swimsuits, cigars, sandals, and skin-care products are all homemade in the Keys. Other bargains include paintings, sculptures, and sketches from local artists, or rarer finds such as conch pearls.

INDOOR MALLS

Bal Harbour Shops
9700 Collins Ave., Bal Harbour.
Tel 305/866-0311.
Exclusive mall specializing in designer shops such as Tiffany, Chanel, Prada, Gucci, Cartier, Hermès, and Bulgari, as well as Florida's largest Neiman Marcus and Saks Fifth Avenue.

Village of Merrick Park
Coral Gables
Tel 305/529-0200.
Neiman Marcus, Nordstrom, and 115 designer boutiques and spas.

Dolphin Mall
11250 NW 25th st., Miami.
Tel 305/DOL-PHIN
One of Miami's largest shopping, dining, and tourist attractions, Dolphin Mall offers visitor-friendly shopping and family entertainment, including restaurants, a 19-screen cinema, and designer outlets, as well as retail and specialty shops.

OUTDOOR MALLS

Bayside Marketplace
401 N. Biscayne Blvd., Miami.
Tel 305/577-3344.
An outdoor mall on the waterfront, with sight-seeing boat tours, street performers, Miami's Hard Rock Café, and a variety of shops.

CocoWalk
3015 Grand Ave., Coconut Grove. Tel 305/444-0777.
Funky, multistory, semi-outdoor mall. Lots of cafés with terrace seating and a 16-screen cinema, but retail outlets go no further than Gap and Victoria's Secret.

Downtown Miami Shopping District
Biscayne Blvd. to 2nd Ave. W. and S.E. 1st St. to N.E. 3rd St., Miami. Tel 305/379-7070.
More than 1,000 shops including the second largest jewelry district in the country, hundreds of electronics, sporting goods, clothing, and shoe stores.

Prime Outlets at Florida City
250 E. Palm Dr. (S.W. 344th St.), Florida City.
Tel 305/248-4727.

Only 30 minutes' drive south of Miami, in a lush tropical village setting with more than 60 manufacturers' factory outlet stores, ranging from Nike and OshKosh B'Gosh to Levi's Outlet by Designs.

Mayfair in the Grove
2911 Grand Ave., Coconut Grove. Tel 305/448-1700.
Mediterranean-inspired town square in the heart of Coconut Grove, with outdoor cafés, nightspots, movie theaters, restaurants, and nationally known retailers.

ARTS & ANTIQUES

The Americas Collection
2440 Ponce de Leon Blvd., Coral Gables. Tel 305/446-5578.
One of the most reputable in Miami, the gallery is dedicated to contemporary Latin American art with the inclusion of some European and American works.

Gotta Have It! Collectibles
4231 S.W. 71st Ave. Coral Gables. Tel 305/446-5757.
Closed Sat.–Sun.
Vintage autographs and memorabilia from sport, Hollywood, and rock music.

Haitian Art Co.
600 Frances St., Key West.
Tel 305/296-8932.
Brilliant, colorful artworks, artifacts, and sculpture from Haiti.

Lincoln Road Shopping District
Lincoln Road, Miami Beach.
Tel: 305/673-7010.
Impressive, upscale 12-block shopping district with individual shops, fine art galleries, and artists' studios, as well as acclaimed restaurants and cafés. Individual merchants' hours vary. Home also to Miami City Ballet and New World Symphony.

BOOKSTORES

Even the coolest people need something to read on the beach.

Barnes and Noble Booksellers
7710 N. Kendall Dr., Miami.
Tel 305/662-4770.
152 Miracle Mile, Coral Gables.
Tel 305/446-4152.
18711 Biscayne Blvd., North Miami Beach. Tel 305/935-9770.
12405 S.W. 88th St., Miami.
Tel 305/598-7727.
More than 17,000 titles including subjects by local authors.

Books & Books
933 Lincoln Rd., Miami Beach.
Tel 305/532-3222.
358 San Lorenzo Ave., Coral Gables. Tel 305/529-4567.
Great range of titles, plus readings by authors.

Borders Books
19925 Biscayne Rd., Aventura.
Tel 305/935-0027.
3390 Mary St., # 116, Coconut Grove. Tel 305/447-1655.
Poetry and book readings; wide range of titles.

Kafka's Used Book Store
1464 Washington Ave., Miami Beach. Tel 786/348-0901.
Mostly used paperbacks.

SMOKING MATTERS

Deco Drive Cigar East
1436 Ocean Dr., Miami Beach,
Tel 305/672-9032.
1650 Meridian Ave., Miami
Tel 305/674-1811.
Open 7 days a week
Buy cigars from Honduras, Nicaragua, and the Dominican Republic. You can also watch cigars being rolled in the store.

Cuban Leaf Cigar Factory
310 Duval St., Key West.
Tel 305/295-9283.
Everything you want to know about cigars, including watching them being made before buying.

El Credito Cigars
1106 S.W. 8th St., Little Havana.
Tel 305/858-4162.

Closed Sun.
Cuban-owned cigar factory.

Key West-Havana Cigar Company
1117 Duval St., Key West.
Tel 305/296-1977
or 800/217-4884.
Huge selection of cigars.

Macabi Cigar Factory Shop
3475 S.W. 8th St., Miami.
Tel 305/446-2606.
More than 100 different brands at five shops throughout the area.

JEWELRY

Jewelry Station
626 Duval St., Key West
Tel 305/294-0027

Kirk Jewelers
132 E. Flagler St., Miami.
Tel 305/371-1321.
Closed Sun.
Wide selection of brand-name watches, 14-carat, 18-carat, and platinum jewelry.

Rainbow Jewelry
101 N.E. 1st St., Miami.
Tel 305/371-2289.
Closed Sun.
Large selection of Cartier products. Also Hermès, Carrera y Carrera 18-carat gold jewelry, and Mont Blanc pens.

Seybold Building
36 N.E. 1st Street, Miami. Tel 305/374-7922.
The historic downtown building has almost 300 jewelers.

DRESSING UP

Miami and the Keys are the places to reinvent yourself.

Carroll's Jewelers
365 Miracle Mile, Coral Gables
Tel 305/446-1611
The Gables' oldest jewelry store has featured handcrafted pieces for more than 60 years.

Armani Exchange
760 Collins Ave., Miami Beach.
Tel 305/531-5900.
Giorgio Armani's newest, edgiest apparel.

SPORTS EQUIPMENT

For the sports enthusiast South Florida has everything.

Alf's Golf Shop
524 Arthur Godfrey Rd., Miami Beach.
Tel 305/673-6568.
Closed Sun.
Golf equipment, shoes, apparel, and bags.

Capt. Harry's Fishing Supplies
100 N.E. 11th St., Miami.
Tel 305/374-4661.
Closed Sun.
Wide range of fishing tackle.

Tarpoon Lagoon
300 Alton Rd., Miami Beach.
Tel 305/532-1445
One of Miami's oldest scuba dive shops.

South Beach Dive & Surf
850 Washington Ave., Miami Beach. Tel 305/673-5900.
Closed Sun a.m.
Large range of surfboards as well as scuba diving gear, and lessons available for both sports.

SPECIALTY SHOPPING

Key West Aloe
524 Front St., Key West.
Tel 800/445-2563.
More than 300 aloe products, including a line of original fragrances.

Key West Hand Print Fabrics
201 Simonton St., Key West.
Tel 305/294-9535.
Unusual tropical apparel for men and women.

ENTERTAINMENT

During the day, Miamians have an excess of outdoor pleasure to pursue; by night the lure of some of the trendiest bars, restaurants, and nightclubs is hard to resist. And when the money runs out, people-watching from a South Beach or Coconut Grove sidewalk café can be very entertaining. What suffers? Cinemas, for instance, show the blockbuster hits, but smaller, independent films struggle to attract audiences, and theater and classical music do not have the focus of Los Angeles or New York.

However, for details of concert and theater times, complete movie listings, rock and jazz venues, and nightclubs, buy the Friday edition of the *Miami Herald* for its very comprehensive "Weekend" listing section.

Visitors to Key West should check the arts and entertainment section in the Friday edition of the *Key West Citizen* for a listing of the latest cultural events.

CINEMAS

It is customary to pay cash for tickets at the box office just prior to the start of the film, but book in advance for much-hyped opening nighters. Prices are often reduced for early afternoon showings, and most cinemas offer discounts for students (with college ID) and senior citizens.

AMC CocoWalk 16
3015 Grand Ave., Coconut Grove.
Tel 305/448-7075.
Multiplex with 16 screens, and a policy of showing art-house and independent films among the new releases.

AMC Sunset Place
5701 Sunset Drive, South Miami.
Tel 305/466-0450.
With 24 screens you'll miss nothing at this multiplex theater. New releases only.

The Miami Beach Cinematheque
512 Española Way, Miami Beach,
Tel 305/673-4567.
Miami Beach's best venue for alternative and foreign films.

Regal South Beach 18
1100 Lincoln Rd., South Beach.
Tel 305/674-6766.
Although part of a chain, this giant glass-walled theater dares to mix big-budget studio films with low-budget art and foreign films.

Sunrise Cinemas Intracoastal
3701 N.E. 163 St., Miami
Tel 305/949-0064.
Sunrise Cinemas Intracoastal has 8 screens that show big-budget, independent, and foreign films.

CLUBS & BARS

MIAMI

Miami is known for its nightlife. Indeed, Miami's clubs are often compared to New York's: nocturnal, sleep deprived, and driven by relentless energy. It is not done to be seen at a club before 11 p.m., when things really get going. This is especially true of South Beach, the epitome of cool Miami, which plays host to some of Miami's trendiest clubs. You have to be 21 to drink alcohol, so few clubs will admit under-21s. Take photo ID even if you are much older. The law states clubs must stop serving alcohol by 5 a.m. and most close between 3–5 a.m. Cover charges vary, and women often get in for free. Some places don't charge at all and put it on the price of drinks. You will need cash to pay admission, however.

Note that Miami's clubs open and close at will. Always telephone first to see if they are still there, and check dress codes.

The Clevelander Bar
1020 Ocean Dr., South Beach,
Tel 305/531-3485.
This beachside bar/restaurant/hotel has been popular for years, especially with visitors in their 30s and up.

Dek23
655 Washington Ave., South Beach
Tel 305/674-1176.
Another of South Beach's new clubs, this one has a New York-inspired interior but locals DJs play the sounds.

Glass at The Forge
432 41st St., Miami Beach.
Tel 305/604-9798.
Sophisticated club where business suits, celebs, and chic partyers dance the night away.

The Improv
3390 Mary St., Coconut Grove.
Tel 305/441-8200.
Famous comedy club that draws nationally known comics.

John Martin's Irish Pub & Restaurant
253 Miracle Mile, Coral Gables.
Tel 305/445-3777.
Day or night, this is the place to refresh yourself with heavy food and thick ale while you're on Miracle Mile.

Mynt
1921 Collins Ave., South Beach.
Tel 305/532-0727.
The place to hang out with the beautiful people.

Nikki Beach Club
One Ocean Dr., South Beach.
Tel 305/538-1111.
Hedonistic models and international businesspeople thrive at this oceanfront club.

Opium Garden
136 Collins Ave., South Beach.
Tel 305/531-5535.
One of the hottest nightclubs in South Beach. Some might consider it decadent.

Oxygen
2911 Grand Ave., CocoWalk, Coconut Grove.
Tel 305/476-0202.
Chic club where silver and blue tones paint a more laid-back scene, until 11 p.m. when the DJ gets the house thumping.

Set
320 Lincoln Road, South Beach.
Tel 305/531-2800.
SoBe's newest VIP club, teeming with models.

Tamara
1677 Collins Ave., Miami Beach.
Tel 305/532-2311.
Executive chef Frederic Delaire serves a exquisite array of French Fusion dishes.

Tapas & Tintos
448 Española Way, South Beach.
Tel 305/538-8272.
Relaxed eatery that nonetheless uses gourmet ingredients. Name means appetizers and red wine.

Twist
1057 Washington Ave., South Beach.
Tel 305/53-TWIST.
One of South Beach's most popular gay bars, it's actually seven bars in one complex.

KEY WEST
Eating and drinking may seem to be the main cultural activity in Key West. There is an "anything goes" attitude and the numerous bars make up the bulk of nightlife here, clamorous places that are often open until 4 a.m. with live music—folk, rock, country. The best bars are grouped at the northern end of Duval Street.

Sloppy Joe's
201 Duval St., Key West.
Tel 305/294-5717.
Hemingway memorabilia draws the crowds, and they are kept there by a mix of live sounds and lively atmosphere.

Captain Tony's Saloon
428 Greene St., Key West.
Tel 305/294-1838.
The original Sloppy Joe's where Hemingway really did hang out.

Jimmy Buffett's Margaritaville Café
500 Duval St., Key West.
Tel 305/292-1435.
The legend in his own lifetime, Florida crooner Jimmy Buffett lent his name to this great bar. It still draws the crowds, despite the fact that Buffett moved away years ago. Live bands cater to a wide spectrum of tastes, and there is Buffett memorabilia and a tourist shop.

La-Te-Da
1125 Duval St., Key West.
Tel 305/296-6706.
The laid-back lifestyle and tolerant attitude that is part of the Key West experience has encouraged a strong gay community. There are a number of predominantly gay bars along Duval Street, but a more mixed attitude prevails at La-Te-Da. This place is great for poolside drinks and the occasional tea dance.

THEATER, CLASSICAL MUSIC, OPERA, & DANCE

Check the "Tropical Life" section of Friday's *Miami Herald* for up-to-date listings of theater productions and performances by the New World Symphony under Michael Tilson Thomas, and the Florida Grand Opera. Tickets can be obtained from Ticketmaster (for outlets, tel 305/358-5885). Be aware that Ticketmaster charges a service fee when you purchase tickets through the agency.

Unless otherwise stated, all venues are wheelchair accessible.

Miami-Dade County Auditorium
2901 W. Flagler St.,
Tel 305/547-5414.
Home to the Florida Grand Opera.

Gusman Center Olympia Theater for the Performing Arts
174 E. Flagler St., Downtown Miami.
Tel 305/374-2444.
Hosts ballets, orchestras, film festivals, and other events throughout the year.

Jackie Gleason Theater
1700 Washington Ave., Miami Beach.
Tel 305/673-7300.
2,700-seater that's home to Broadway shows, and modern, classical, jazz, and pop concerts.

Adrienne Arsht Center for the Performing Arts
1300 Biscayne Blvd., Miami.
Tel 305/949-6722.
This 570,000-sq.-ft. complex, which premiered in 2006, hosts performances by the Miami City Ballet, the Florida Grand Opera, and New World Symphony.

New World Symphony
555 Lincoln Road, Miami Beach.
Tel 305/5-.
A 90-member orchestral company devoted to training musicians between 21 and 30, it bills itself as America's Orchestral Academy.

Red Barn Theatre
319 Duval St., Key West.
Tel 305/296-9911.
All types of plays from classical English/American playwrights to modern productions.

Tennessee Williams Fine Arts Center
5901 W. College Rd., Key West.
Tel 305/296-1520.
All things musical, from Broadway shows to classical concerts, jazz, and opera.

Waterfront Playhouse
Mallory Sq., Key West.
Tel 305/294-5015.
A combination of classic and modern plays and popular musicals.

MIAMI CALENDAR OF EVENTS

Information available from:
www.miamiherald.com/calendar

JANUARY
Art Deco Weekend
Tel 305/672-2014.
A tribute to Miami's South
Beach art deco architecture,
when the streets are filled with
big-band sounds and hotels are
hard to find.

FEBRUARY
**Annual Miami International
Film Festival**
Tel 305/237-FILM.
A ten-day film show scattered
throughout the city, featuring
world and U.S. premiers of
international and domestic
productions, plus big-budget
movies and more ambiguous
fare produced during the year.

Coconut Grove Arts Festival
Tel 305/447-0401.
Considered the number one
fine arts festival in the country,
attended by up to a million
people, with the work of more
than 300 artists on show.

**Miami International Boat
Show**
Tel 954/441-3220.
More than 2,300 of the world's
leading marine industry manufacturers display the newest
powerboats, engines, and
accessories at the Miami Beach
Convention Center.

MARCH
Calle Ocho Festival
Tel 305/644-8888.
Little Havana's week-long
celebration of Latin food, music,
drama, and dance. The highlight
is the final Sunday night street
party known as Calle Ocho.

Sony Ericsson Open
Tel 305/442-3367.
One of the nation's most
popular tennis tournaments is
held at the Tennis Center at
Crandon Park, Key Biscayne. Top
players compete for more than
$7.5 million.

Asian Festival
Tel 305/247-5727.
Held over two days at the Fruit
& Spice Park in Homestead,
where South Florida's thousands
of Asian immigrants celebrate
their food and culture.

JUNE
**Miami/Bahamas Goombay
Festival**
Tel 305/448-9501.
Coconut Grove's Bahamian
community pays tribute to its
roots. Watch Junkanoo parades,
the Royal Bahamian Police
Marching Band, and try some of
the best conch fritters around.

JULY
**Annual America Birthday
Bash**
Tel 305/358-7550.
The state's largest 4th of July
party, held at Bayfront Park.
Something for everyone with an
ethnic food court, three stages,
rock bands, Latin musicians, and
great fireworks.

AUGUST
**Annual Miami Reggae
Festival**
Tel 305/891-2944.
The entire Jamaican community
turns out for local, national, and
international musicians at this
two-day event in honor of
Jamaica's Independence Day.

NOVEMBER
**Miami Book Fair
International**
Tel 305/237-3258.
Week-long literary extravaganza
that features appearances and
readings by authors of local,
national, and international
standing.

NASCAR Championship
Tel 866-989-RACE.
The NASCAR Ford 200, 300,
and 400 Championships take
place at Homestead-Miami
Speedway, ending the racing
season.

DECEMBER
Annual King Mango Strut
Tel 305/444-7270.

Local and national events and
characters are satirized in this
wacky Coconut Grove parade.

Art Basel Miami Beach
www.artbasel.com.
This four-day event is the
American sister of Art Basel in
Switzerland, perhaps the world's
most presitgious annual art
show. Art Basel Miami Beach
showcases 1,000 artists from
around the world as well as
music, film, and other events.

ING Miami Marathon
Tel. 305/278-8668.
A marathon, half marathon, and
smaller races plus a giant health
& fitness expo at the Miami
Beach Convention Center. Tens
of thousands participate.

KEY WEST SPECIAL EVENTS

Sunset in Key West
Sunset at the southernmost city
in the United States is renowned
as a spectacular sight. Each day,
as sunset draws near, crowds of
locals and tourists make their
way to Mallory Square, where
celebrations take place as the
sun seems to drop off the edge
of the world into the Gulf of
Mexico, to the accompaniment of
entertainment, food, and music,
and applause from the crowd.

**Conch Republic
Independence Celebration**
A ten-day festival celebrating the
Conch Republic's mock secession
from the Union, based on the
area's "insurrection" against a
United States Border Patrol's
alien and drug search road-block
that jammed the Keys' roadways
in 1982. This is reenacted each
year on April 23, recalling the
republic's motto:"We seceded
where others have failed."

Fantasy Fest
A ten-day event held in late
October, which marks the start
of the autumn/winter season.
It embraces Halloween, and is Key
West's answer to New Orleans'
Mardi Gras and Rio's Carnival.
Centered around the Old

Town, food festivals, street fairs, concerts, art and craft shows, a "Pretenders in Paradise" costume contest, pet masquerade, and parade, culminate in a Twilight Fantasy parade of spectacular floats and costumes.

Old Island Days
Beginning in December, Old Island Days takes place over a four-month period. It looks back at Key West's unique history, heritage, and traditions with tours of hibiscus and bougainvillea-adorned houses and gardens, and a conch shell blowing contest.

Hemingway Days Festival
Dozens of square-jawed, white-haired gents turn up for the Lookalike Contest that is the festival's highlight.

SWIMMING WITH THE DOLPHINS

To swim with dolphins, you must make reservations in advance and adhere to a few simple rules. Nothing can compare with the wonder of being close to these extraordinary mammals, and many children who are ill or have disabilities benefit greatly from dolphin encounters.

There are three main "dolphin experience" locations in the Florida Keys:

The Dolphin Research Center
Grassy Key, Marathon Shores, FL 33052. Tel 305/289-1121.

Dolphin Plus
P.O. Box 2728, Key Largo, FL 33037. Tel 305/451-1993.

Theater of the Sea
MM 84, Islamorada, FL 33036. Tel 305/664-2431.

NEW SOUTH FLORIDA CUISINE

Many of Miami's new residents are Spanish-speaking. A large number are refugees from Cuba. Others fled violence in Central America, poverty in the Caribbean, or are affluent Brazilians, Venezuelans, and Colombians who maintain holiday homes in Miami. With Miami becoming the crossroads of Cuba, the Caribbean, and Latin America, the ethnic diversity has caused its own culinary revolution.

Floridian fusion cooking, or the New World cuisine, is the result of Floridian chefs finally becoming aware of the gastronomic cornucopia growing in their own backyards, after decades of dishing up International and California fare as early bird specials (cheap 4–6 p.m. meal deals).

The result is a cuisine that bursts with tropical flavors and vibrant combinations, with the upbeat Latin American tempo bringing style, and the Caribbean Basin contributing most in terms of ingredients and inspiration. Salt cod, tamarind, guava, plantains, conch, and even the hottest chili pepper known, the Caribbean scotch bonnet, are all considered everyday fare.

Superb local raw ingredients also play a part: seafood from the Atlantic Ocean and Gulf of Mexico; exotic natives such as stone crabs, snapper, catfish, frogs' legs, alligator, blood oranges, and hearts of palm; along with the luxuriant subtropical climate that supports a year-round growing season.

Homestead, a farming community near Miami, has become the nation's exotic fruit capital, noted for lychees, passion fruit, mameys (looks like an elongated coconut and tastes like baked sweet potato), and mangoes.

South Florida restaurant-goers have an incredible choice of Jamaican, Trinidadian, Cuban, Haitian, Argentinian, Peruvian, Nicaraguan, Colombian, and Honduran restaurants. Most street corners in Miami have their *loncherias* (Cuban snack bars), and major supermarkets sell plantains, boniatos (sweet potatoes), cassavas, and other Hispanic produce.

MENU READER
Florida natives

Alligator—farm raised, not from the wild. A smooth, very lean meat that can be tough if not carefully prepared and cooked—best battered and deep-fried. Alligator stew is an old Florida specialty.

Citrus fruits—largest cash crop in Florida, producing more than 80 percent of the nation's limes, 50 percent of the world's grapefruits, and 25 percent of the world's oranges.

Conch (pronounced conk)—a Bahamian specialty, a giant edible sea snail, firm textured, similar to abalone, shrimp, and scallops. Their huge, flaring conical shells that you can blow as a horn or put to your ear to hear the ocean need no introduction. High in protein, low in fat, and usually served as an appetizer, perhaps in a ceviche or in a chowder, or battered and fried as fritters.

Key lime—small, yellow, and indigenous to South Florida and the Florida Keys. Key lime pie is the region's most famous dessert. In an authentic form it is sweetened with condensed milk, has a yellow, puddinglike filling, and a Graham cracker crust.

Florida catfish—a specialty of Lake Okeechobee, northwest of Palm Beach, where it is filleted, sprinkled in cornmeal, and deep-fried. However, more and more Florida catfish is farmed.

Florida lobster—the formidable looking spiny lobster is a crustacean with giant antennae, a barb-covered carapace, but no claws. All the meat is in the tail. Abundant in Florida waters, it's smaller and sweeter than the bi-clawed Maine lobster. In season from the end of August to April.

Florida mangoes—short season, roughly May–Aug., but used in salsas and chutneys throughout the year. Hundreds of varieties grow in yards and along roadsides during the season.

Frogs' legs—hunted wild in the Everglades. Prized as much by backwoods fishermen as by gifted chefs for meat that is tender, succulent, mild-flavored, and sweet.

Swamp cabbage or *hearts of palm* —once the mainstay of the pioneer diet. Popular in rural areas, and with creative chefs.

Stone crab—in season from Oct. to April. The claws are the only part you can eat; crabbers clip one of the two claws and toss the creature back into the water so it can grow a new claw in 12–18 months. Traditionalists serve the claws with melted butter or mustard sauce, but Florida's new generation of chefs is experimenting with novel ways to serve this delicacy.

Florida fish
Amberjack—large, firm-fleshed, deep-water fish with a mild flavor similar to grouper.

Cobia—large warm-water fish that resembles a shark. Has a mild-flavored, firm flesh that works well in chowders and ceviche.

Dolphin—also known as *mahi mahi*, a white-meat saltwater fish, not the sea mammal, that is at its best simply either blackened or plain grilled.

Grouper—large, firm, sweet, white-fleshed fish; it can weigh up to 80 pounds.

Kingfish—dark-fleshed fish popular with Cubans and Central Americans. The traditional fish for making *escabeche* (pickled fish).

Mullet—the number-one cash fish in Florida, caught in great quantities off the west coast. Rich and oily, ideal for smoking.

Pompano—a flat, silvery fish that's highly prized for its mild-flavored fillets.

Snapper—flourishes in the shallow waters off the Keys. Florida's most popular fish, sweet, mild flavored, and tender.

Tuna—both the 500- to 600-pound yellowfin tuna and the 20- to 40-pound blackfin tuna are caught off the Florida coast.

Wahoo—the name is Hawaiian and means "sweet." A particularly prized Florida game fish, it is dark, with a firm bite and a robust, dulcet flavor. The tropical fish belongs to the mackerel family, but has a gray/white flesh.

Floribbean menu
Adobo—Cuban marinade of sour orange juice, garlic, cumin, and oregano.

Batido—Hispanic milkshake of fruit, ice, and sweetened condensed milk.

Boliche—Cuban pot roast.

Bolo—Cuban cooked-ham sandwich.

Chimichurri—Nicaraguan condiment that originated in Argentina, made from parsley, garlic, and olive oil, and served with grilled meats.

Churrasco—Nicaraguan grilled marinated beef tenderloin.

Emparedado—Cuban sandwich of cooked ham, roast pork, cheese, and pickles on Cuban bread rubbed with garlic.

Enchilado—seafood in Cuban-style Creole sauce.

Frijoles negros—black beans.

Lechón asado—roast suckling pig.

Mojito—Cuban cocktail of rum, lime, yerbabuena (mint), and soda water.

Mojo—wonderful Cuban sauce with garlic and sour orange or lime juice.

Picadillo—ground beef served with olives, capers, and raisins.

Tamal—cornmeal pastry cooked in a corn husk.

Yuca—cassava root.

ANNUAL MIAMI FOOD FESTIVALS

Taste of the Grove
Peacock Park.
Tel 305/444-7270.
Held mid-January. Two-day food and music fest with Coconut Grove's most popular restaurants offering samples of their finest foods.

South Beach Wine & Food Festival
Tel 305/625-4171.
Each February, this annual celebration presented by the Food Network attracts tens of thousands of visitors.

Carnaval Miami International
Calle Ocho, Little Havana.
Tel 305/644-8888.
Part of the Calle Ocho Festival held in March. Massive nine-day celebration of Latino food and culture extending 23 blocks.

Taste of the Beach
Lincoln Road Shopping District, Lincoln Rd.
Tel 305/672-6050.
Held in April. Two-day fest offering the chance to check out the best Miami Beach has to offer.

CREDITS

ILLUSTRATIONS CREDITS

Abbreviations for terms appearing below: (t) top; (b) bottom; (l) left; (r) right; (c) center

Cover (l), Powerstock/Zefa; (c), Image Bank; (r), The Stockmarket Photo Agency Inc. Spine, Powerstock/Zefa. Back cover: Robert Harding Picture Library.

1, Glowimages/age fotostock. 2/3, Tony Stone Images. 4, Innerspace Visions/Doug Perrine. 9, Chris Gordon/Getty Images. 11, Robin Hill. 12/13, Alan Schein Photography/CORBIS. 14/5, Catherine Karnow. 17, Paul Chesley/National Geographic Image Collection. 19, Historical Museum of Southern Florida. 20, Peter Newark's Pictures. 22, Flagler Museum Archives. 23, Magnum Photos/A Abbas. 24/5, Maggie Steber. 27, Robin Hill. 28/9, Courtesy Adrienne Arsht Center for the Performing Arts of Miami-Dade County/Robin Hill. 30, Marc Serota. 3l, Robin Hill. 34, AA Photo Library/ P Bennett. 35, Robin Hill. 36, Robin Hill. 38/9, Miami-Dade Public Library. 39, AA Photo Library/P Bennett. 40, Robin Hill. 41, Lanny Provo. 42, Robin Hill. 44, Robin Hill. 45, Tony Arruza. 46/7, AA Photo Library/P Bennett. 48, Robin Hill. 49, Magnum Photos/Alex Webb. 51, AA Photo Library/P Bennett. 52, Maggie Steber. 55, Norman Van Aken. 56, Xavier Cortada Studio. 57, Lanny Provo. 58, Robin Hill. 59, AA Photo Library/P Bennett. 61, Lanny Provo. 62, Lanny Provo. 63, Steven Brooke Studios. 64, Robin Hill. 65, Robin Hill. 67(t) Robin Hill. 67 (cl) AA Photo Library/P Bennett. 67(cr), Robin Hill. 67(b), Tony Arruza. 68, AA Photo Library/P Bennett. 70, Club Pearl. 71, Robin Hill. 72 Courtesy Miami Jai-Alai. 73 (lt), Courtesy Seminole Hard Rock. 73 (rt) Courtesy Seminole Hard Rock. 73 (b), Justin Dernier/ EQUI-PHOTO, Courtesy Gulfstream Park. 75, Robin Hill. 76/7, Rex Features. 78, Lanny Provo. 79, Images Colour Library. 81, AA Photo Library/P Bennett. 82/3, Robin Hill. 84, Jeff Greenberg /age fotostock. 86, AA Photo Library/P Bennett. 87, AA Photo Library/P Bennett. 88, Robin Hill. 89, Tony Arruza. 91, Robert Harding Picture Library. 92(t),

Robin Hill. 92(b), Mitchell Wolfson Jr. Collection, The Wolfsonian-Florida International University, Miami Beach, Florida. 93, Bass Museum of Art. 94, Sanford L. Ziff Jewish Museum of Florida. 95(l), Lanny Provo. 95(r), AA Photo Library/ P Bennett. 96/7, Robin Hill. 98, The Ritz-Carlton, South Beach. 99, Robin Hill. 100, Robin Hill, 101, Innerspace Visions/Doug Perrine. 102/3, Innerspace Visions/Doug Perrine. 104, Jodi Cobb/National Geographic Image Collection. 105, Robin Hill. 106/7, Robin Hill. 107, AA Photo Library/ P Bennett. 108, Robin Hill. 109, Robin Hill. 110, Pictures Colour Library. 111, Robin Hill. 113, Robin Hill. 115, World Pictures. 116, Robert Harding Picture Library. 118, Robert Harding Picture Library. 119, Miami Museum of Science & Planetarium. 120, AA Photo Library/P Bennett. 121, Historical Museum of Southern Florida. 122, Robin Hill. 123, Miami Museum of Science. 124, Robin Hill. 125, AA Photo Library/P Bennett. 128, Tony Arruza. 129, Robin Hill. 130, Coral Gable Venetian Pool. 131, Robert Harding Picture Library. 132, Robin Hill. 133, Robin Hill. 135, Robin Hill. 136, Robin Hill. 137, AA Photo Library/P Bennett. 138, AP Photo/Wilfredo Lee. 139, Robin Hill. 140, Robin Hill. 141, Robin Hill. 142, Robin Hill. 143, AA Photo Library/J A Tims. 145, Everglades Safari Park, Miami, FL 147, Pictures Colour Library. 148/9, Chris Johns/National Geographic Image Collection. 149, James Richardson. 151, Bruce Coleman Collection. 152, AA Photo Library/J A Tims. 153(l), Pictures Colour Library. 153(r), AA Photo Library/P Bennett. 154/5, Tony Stone Images. 156, AA Photo Library/J A Tims. 157, Innerspace Visions/Masa Ushioda. 158, "Andy Newman, Florida Keys & Key West Tourism Development Council." 160, Clara Taylor. 161, Stephen Frink/stephenfrink.com. 162, Robert Harding Picture Library. 163, Robert Harding Picture Library. 164, AA Photo Library/J A Tims. 165, Robin Hill. 166/7, James G. Duquesnel, Biological Scientist II. 168, Lanny Provo. 169, Lanny Provo. 171, Innerspace Visions/Doug Perrine. 172, Clara Taylor. 173, Clara Taylor. 174, Robert Harding Picture Library. 175, Robert Harding Picture Library. 176, Clara Taylor. 177, AA Photo

Library/J A Tims. 178, Clara Taylor. 179, Tony Arruza. 180, Clara Taylor. 181, Clara Taylor. 182, Pictures Colour Library. 183, Picture Quest. 185, AA Photo Library/J A Tims. 187, Clara Taylor. 188(t), Robert Harding Picture Library. 188(b), Clara Taylor. 189, www.photography byrebecca.com. 190, Robert Harding Picture Library. 19l, Clara Taylor. 195, "Andy Newman, Florida Keys & Key West Tourism Development Council." 196, Clara Taylor. 197, Innerspace Visions/Doug Perrine. 198, AA Photo Library/ P Bennett. 199, Clara Taylor. 201(tl), Tony Arruza. 201(tr), Lanny Provo. 201(b), Tony Arruza. 202, Clara Taylor. 203, Catherine Karnow. 204, Clara Taylor. 205, Robert Harding Picture Library. 207, Robert Harding Picture Library. 208/9, Pictures Colour Library. 210, Robin Hill. 211, Lanny Provo. 213, Patrick Ward/CORBIS 214, "Andy Newman, Florida Keys & Key West Tourism Development Council." 215(t), Clara Taylor. 215(b), Clara Taylor. 217(t), Lanny Provo. 217(b), AA Photo Library/ J A Tims. 218, Tom Greenwood. 219, Bill Keogh Photography. 220/l, Clara Taylor. 222, Pictor International, London. 223, Clara Taylor. 224, Clara Taylor. 225, AA Photo Library/J A Tims. 226, AA Photo Library/P Bennett. 227, AA Photo Library/J A Tims. 229, Spectrum Colour Library. 230, Clara Taylor. 231, Clara Taylor. 232, Clara Taylor. 233, "Andy Newman Florida Keys & Key West Tourism Development Council." 235(t), Bob Krist/CORBIS. 235(b), Tom Melham. 236, Clara Taylor. 237, Clara Taylor. 238, Clara Taylor. 239, Robin Hill.

Founded in 1888, the National Geographic Society is one of the largest nonprofit scientific and educational organizations in the world. It reaches more than 285 million people worldwide each month through its official journal, National Geographic, and its four other magazines; the National Geographic Channel; television documentaries; radio programs; films; books; videos and DVDs; maps; and interactive media. National Geographic has funded more than 8,000 scientific research projects and supports an education program combating geographic illiteracy.

For more information, please call 1-800-NGS LINE (647-5463) or write to the following address: National Geographic Society 1145 17th Street N.W. Washington, D.C. 20036-4688 U.S.A.

Visit us online at www.national geographic.com/books

For information about special discounts for bulk purchases, please contact National Geographic Books Special Sales: ngspecsales@ngs.org

For rights or permissions inquiries, please contact National Geographic Books Subsidiary Rights: ngbookrights@ngs.org

Order Traveler today, the magazine that travelers trust. In the U.S. and Canada call 1-800-NGS-LINE; 813-979-6845 for international. Or visit online at www.nationalgeographic.com/traveler and click on SUBSCRIBE.

Published by the National Geographic Society
John M. Fahey, Jr., *President and Chief Executive Officer*
Gilbert M. Grosvenor, *Chairman of the Board*
Tim T. Kelly, President, *Global Media Group*
John Q. Griffin, *President, Publishing*
Nina D. Hoffman, *Executive Vice President;*
    President, Book Publishing Group

Prepared by the Book Division
Kevin Mulroy, *Senior Vice President and Publisher*
Leah Bendavid-Val, *Director of Photography Publishing*
    and Illustrations
Marianne R. Koszorus, *Director of Design*
Barbara Brownell Grogan, *Executive Editor*
Elizabeth Newhouse, *Director of Travel Publishing*
Barbara A. Noe, *Series Editor*
Carl Mehler, *Director of Maps*
Jennifer A. Thornton, *Managing Editor*
R. Gary Colbert, *Production Director*

2005 and 2008 updates by David Raterman

Edited and designed by AA Publishing (a trading name of Automobile Association Developments Limited, whose registered office is Norfolk House, Priestley Road, Basingstoke, Hampshire, England RG24 9NY. Registered number: 1878835).
Betty Sheldrick, *Project Manager,* David Austin, *Senior Art Editor*
Allen Stidwill, Karen Kemp, *Editors*
Phil Barfoot, Mike Preedy, Bob Johnson, *Designers*
Avril Chester, *Assistant Designer*
Simon Mumford, *Senior Cartographic Editor*
Helen Beever, Amber Banks, *Cartographers*
Richard Firth, *Production Director,* Wyn Vosey, *Picture Researcher*
Drive maps: Chris Orr Assoc., Southampton, England
Cutaway illustrations drawn by Maltings Partnership, Derby, England

Staff for 2008 update
Lawrence Porges, *Project Editor*
Richard S. Wain, *Production Project Manager*
J. Hunter Braithwaite, Bridget English, Caroline Hickey, Paula Kelly,
    Elliana Spiegel, Ruth Thompson, Meredith Wilcox *Contributors*

Third edition 2008

The Library of Congress has cataloged the first edition as follows:
Miller, Mark.
    The National Geographic traveler. Miami & the Keys / Mark Miller.
        p.   cm.
    Includes index.
    ISBN 0-7922-7433-4
    1. Miami (Fla.) Guidebooks. 2. Florida Keys (Fla.) Guidebooks.
    I. Miller, Mark. II. Title. III. Title: Miami & the Keys.
F319.M6A78 1999
917.59'3810463—dc21   99-40354
                                        CIP

National Geographic Traveler: Miami. Third edition 2008
ISBN: 978-1-4262-0323-7

Printed in China

Visit the society's Web site at http://www.nationalgeographic.com

NATIONAL GEOGRAPHIC
TRAVELER
A Century of Travel Expertise in Every Guide

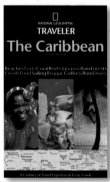

- **Alaska** ISBN: 978-0-7922-5371-6
- **Amsterdam** ISBN: 978-0-7922-7900-6
- **Arizona** (3rd Edition) ISBN: 978-1-4262-0228-5
- **Australia** (3rd Edition) ISBN: 978-1-4262-0229-2
- **Barcelona** (2nd Edition) ISBN: 978-0-7922-5365-5
- **Beijing** ISBN: 978-1-4262-0231-5
- **Berlin** ISBN: 978-0-7922-6212-1
- **Boston & environs** ISBN: 978-0-7922-7926-6
- **California** (3rd Edition) ISBN: 978-1-4262-0324-4
- **Canada** (2nd Edition) ISBN: 978-0-7922-6201-5
- **The Caribbean**
  (2nd Edition) ISBN: 978-1-4262-0141-7
- **China** (2nd Edition) ISBN: 978-1-4262-0035-9
- **Costa Rica** (2nd Edition) ISBN: 978-0-7922-5368-6
- **Cuba** (2nd Edition) ISBN: 978-1-4262-0142-4
- **Dominican Republic** ISBN: 978-1-4262-0232-2
- **Egypt** (2nd Edition) ISBN: 978-1-4262-0143-1
- **Florence & Tuscany**
  (2nd Edition) ISBN: 978-0-7922-5318-1
- **Florida** ISBN: 978-0-7922-7432-2
- **France** (2nd Edition) ISBN: 978-1-4262-0027-4
- **Germany** (2nd Edition) ISBN: 978-1-4262-0028-1
- **Great Britain** (2nd Edition) ISBN: 978-1-4262-0029-8
- **Greece** (2nd Edition) ISBN: 978-1-4262-0030-4
- **Hawaii** (2nd Edition) ISBN: 978-0-7922-5568-0
- **Hong Kong** (2nd Edition) ISBN: 978-0-7922-5369-3
- **India** (2nd Edition) ISBN: 978-1-4262-0144-8
- **Ireland** (2nd Edition) ISBN: 978-1-4262-0022-9
- **Italy** (3rd Edition) ISBN: 978-1-4262-0223-0
- **Japan** (3rd Edition) ISBN: 978-1-4262-0234-6
- **London** (2nd Edition) ISBN: 978-1-4262-0023-6

- **Los Angeles** ISBN: 978-0-7922-7947-1
- **Madrid** ISBN: 978-0-7922-5372-3
- **Mexico** (2nd Edition) ISBN: 978-0-7922-5319-8
- **Miami & the Keys**
  (3rd Edition) ISBN: 978-1-4262-0323-7
- **New York** (2nd Edition) ISBN: 978-0-7922-5370-9
- **Naples & southern Italy**
  ISBN 978-1-4262-0040-3
- **Panama** ISBN: 978-1-4262-0146-2
- **Paris** (2nd Edition) ISBN: 978-1-4262-0024-3
- **Piedmont & Northwest Italy**
  ISBN: 978-0-7922-4198-0
- **Portugal** ISBN: 978-0-7922-4199-7
- **Prague & the Czech Republic**
  ISBN: 978-0-7922-4147-8
- **Provence & the Côte d'Azur**
  (2nd Edition) ISBN: 978-1-4262-0235-3
- **Romania** ISBN: 978-1-4262-0147-9
- **Rome** (2nd Edition) ISBN: 978-0-7922-5572-7
- **St. Petersburg** ISBN 978-1-4262-0050-2
- **San Diego** (2nd Edition) ISBN: 978-0-7922-6202-2
- **San Francisco**
  (3rd Edition) ISBN: 978-1-4262-0325-1
- **Shanghai** ISBN: 978-1-4262-0148-6
- **Sicily** (2nd Edition) ISBN: 978-1-4262-0224-7
- **Spain** (3rd Edition) ISBN: 978-1-4262-0250-6
- **Sydney** ISBN: 978-0-7922-7435-3
- **Taiwan** (2nd Edition) ISBN: 978-1-4262-0145-5
- **Thailand** (2nd Edition) ISBN: 978-0-7922-5321-1
- **Venice** ISBN: 978-0-7922-7917-4
- **Vietnam** ISBN: 978-0-7922-6203-9
- **Washington, D.C.**
  (3rd Edition) ISBN: 978-1-4262-0225-4

AVAILABLE WHEREVER BOOKS ARE SOLD